HEROES, FOOLS & OTHER DREAMERS

A Sportswriter's Gallery of Extraordinary People

DAVE KINDRED

LONGSTREET PRESS

Atlanta, Georgia

Published by
LONGSTREET PRESS, INC.
2150 Newmarket Parkway
Suite 102
Marietta, GA 30067

Printed in the United States of America

2nd printing, 1989

Library of Congress Catalog Card Number 88-081800

ISBN 0-929264-02-9

This book was printed by R. R. Donnelley and Sons, Harrisonburg,
Virginia. The text type was set in Goudy Old Style by Typo-Repro
Service, Inc., Atlanta, Georgia. Design by Paulette Lambert.
Cover Illustration by Wayland Moore.

For my father and my son,
the greatest heroes of all

Contents

HEROES, FOOLS & OTHER DREAMERS

A Sportswriter's Gallery of Extraordinary People

Introduction

June 16, 1988

I n case a ground ball comes bouncing through the house, I have my old baseball glove within reach. My wife one day said, "Why do you keep that glove on your desk? And don't give me that stuff about ground balls rebounding through the house."

The Wilson A2000 sits on an antique walnut jewel box, as if enthroned. As to why it is there, I told my wife, "Beats me."

The glove is beautiful. It is the best baseball glove ever made. After all this time the leather is a golden color under a patina of dirt carried away from infields all over Illinois. Slide your hand in there. The leather is a little dry but it's soft. It's soft enough that when you feel it against your palm you remember a kid's dreams. To feel the A2000 is to imagine it carrying you toward a sharply hit ground ball behind second base. To touch the glove now . . .

"Honey, I've figured it out, about my ball glove."

"And?"

"It reminds me of when I had hair."

I am not one of those people who fret about age. But there is pain which comes with knowing my baseball glove is 26 years old. That makes me 47. I am a very young man in every sense except athletically. The pain comes from that last part, because probably, if it hasn't happened yet, the chances are — well, I may not get to the big leagues after all. Even the example of Satchel Paige is no longer inspirational. Bill Veeck called the great pitcher to the Cleveland Indians at the antiquarian age of 42. As best I can remember, I passed that number at a high rate of speed.

I'm wondering something. Why can I tell you 26 years later the

1

name of the salesman who sold me that ball glove? He was Red Ringheisen. The glove cost $35. That was real money at the time; my job paid $50 a week. Even today, if you hold the glove to the light just so, you still can make out in the pocket the words which persuaded me to spend my life savings: "Pro Model." On the outside of the glove's thumb, printed carefully in inky block letters is: KINDRED. Big leaguers did it that way.

Had God been kinder to my body, which is to say had He arranged for bigger pieces in some places and smaller pieces in other places, by now I would be a retired big-league shortstop. I became a sportswriter the day my father outran me to first base.

That day I was 17 years old, an age at which young men are sure of nothing and sure of everything. Immortality and omniscience hold sway at twilight only to be replaced the next morning by the certain knowledge that she will never talk to you again. You fool. She's gorgeous. She's smart. She's the only girl who ever kissed you without first waiting for you to get the infield dirt washed away. She said she didn't care how dirty you were; she even seemed to like it because the grime was well earned. "Anybody can be clean," she said. Now, there's a girl to take home to Dad. There's a girl who will understand about old baseball gloves.

One afternoon in the time of my greatness, Dad said he would race me to first base. He was an old man, really old, older than dirt, a decrepit (even balding) gentleman who should have been whittlin' on twigs at the courthouse square instead of daring his speedburner son to a footrace. I have since figured out exactly how old Dad was. He was 47, which is, as I now know, younger than springtime. Dad wore khaki work trousers the day of the race. He had on his carpenter's cap with a stub of a yellow No. 2 pencil stuck upside down under the right side. I took a sly glance at his shoes. They were heavy brown things which he called clodhoppers. On my flying feet were Rawlings' best baseball spikes, the Fleetfoot model, with the tongue flap turned down over the laces the way the big-league players did it.

Practically everything I did as a young man was designed to make me a big-league baseball player: every book I read, every step I ran, every trip to the sporting goods store (where to this day the smell of new baseball gloves is a sensation so pleasurable I find myself standing in front of the display until a fresh-faced young woman — the Red Ringheisens are gone now, replaced it seems by young women in coaching shorts — breaks the spell by saying, "Sir. Oh, sir. Are you looking for someone?").

Because our home sat on one corner of an otherwise vacant block, my father mowed a weedy lot out back, carried away stones, chopped out stumps and put down a ballfield. For home plate we used a concrete block imbedded in the black Illinois soil. During a period when I thought to be a pitcher, Dad contrived to build an aid to my control. He simulated the strike zone by driving wood lathings into the ground and then stretching two strands of twine between the stakes. The twine was tied one at shoulder height and and one at the knees with two more pieces of string set 17 inches wide to connect the top and bottom strands. A strike, then, was any pitch inside the twine rectangle. (Much later I saw a newsreel film of the old Brooklyn Dodgers working out under the stern eye of the genius Branch Rickey; his pitchers threw at a stringed rectangle. Until someone persuades me otherwise, I will believe Rickey, on his way to St. Louis one day, stopped by and asked Dad if he'd had any good ideas lately; that's when Dad took the Mahatma out back.)

As his father had done for him, my father pitched corn cobs to me at bat. Anyone who has ever tried to hit a thrown corn cob knows the cobs are dark and erratic in their flight. You might as well try to hit a bumblebee in a hurricane. We did this in the evenings after Dad came home from work; I would wait by the kitchen window because from there I could see his truck raising a dust storm on the road from McLean. To work on my fielding, I hurled a golf ball against our concrete porch steps and dared the ricocheting pellet to elude my glove. I was, in those moments, Pee Wee Reese. There was a railroad track by our house; I took a broken bat up there and hit rocks from the track bed for hours to make my wrists stronger. You needed strong wrists to play in the big leagues. I had read that somewhere.

I read about Stan Musial of the St. Louis Cardinals. The great left-handed hitter of the 1940s and '50s had a curious batting stance in which his back was nearly turned to the pitcher. He hit from a deep crouch as well, and the effect was such that someone described Musial at bat as "a small boy looking around a corner." That was good enough for me. Though I was a natural right-handed hitter, I thought perhaps I had untapped power from the left side, particularly if I used a deep crouch with my back nearly turned to the pitcher.

What happened in the Musial stance is painful to recount even in middle age. I did an unusual thing when a ball was thrown at me. I stood there and let it hit me. I couldn't get out of the way. The paralysis, I now know, was symptomatic of what kinesiologists might call a neuro-motor deficiency; the nerves send a message which the muscles receive in garbled form the next day. Such a deficiency suggests a low ceiling on the heights to which an athlete can aspire. That was too complex an insight, and too real a summation of my athletic dreams, to have been made at age 17. On the other hand, a footrace with your father is a simple thing.

We raced one evening at the ballpark down the street from home. I should have known bettter. On a bookcase in my study, I have two blue ribbons which my father won at a school track meet in Logan County, Illinois. The ribbons are in shreds now, but if you put the pieces together you can see the year, 1928, when he was 16, and you can see he won both the 220- and 440-yard dashes. I remember his being proud of one thing. He high-jumped over a bar one day and walked back under it. Knowing some of this and yet knowing that no doddering carpenter could outrun a future major-league shortstop, indeed the next Pee Wee Reese, I suddenly found myself a step behind the old fellow when we sprinted away from home plate. Dad beat me to first base by that step and part of another. As we caught our breath on the outfield grass, I did that afternoon what any 17-year-old immortal would have done.

Without hesitation and with no remorse whatsoever, I lied. Though both of us knew the truth, I said, "Next time, I won't let you win."

The truth was plain. Either Dad was the world's fastest geezer, or, o diary, I wasn't so quick after all.

That afternoon I decided that maybe, possibly, even probably, I should make at least tentative plans to earn a living at something other than big-league ball. I was small and only ordinarily strong. Adding slow to that mix didn't make me a better prospect. Had Stan Musial been traded to the cursed Cubs, I could not have been more depressed.

As I said a few minutes ago, I am wondering something.

I am wondering why our games have this hold on us.

A grown man keeps his old ball glove where he can see it every day. Nearly 30 years later, he slips his hand into the A2000 and feels young enough to go deep in the hole and throw out anyone, even his fleetfooted father. Why?

Once a benchwarming end at Whittier College, Richard Nixon later suggested plays to the Washington Redskins. An offensive guard at Eureka College, Ronald Reagan says games are good because they're clean hate. (Including halfback Dwight Eisenhower and the center Gerald Ford, every Republican president lately played football as a kid. I'm not sure what the trend means, but Lyndon Johnson once said, "The trouble with Ford is he played too many years without a helmet.")The Spanish philosopher George Santayana said in the 1920s that his three favorite things about America were our kindness, our jazz bands and our football. Historian Jacques Barzun said anyone who would understand the heart and mind of America first must learn baseball.

The appeal of our games is literally sensational. The action resounds against our senses, even the sense of touch as applause and cheers vibrate against our chests. The appeal is increased by being cerebral as well. Sports engages our whole being. "Games are beautiful in their complexity, their rhythm, as well as in the beauty of their players," wrote the Rev. Timothy S. Healy, president of Georgetown University. "The ancient Greeks knew that it was a good thing for all of us to watch beauty, above all when that beauty involved movement, suddenness and improvisation. . . . Watching anyone do anything well enlarges the soul."

On a spring night in 1988 Larry Bird of the Boston Celtics had the basketball in his hands. He was about to do something very well indeed. With a game to be won or lost, he did what you thought couldn't be done — except by him. A man did a thing nearly impossible, and you expected him to do it. Of how many people can such a thing be said? That, oh no, it can't be done but, oh yes, wait a second and Larry'll do it. He had the basketball in his hands — this against the Atlanta Hawks (no need to limit Bird by details; it could have been anytime, anyone, any game) — and what he did next was throw in a lurching, stumbling, wrong-handed hook shot to put the Celtics ahead for good. He did it this way . . .

Bird had no room to move, so good was the defense. Cliff Levingston of Atlanta pressed his body against Bird's, the men 20 feet from the basket, with their backs to it, out on the right side of the Boston Garden parquet floor. Score tied, 90-all. Playoff tied, three games apiece. There were eight minutes to play, and there would be another 54 points; still, Bird's work would mark this as a sweet spot in time, for after he did it the Celtics always were in the lead. With no room to move, yet knowing that move he must — "It always comes back to Larry," his coach would say — Bird took a long, reaching first step to Levingston's right side.

Because Bird is slower in movement than most great basketball players, he depends on guile and, to a lesser extent, on strength. However efficient Levingston's defense was, it had no answer for all of Bird's offense. To stop Bird's long-distance shooting, Levingston had to be up on him. The risk of such defense is plain. Bird then is given the opportunity to step past the defender if the defender makes even the smallest error in judgment. In this case, Levingston made no error; he played wonderful defense against a man every NBA player respects with the game to be won or lost. ("Times at the end of big games with Larry, you're staring into the eyes of an assassin," Dominique Wilkins said.) Levingston is a 6-foot-7 leaper so quick into the air that his presence denied Bird the outside jumper. By positioning and footwork, the defender kept such balance that he also denied Bird any dribble toward the basket.

But not everything can be denied. If convention fails, the great ones go for invention. "Every time a basketball player takes a step," John McPhee wrote in his 1965 essay on Bill Bradley, "an entire new geometry of action is created around him. In ten seconds, with or without the ball, a good player may see perhaps a hundred alternatives and, from them, make half a dozen choices as he goes along. A great player will see even more alternatives and will make more choices." Of Bradley's reverse pivot — the move favored by Bird in serious situations because it presents so many possibilities: the spin move around the defender, the fall-away jumper, the fake and pass followed by a cut to the basket for the ball given back — McPhee wrote that Bradley, by continuing his dribble to the basket, often made the defender "look like a pedestrian who has leaped to get out of the way of a speeding car."

Nothing so elegant, nothing so pure for Larry Bird this time. With a spin move and one reaching step to Levingston's right, Bird didn't so much put down a dribble as he pushed it ahead of him; not putting the ball on the floor at his feet, but tossing it ahead and relying on the centrifugal force of his spin to take him to a meeting place with the ball, maybe five feet past Levingston. Bird chased after the lonely ball, lunged after it, stumbling as if about to land on his nose. Had the game meant less, had there been time to do it another way, Bird would never have tried the move; too near impossible for even Larry Bird.

One stumbling step. Two. Three now, the third step taking him into the paint. Bent forward now, falling, desperate. Bill Bradley told McPhee it wasn't necessary to see the basket before you shoot. By a lifetime's work, he said, you come to know every spot on the basketball floor. You see painted lines. You see cracks in the wood. He said, "You develop a sense of where you are."

Stumbling, blind to the basket, bent at the waist, Bird put up a left-handed hook shot (though to call it a hook shot is to give it distinction it lacked; rather, imagine a dogface soldier dragging his hind end through the mud until he is against a sandbagged bunker, where with his head down he stiff-arm lobs in a grenade). Put up softly, Bird's shot banked against the glass, above the painted square, and fell into the basket. Two points. And Bird was fouled. A free throw as well. Three points when anyone else would have had none — three points that turned the game, points hard earned because, as Bird has said, "I'm someone who works for everything he gets."

Three points. One play. One man's life. Larry Bird's mother raised six children as a $2-an-hour short-order cook in French Lick, Indiana. His father had been something of a hotshot kid basketball player until he quit school after the eighth grade. Between drinks, Bird's father was said to be the best piano tuner in French Lick. He killed himself a year after the divorce. The boy was 17. He went from his little nowhere town to the big state school, Indiana University, only to leave the first month when he looked in his roommate's closet and saw all the new clothes he could never have. "The hick from French Lick" (as he called himself, even after making a million or two a year with the Celtics) said he'd never thought much about life after high school. He guessed he would work construction, pour concrete, something. All he cared about was basketball, "but I went to class and did my homework," because he believed it would catch up to you if you didn't do it, even on the basketball court.

"The guy who won't do his schoolwork misses the free throw at the end," Bird once told Tom Callahan of *Time* magazine. "In high school we used to shoot fouls at 6:30 in the morning before class, but one of my best friends never showed up. In the regional finals our senior year, he missed three one-and-ones in a row, and we lost in overtime. I never said nothing to him. I just looked at him, and he knew."

On that spring day of 1988 in Boston Garden, Bird tossed in the stumbling hook shot and by looking at his face you would never have known he had done anything at all, *anything,* let alone this thing so nearly impossible. Beyond a weariness not so much seen as sensed in the dead chill of his face, Bird betrayed no emotion. The face could have been that of a French Lick roofer who had hammered in the 1,765th nail of a 3,000-nail day. Around Bird, the fabulous Boston basketball arena filled with the thunder and screams of partisans. Bird's face revealed neither joy nor relief. John Riggins once explained his policy of no celebrations after touchdowns by saying, "I expect to score." Bird considers it his job to make every shot, however unlikely. It would be no surprise to learn that on summer days in French Lick, on the basketball court at his house, he practiced that running, stumbling, left-handed grenade toss.

Bird's face revealed nothing because, in his mind, nothing had been done yet. To celebrate would be to lie. The game was still to be won; and such work is too important to interrupt it for a smile. Bird wants to win. A man with his losses in life may even need to win. Later in that game Bird made a three-point shot from a spot not a foot away from Atlanta's bench. That made it 112-105 with less than two minutes to play. It was an assassin's killing shot. And still not a flicker of emotion from Bird. *Just go to class. Do the homework. Shoot the fouls at 6:30 in the morning. Don't say nothing to your buddy who screwed up by screwin' off. Just look at him, and he'll know.* Bill Russell, as mean as they come, decided to quit coaching the Celtics when one night he looked around to see who was laughing in the huddle — and discovered it was him. The game had been his way out of dirt poverty. It had given him fame and wealth. These things are not the same as happiness; and perhaps his life as a black man in one of America's virulently racist cities made it impossible for Russell ever to be happy. Then one night it all seemed so . . . foolish. Why should a grown man scream at other grown men over a kid's game which they play in their underwear? At that moment, for Bill Russell, the game became a waste of energy and talent. For one man, the game had become a lie, ugly as all lies.

For Larry Bird, happily, the game is the truth, and with only a modest blush I can write of sports as Keats wrote of an urn . . .

> *"Beauty is truth, truth beauty,"* — *that is all*
> *Ye know on earth, and all ye need to know.*

Ye need to know, too, Pete Rose. The bristly flat-top version of Peter Edward Rose, working on his first thousand hits and determined to be baseball's "first $100,000 singles hitter," spent a day at the Ohio State Fair and a Dayton county fair during the 1969 season. He did a radio show, a TV show and a question-and-answer session with fans. To make the Cincinnati-Columbus-Dayton swing and get back for that night's game, Rose had been in an airplane, a helicopter, a bus and three automobiles. He sat on the rickety steps of a dank clubhouse in the innards of Crosley Field, a lovely decrepit place. Rose rubbed a ham bone over the barrel of his Louisville Slugger, "to tighten the wood," and then he allowed as to how all the moving around that day had left him tired.

With a wry bow to commercialism, I asked Rose what he'd been selling at the State Fair.

He stopped the bone's movement and said, "Baseball."

Almost two decades later, with Rose in a Buster Brown haircut (heavy on the Grecian Formula) and working toward his 4,000th hit, I asked one of those fantasy questions we dream up when the real questions have been asked a hundred times. "If you could be any player in baseball history," I said, "who would you be?"

Not a second's hesitation preceded Rose's answer, which was, "Me."

What an odd piece of work, Pete Rose. He had a fullback's body, thick in the wrong places for baseball. Some athletes seem above the law of gravity when running, their feet winged; Rose hammered his size 10s against the earth with a Clydesdale's resolve. His face was so rough it seemed the first cut by a rookie sculptor trying for an old bulldog. Rose's speech ran the gamut from coarse to vulgar with an occasional stab at scatology. His wives could have been Roller Derby queens. His first, Karolyn, wore a diamond ring in the shape of Rose's uniform number, 14, and during a stint as a radio sports announcer was heard to say of a Cincinnati Stingers hockey game, "Puck-off is at 7:30."

His rival for attention, Cincinnati catcher Johnny Bench, called Rose "the most selfish player I've ever seen — and we need eight just like him." Nothing you could tell Rose about Rose that Rose didn't know. I once tried. I began, "Did you know that you've had 200 hits in a season seven times — and anybody who ever did that is . . ."

"In the Hall of Fame," Rose finished.

Rose ran to first base on walks. He ran over catchers to score. He slid head-first. ("What could hurt this face? Pretty don't help you hit.") Relief pitcher Tug McGraw said, "If anybody plays harder than Pete Rose, he's gotta be an outpatient."

Ty Cobb used baseball as an instrument of revenge against a world he hated. His mother, by accident apparently, had killed his father as the man, for reasons unknown, tried to climb in her bedroom window. Cobb came to the game as he came to life, a mean curl to his lip. For Rose, as for Bird, his game is sweet life itself.

Late in the classic sixth game of the 1975 World Series — won by Boston on Carlton Fisk's foul-pole home run in the 12th inning — Rose turned to Fisk behind the plate and said, "Ain't it great?" He meant the game they were in. Who else but Rose would have said such a thing at such a time? Who else would have the sense of place and history? He recognized the beauty of the moment even as he helped create its truth. *Ain't it great?* Damn right it's great, and if you open your heart to the games, they will never fail you, for they are solid and true, pure and precious. Scandal and poisonous characters come and go. They change nothing that matters because the games contain truths which are eternal, and it is to those truths that we form our attachments. Al Campanis of the Dodgers spoke of immortality on first seeing the young Sandy Koufax throw; he said, "The hairs came up on my arms. The only other time that happened was when I saw the Sistine ceiling." Novelist W. P. Kinsella wrote, "Within the baselines, anything can happen. Tides can reverse, oceans can open. That's why they say, 'The game is never over until the last man is out.' Colors can change, lives can alter, anything is possible in this gentle, flawless, loving game."

Why sports?

Because we're connected to the games. We're connected in ways we seldom acknowledge and may never understand. We may get no further as a player than the backyard games in which aspirants to Pee Wee Reesedom throw a golf ball against the concrete steps. We may race our fathers one day and discover we're not all we hoped to be. But when we go to the ballpark, the place of our dreams, we feel a connection to the game. We vibrate in tune to the game's eternal

11

rhythms. It all feels right, as few things in life feel all right. The umpire's declaration of balls and strikes, the white lines, the sounds of leather and wood, the dance of teams trading turns at bat — all of it has been so much a part of our lives for so long that we feel warm and safe in its company. We *are* the game in ways that we are few other things. To see Ozzie Smith diving for a ground ball is to feel our bodies crash to earth with his. What Stan Musial did, we had done (well, sort of).

Though we journalists like to strut around in our best new suit of objectivity, everyone knows we are romantics in hot pursuit of subjectivity. Certainly I am not so vain as to deny the appearance of objectivity in my reports; after all, when dullness is called for, I can fake it as well as any political scribe. But I am here now to tell as near to the truth as I am capable of doing. And the truth is, I love our games because they touch my soul in ways no preacher's sermon ever has; they lift me up by showing me how good we can be, and by that I mean good in every way: morally, spiritually, physically. To see Dale Murphy in motion, that great, angular body sprinting across a timelessly beautiful field — to see Murphy running down a fly ball in the gap is to know that God's in His heaven and well pleased. "Dale's still got the wheels," God'll say to a buddy. "Let's check in on Michael Jordan now. I sent him some new shoes the other day."

Murphy is a Mormon, baptized at age 19. "I knew there was more to this existence than just day-to-day playing baseball. Playing baseball's never been work for me. I feel that's one of the things I've found. You're not here by accident."

"What I'm wondering," I said, "is about guys who testify, testify, testify. Some guys get a fat pitch and they say, 'I thank God for that fat pitch.' That seems out of place. I don't hear you saying that."

"There was a quote in *The Sporting News*. 'Dale Murphy says God isn't really interested in batting averages.' I meant a lot of things by that. He's not interested in batting averages, obviously. He's more interested in what kind of fathers or people or husbands we are. He still is concerned with what you do with your abilities. As far as baseball is concerned, it is a God-given talent because why can't everybody do it? Why can't I write? When I get out there, some of that stuff I do is my fault or my doing. But ultimately, the ability, the hand-eye coordination, the gift of sight — I really feel it's given to us."

I write about different sports in different tones of voice. For golf, I am soft and pastoral. Football makes me angry. Basketball quickens the heart. Boxing scares me. These moods then are reflected in what I write. As natural and predictable as that may sound, the connection never occurred to me until I'd been writing for 20 years, until one day I tried to figure out why I feel so good at the Masters and so lousy at the Super Bowl. The golfer Mac O'Grady says he is awed by the "beautiful biophilia" at Augusta National (he defined that as the sensory perceptions created by the flora, fauna and geography of the place). There's that. But not that alone. Golf is poetry, football is war. I like poetry better.

So the games changed me, even as a spectator, even as an objective reporter. They changed me by seducing me into their rhythms. It seems only natural and predictable, then, that the games would have touched me in more substantive ways which similarly have gone unnoticed. If I am changed by the casual rhythms of golfers and the simple geography of 200 acres, then how am I changed by the senses of order, fairness and justice which are the taken-for-granted underpinnings of our games? For the better, I would hope. Perhaps consciously but much more likely by simple exposure to goodness, we come away from games feeling better about ourselves. We see Greg Norman striding down the fairways at Augusta, striding so purposefully, that great white shock of hair all but glowing, the man's stride so . . . so *positive* that he seems to be walking not on the fairway but above it, lifted up there by the power of his talent. We see Norman and we draw from his example a feeling of his strength and excellence; and we put that feeling to our own uses, perhaps in work as difficult as a mother's rearing a child, perhaps even in the writing of a sentence. We would be as good in every way as our games have shown it is possible to be. Not to brag on myself, but I have been a very good boy lately; I have stayed in out of the rain, I have come to a complete stop at most stop signs and I have torn at the perforation when my creditors so ordered. For this, and more, Dale Murphy and Greg Norman get some credit.

The world, an imperfect place, seeks harmony above all. Our games have it already. Rhythm and harmony flow from order, and games demand order which is absolute. The German sociologist Johan Huizinga in *Homo Ludens*, a study of play, wrote, "Inside the playground an absolute and peculiar order reigns. Here we come across another, very positive feature of play; it creates order, *is* order." Huizinga believes order and games are inseparable, that they are mutually dependent and mutually nurturing. One cannot exist without creating the other.

The games are played before our eyes according to rules we've known forever, catechisms memorized in childhood, an order we accept without question because it has always been good to us. Unlike laws, the foundation rules of our games are immutable. (Baseball once tinkered with the height of the pitcher's mound, letting home-field groundskeepers tailor it to their pitchers' preference, often raising it past the rule's limit. Batting averages fell. In 1968 Carl Yastrzemski won a batting title at .301. Well, enough. Baseball began to enforce its rule on mound height. As mounds were lowered, averages climbed to proper standards. Blessed order was restored to the universe. It can be argued that not even the Curt Flood and Andy Messersmith legal wars changed baseball as much as the seemingly trivial act of lowering the mound. "Ninety feet between bases," Red Smith said, "is the nearest to perfection that man has yet achieved." You don't add an earring to the Mona Lisa. You don't tamper with baseball's rules.)

Truth is all we want from this world. Finding it at the ballpark gives us reason to think we can find it somewhere else.

Why sports?

Kennedy's presidency fired me with youthful idealism. Even as I walked the sidelines at football games, I wanted to walk with the brave men and women of the civil rights movement. I wanted to be in Chicago, but not with the Cubs. Give me the Democratic convention; give me the rapscallion Richard Daley, not the cuddly Ernie Banks. My generation slogged through Vietnam. I took my pen and notebook to an eastern Kentucky mountain village named Kingdom Come for a high school basketball game.

Kingdom Come High School was a little box of a sandstone building, three stories high. The basketball team played upstairs on a court so tiny that players driving for a layup were in danger of falling out a window (which explained the safety net of chicken wire tacked over the windows).

Kingdom Come. The school took its name from a children's book, *The Little Shepherd of Kingdom Come*. I asked the team's star, Junior Halcomb, what it was like to play on the third floor with chicken wire over the windows and the court so tiny that the out-of-bounds stripes were painted right against the walls. "Hit's hail, man," Junior said.

We ate that night at the coach's home. Jerry Coots, 22, said Kingdom Come wasn't much of a place, typical of Appalachia where some people were poor and the rest poorer. When Lyndon Johnson declared his war on poverty, he helicoptered into eastern Kentucky for a photo opportunity. Only 30 percent of the fathers in Kingdom Come's valley had jobs. Boys left school early for the Army or they caught a bus to Cincinnati or Detroit or Dayton, anyplace north, just to get out.

While we talked, I heard an odd noise in the room. The noise came every two or three seconds, like someone breathing, except this sounded like dirt rattling through a sifter. I looked around the table and saw that the sound came from Coots's father, a small man made to seem smaller by the curvature of his back between his shoulders. A coal miner's back. He had spent his life bent double bringing up coal from three-foot-high mine shafts under a mountain. His terrible and terrifying work never got Mr. Coots enough money to move away from Kingdom Come. What he got, by breathing coal dust, was black lung disease.

Kingdom Come. I learned something there. Twenty years later, I can hear the old coal miner breathing. I went to the mountain to write about basketball. I left having written about the suffocating terror of no escape except the next Greyhound out of town. I wrote about a place named Kingdom Come which a young boy called hell.

Ever since then, from Kingdom Come to the Kremlin, of heroes, fools and other dreamers, I have written about sports as sports touches people. Sports is the human spirit made real. A professor of religion, Michael Novak, author of *The Joy of Sports*, has written, "Most of what Americans know about the humanistic traditions — about excellence in act, about discipline, about community, about unity of body and will and spirit — they learn first-hand from their experiences in sport."

Ordinary people in ordinary places teach us that courage is not limited to soldiers in Da Nang and marchers in Selma. Jerry Coots's father, when I asked about coal dust in his lungs, said, "Got my children through school, got grandchildren on the way. I'm all set." So the dust didn't bother him? "Didn't say that, now did I? But what you can't do nothin' about, you let it lay."

Why sports?

To see Ozzie Smith at work. The St. Louis Cardinals' shortstop should work in a tux. The man is music. He is soft lyrics and a gentle melody. Put him in a tux and give him some tap shoes for the dance at second base. "We're here to entertain," Smith says. "Not hot dogs. It's a flair. Flair more than anything else."

As a child, Ozzie Smith didn't have a ball glove. He slipped his hand inside a brown paper bag. He bounced a rubber ball off a wall. Sometimes he would lie on the floor, toss the ball high and see if he could catch it with his eyes closed. (He could.) As a big-leaguer, Smith once leaped over a diving left fielder to catch a fly ball for "my second-best play ever."

The best play came on a ground ball hit by Jeff Burroughs in 1978. "Burroughs hit a ball up the middle," Smith said. "I took four or five steps in that direction. That tells me I have to dive." As he left his feet, flying toward right field, Smith saw the Burroughs ground ball take a bad hop. It bounced to the left, going behind him.

"My glove is gone now," Smith said, meaning it was useless against a ball behind him. So Smith threw his bare hand up and back where the bad-hop grounder soon would bounce over him for a single. "All I can do now is hope the ball sticks in my hand . . . ."

Here Smith smiled at the wonders of man.

". . . which it did."

Then Smith bounced up off the dirt. (No one ever dove for a ball and bounced up as quickly as Smith, who says he has studied his body action on video tape and discovered that he arches his back so that as his chest collides with the Earth his feet and arms will snap down and pop him up, like fresh toast in the morning.) And he threw Burroughs out.

"Manifest destiny," Smith said with a wink. "Some things are meant to be," and though the amazing shortstop played with words there, who would deny that something mysterious, something outside us, is at work here? The late Kentucky basketball coach Adolph Rupp said of All-America guard Louie Dampier, "God taught Louie how to shoot. I just took credit for it."

Tom Callahan, *Time* magazine's sports columnist: "There's something there that buoys people. I take sports seriously. I like to be funny about it, wisecracks and all. But basically I take it seriously. It's not nuclear physics. You always remember that. But if you write about sports long enough, you're constantly coming back to the point that something buoys people, something makes you feel better for having been there. Something of value is at work there, and it's a value beyond the cheap, tawdry value ABC and Calvin Griffith and all the money-changers put on it. Something is hallowed here. I think that something is excellence."

It's Ted Williams at bat. It's Vince Lombardi and Bob Knight creating teams of simple purity. It's Larry Bird inventing a wonder when a wonder is the only answer. It's Walter Payton running, Ozzie Smith diving. It's Muhammad Ali floating like a butterfly. It's ordinary people doing extraordinary things and extraordinary people doing unimagined things. We see these things done by men, the Sistine ceiling painted by a man, and we know, as surely as we know when we read Frank Deford's book on his daughter Alex, who was a piece of God's beauty dying before her father's eyes — we know at these moments that we are part of something greater than ourselves.

Like Dickens's novel *Nicholas Nickleby* but unlike so much else, our games have a moral center, an identifiable and undeniable sense of right and wrong. Winners and losers are decided by merit, not by feckless politicians or by witless fate. (Caprice raises her pretty head often enough to keep the underdogs full of hope. Bless 'em all.) In our games, talent has something to do with winning; even fairness, so little noticed these days, has its say. Our games have agreed-upon rules and are enforced by judges in whom we place total faith (holding back only the right to boo the purblind incompetents).

Where can we get a better deal than that? A drama filled with Truth, Justice and Beauty — all played out under familiar rules, right before our eyes, with no script, with improvisation the thrilling norm. Our games are spontaneous combustions, each set off by events unimaginable until we see them done by a Larry Bird or a Michael Jordan. Anyone who saw it will forever see Bob Welch bringing fast balls to Reggie Jackson in the 1978 World Series, power against power, a test of strength, talent and will as searching as anything Shakespeare asked of Macduff. I can still see John Riggins pull his body from Don McNeal's grasp and outrun every little man to the end zone. Riggins at 240 pounds, Riggins flying. To see this massive sprinter win a Super Bowl game with an incomparable, unrepeatable and unimagined run — a run that was as much a product of the man's life as of the moment, a run done before our eyes under the rules of good and bad which we learned as children and took with us into the world — to see John Riggins's run was to come away from that football game as the British essayist Bernard Levin came away from a production of *Nicholas Nickleby*:

"Not merely delighted but strengthened, not just entertained but uplifted, not only affected but changed."

Dad

November 23, 1978

Atlanta, Illinois

It was a Sunday, 15 years ago, the Sunday before Thanksgiving. Down by a twisting creek, off in a flat and treeless corner of a farmer's pasture, a handful of men had come together, as they did every Sunday before Thanksgiving, for a turkey shoot.

The men carried old guns, the kind they call muzzle-loaders. They shot at bull's-eye targets set up by the creek, and on this day, chill and still in the country, the report of a shot rang across the hills. In an ambulance, coming over the hills toward the creek, the man heard the shots, and he smiled.

The man brought these shooters together over the years. There weren't many, no more than 20. But every Sunday, they came to shoot their muzzle-loaders. If it snowed, they wore gloves and cursed the weather, but they came anyway. They shooed away the cows down by the creek, and they shot until the daylight, or the coffee, ran out.

The man who started them shooting was always the first there and the last to leave. He brought the targets and took them home. He kept them in his garage and he kept them in his house, and, finally, he built a room inside his house for the guns and targets and the pounds of lead (he made bullets on his wife's stove).

The man had always been a sports fan. In grade school he was a runner and high jumper. Once, he was proud to say, he made it over the high jump bar and was able to walk back under it without stooping. He played baseball, too, and basketball, but not much. His father died at 41, and he went to work when he finished the eighth grade. He drove trucks for a while, and he was in the Army

19

for a while, and then he was a carpenter.

The man was caught up by guns when he moved his wife, son and daughter into a big, old house and, cleaning it, found a rusting handgun. Later he began buying the muzzle-loaders, one here for $10, one there for $25, and, tired of driving a hundred miles every Sunday to shoot, he made up his own muzzle-loading club.

The man ran advertisements in shooting journals, setting down the dates for his club's shoots; he took to wearing a buckskin jacket when he shot, and he always wore a black mountaineer's hat with a pheasant feather stuck in the band; he made, with his own hands, muzzle-loading guns of such precision and beauty that men offered him hundreds of dollars for them, all the while knowing the man would as soon sell his right arm as his guns.

Every spring the man made the pilgrimage to Friendship, Indiana, 300 miles from home, for the national championship muzzle-loading matches. He drove a pickup truck, and his wife sat in the front with him, and his son and daughter rode in the back in a cabin he built for them. He entered the bench-rest matches, those in which the shooters put their guns on a table to shoot them. He never won, but he never cared, and in the winter, looking at his magazines, he would announce to his family the dates for the spring nationals.

And then, 15 years ago, when the doctors told him he had cancer and told him he had two weeks to live, no more, the man thought of his turkey shoot down by the creek. He would go, he said, to the turkey shoot if he had to go in an ambulance. And on that Sunday before Thanksgiving, he went.

Coming over a hill in the pasture, the ambulance rolling silently over a path worn dusty by the shooters' cars over the years, the man heard the guns of his friends and he smiled. He wore his black mountaineer's hat (his wife once caught him unawares and took his picture when he wore white longjohns and the black hat). And when they lifted him out of the ambulance on a stretcher, he told his son he wanted to sit up, so he could see.

He hadn't spoken in the ambulance during a half-hour's drive to the shooting range. Once there, he laughed and talked and had his picture taken with his friends and family making a semicircle on either side of his stretcher.

He didn't talk going back to the hospital that Sunday before Thanksgiving, and he died on Tuesday, and I thought of all this again on another Sunday before Thanksgiving when, late at night, my son, 16, said, "I love you, daddy." That's what I said, on that ambulance ride 15 years ago, to my father.

Walter Payton

January 11, 1988

Chicago

Sweetness no more. Walter Payton is gone. The ball last settled into his hands on a little pass when the Bears asked him to do one more miracle, after all these years one more miracle, a little one, a matter of eight yards for a first down in the last minute. And when Payton made seven yards — forced out of bounds by tacklers closing down on him — it was over, a man's lifework done.

A life's work, running with a football in your hands? Yes, if you're Walter Payton. If you came from the hardscrabble nowhere of Mississipppi, if in 13 pro football years you became the greatest runner ever, if your dignity graced the game more than any game deserved, then, yes, a life's work not only well done but uniquely done, a work of immortality.

Whatever the score on this icicle of a January day, it doesn't matter. Nor does it matter that the Redskins and not the Bears have moved nearer the Super Bowl. We have seen the last day's football work of Walter Payton, a runner of heavenly gait, a man they called "Sweetness," whose gentle manner and lilting voice belied the iron of his will and body.

A yard short, the game lost, Walter Payton walked off a football field for the last time. Players from both sides touched him, no words needed, for everyone knew this was it, the 13 years done, Payton retiring at age 33, a young man but still an old runner, the quickness that delivered so many miracles now gone.

The game ended around him. Payton alone stayed on the Bears' bench. In massive old Soldier Field with its Roman columns, a single man sat on the bench. Payton let his hands fall together between his knees. He tugged at the fingertips of the gritty gloves a ballcarrier wears on wintry days by the Chicago lakeshore. He sat with his head bowed, and from behind him came the voices of fans: "We love you, Walter." . . . "Thank you, Walter." An old man raged against the dying of the light, "One more year, Walter. You can still do it."

Walter Payton, a millionaire, has talked about buying an NFL franchise. The Bears have invited him into the front office. There's a world out there for him. So when he saw the sidelines of time and age closing down on him, he decided it was time to go. He shares the NFL rushing record of nine straight 100-yard games; he has done it 77 times, but not once in his last 20 games.

He had 85 yards this day on 18 carries. For a step here, a step there, the years fell away, and we saw what Walter Payton had been when every step was taken with a winged foot. This day's work done, a life's work done, the workman sat on his team's bench at the side of an empty field in a great stadium. He would say, "I didn't want to hurry the moment."

From somewhere behind him came a woman's shout, "Chicago loves you, Walter." And he rose to leave, with 25,000 people chanting in farewell, "Wal-ter . . . Wal-ter."

As if by habit, Payton moved onto the field, walking near the hashmark, one last time moving toward the end zone. He never looked up, never raised his eyes, until he entered a dark tunnel. Then he blinked against tears. He had left records everywhere. Now he had left himself behind. Sweetness no more.

He came to his locker in a corner of the Bears' room. He sat in his uniform. He still wore his helmet. He let his head fall back against a wall, and a teammate said, "You OK?"

Payton's tiny voice, his eyes closed, still in his uniform: "I'm just taking my time taking it off. This is the last time I take it off."

An old Chicago newspaperman, Bill Gleason, Payton's friend, sat by him. Of two dozen reporters there, none spoke. Then Payton said to Gleason, "You going to miss me?"

"Absolutely," Gleason said. "What I'm going to remember is how much fun you were."

Payton said, "That's the main reason I was playing, to have fun."

He later would stand in front of a press conference and say, "The last 13 years for me have been a lot of good times and a lot of bad times. There were times when I wanted to quit and times when there'd be no quit in me. . . . The bottom line is, God blessed me. I've truly been blessed."

Ready to leave the locker room a last time, Walter Payton put his gear into a bag slowly. He clicked shut the clasp of a watch heavy with diamonds. He touched his neck with a spray of perfume, and then, with a little laugh, sweetness indeed, he sprayed a few puffs of the stuff on the sportswriters at his side, the perfume battling Bill Gleason's cigar.

Ben Crenshaw

April 16, 1984

Augusta, Georgia

His boy would win the Masters and Charlie Crenshaw loved it. He's an old man now, 70, who has seen his boy hurt too many times. Ben Crenshaw was to be the next Nicklaus. He won the first pro tournament he played. But in a decade of frustration, he never won a major championship. No Opens, no PGAs, no Masters. His marriage fell apart and Ben blamed himself because he gave his heart more to the game than to his marriage. His swing fell apart and a hundred friends tried to help put it back together. Then, late on a lovely Sunday afternoon, Charlie Crenshaw knew his boy would win the Masters and the old man wept.

Spring days die softly here. Sunlight fades to the pink of a baby's cheeks. When the sun goes down behind a stand of strong pine trees, the dying light moves across the ground in random patterns that, if we are lucky, paint a picture we will remember always. Such a light, filtered through the pines, fell across Ben Crenshaw's face shortly after 5 o'clock Sunday afternoon. The light touched Ben's blond hair. For a moment, he was golden.

He had won the Masters. There were three holes to play, but he had won it. He had a three-stroke lead. He had made a 12-foot birdie putt at the 15th hole. There his father, Charlie, a Texas lawyer, beefy and rough-cut, allowed himself a small celebration. Walking behind the huge gallery, walking alone, he threw his fists wide, for just a second, and then clasped his hands behind his back again, walking on.

Only three holes to go then, and Charlie Crenshaw stood by a

25

pine tree a dozen yards from the 16th green. It's a 170-yard hole with a pond guarding its left side. "Keep this one dry, baby," Charlie Crenshaw said. He said it aloud, but he said it to no one. He said it to himself and he said it to his boy 170 yards away. Ben Crenshaw would win his first Masters unless, by his own failings, he lost it.

He had lost other big ones he wanted. He came to his game loving it. He ran his hands over maps of the Old Course at St. Andrews, where the game was born. He knows about Old Tom Morris and Young Tom Morris, Francis Ouimet and Bobby Jones. He can show you the spot at Augusta where Gene Sarazen did it. But it seemed, in the cruelest turn, that this gentle little man loved too much. Maybe it would be easier to win if he came to work stone ignorant rather than knowing where the footprints led.

"When you lose the PGA in a playoff . . . when you hit it into the water on the 71st hole of the U.S. Open and miss a playoff by a shot . . . when you double-bogey the 71st hole of the British Open to lose that tournament, you start wondering."

Ben Crenshaw said those words an hour after winning the Masters this time. He spoke of 1975 in the U.S. Open at Medinah, 1979 in the PGA at Oakland Hills and '79 in the British Open at Royal Sandwich. Six times in the majors, twice in the Masters, Crenshaw has finished second.

"You start wondering if you can hold yourself together."

Keep this one dry, baby.

Charlie Crenshaw stood by the 16th hole. His boy put his tee shot on dry land. Then Ben Crenshaw walked to the green. With thousands of people applauding, with the sweet sound washing over him, with the dying sunlight golden on his face, Ben Crenshaw smiled. And his daddy, next to a pine tree behind a thousand people, said, "It's great when they cheer for your kid like that. Man."

With his heavy hands, Charlie Crenshaw wiped away tears.

This was it. "Lady Fate or Dame Fortune takes somebody by the hand and leads them through," Charlie Crenshaw said to a reporter who found him in the crowd. "She's been with Ben all week. He's hit shots through trees and out of trees. . . . He's had the greatest putting round I've ever seen. That one at 10, my Lord. . . . When David Graham made two putts in the '79 PGA just to stay in the playoff, to keep Ben from being a champion, it couldn't have been David Graham by himself. That lady just has to be with you."

Charlie Crenshaw laughed. "That lady has been all over Ben so many times this week."

At the 10th hole, Crenshaw had made a 60-foot putt that broke eight feet, rolling on an arc of improbable design to an intersection with the hole, a dot in the great distance. If Graham beat Crenshaw in '79 with two playoff putts, Crenshaw beat Tom Kite here with that 60-foot improbability. Kite botched the 10th hole five minutes later and dumped a killing shot into Rae's Creek 15 minutes after that.

When the 60-footer at the 10th fell, Ben Crenshaw said he thought, as his father had, "Maybe this is my day." This is what they wanted for 20 years. Charlie, never more than a hacker himself, bought his son a putter for his 15th birthday at home in Austin. Ben still uses it, though with a new shaft ("It got broken when I was 16. It ran up a tree or something").

This is the day Charlie Crenshaw thought of two years ago when his boy was in trouble. Ben had fallen to 83rd on the money list. The boy who would be king was a sad commoner. A hundred friends, earned by his humility and kindnesses, tried to help. He tried a hundred new swings. Then he tried what always had worked. He talked to his father.

Charlie Crenshaw remembers the talk. "I told him the Lord gave him his swing. Just like He gives a gift to a great artist or a pianist. I told him, 'Just go up and hit it, don't analyze it.'"

So in 1983 Ben Crenshaw won his first tournament in three years. And now, at age 32, he has won the Masters. Ben Crenshaw stood in the dusk at a victory ceremony. He thanked his friends. "If I could cut out a piece of my heart and give it to you, I would," he said. And he said, "I am so happy my father is here. I am very fortunate to have the father I do. He's a gentleman and I have tried to live the life he would want me to."

Ben Crenshaw's last piece of golf work Sunday was to sign his scorecard in a tent beside the 18th green. As he came out of the tent, the champion saw his father and walked to him, arms open. They hugged for a long, long time, with the boy burying his face in his father's shoulder.

Bill Veeck

January 4, 1986

To sit with Bill Veeck was to enjoy man at his fullest. He was bright and brave, laughing and conniving, in love with life. In the summer of 1977, when Veeck last ran the White Sox, he sat in the dim light of the ballpark saloon. With both hands he lifted his piratical wooden leg onto a table. He had no use for any newfangled prosthesis that comes with a foot. "See this?" he said, and he meant the blunt end of his oak limb. "Me and Long John Silver. Romantic rogues, the two of us."

His voice came as a train in the night. It rumbled at a distance, far away, until suddenly it thundered past. "Baseball is the least changed thing in our society," Veeck said in that saloon that night. He had a beer in hand and another waited its turn. "In a confused and confusing world in which the underpinnings are less stable than shifting sand, baseball is an island of stability."

By then, at 63, Veeck was deaf in one ear and wore a hearing aid in the other. Sometimes he spoke at a roar because he wanted to hear what he said; most times it was out of passion. He had no interest in being polite; he considered politeness an absence of passion. He smoked four packs of cigarettes a day, he drank a case of beer, he read both Shakespeare and sportswriters ("I am a dispose-all for the written word") — and he worked at baseball with a passion alien to most men.

"These owners today are not career baseball operators," said Veeck, a lifer whose stiff-collared father ran the Cubs from 1917 to '33. "These are successful businessmen from other fields who get into baseball for personal publicity, to buff and burnish their egos."

29

At this point, Veeck's off-center smile rearranged the folds and crevices of his wasted sage's face and he said, "Of course, no one at this table has an overwhelming desire to put a high sheen on his ego. Or on his wooden leg."

Red Smith wrote lovingly of Veeck. The maverick "traduced, debauched and desecrated the national game," Smith wrote, in such a way that the St. Louis Browns' attendance rose from 247,131 to 518,796 in one season. No gimmick was beneath Veeck, who put on Cabdrivers Night, Bartenders Night and Witches Night.

In 1951 Veeck signed the midget. Eddie Gaedel, an actor, was 3-foot-7 and 65 pounds. He met with Veeck the day before the game to talk about the gig. Gaedel felt an urge to enlarge his role and even hefted a toy bat as if eager to get at major league pitching.

"Eddie," Veeck said, "I'm going to be on the roof with a high-powered rifle, watching every move you make. If you so much as look like you're going to swing, I'm going to shoot you dead."

For a radio sponsor's birthday, Veeck wheeled a seven-foot cake to home plate. And out popped Gaedel, to everyone's amusement, a midget in a Brownies' uniform with the number "1/8" on the back. Later, to the astonishment of all, Gaedel came to bat in the ballgame, the only midget ever to appear in a big league game.

"His strike zone was just visible to the naked eye," Veeck wrote. "I picked up a ruler and measured it for posterity. It was 1 1/2 inches."

On four pitches, perhaps mindful of Veeck's rifle, Gaedel drew a walk.

Veeck's teams won two league championships and one World Series. In 1947 he signed the first black player in the American League, Larry Doby. (This after failing three years earlier to make the Philadelphia Phillies an all-black team; baseball historian Robert Smith called Veeck "a fast-buck type who had no patience with prejudice").

Veeck owned and/or operated the Indians ('46-49), the Browns ('51-53) and the White Sox ('59-61, '76-80). The first of baseball's franchise moves — the Boston Braves to Milwaukee — was engineered in 1953 by a cabal which feared Veeck would move the

Browns there first. The ripples of that move still wiggle across the sporting pond.

Two months ago, Veeck savaged players who testified under immunity from prosecution that they had used cocaine. He demanded that commissioner Peter Ueberroth act against these players who, he said, had "a quarter's worth of character."

Veeck's leg was hurt in World War II when an artillery piece recoiled against it. He has lived in pain and sickness, a man keeping score of sodium pentathol shots ("Thirty-two, last count"). A succession of operations moved up the leg. He carved a hole into his first peg leg for use as an ashtray.

"Veeck has measured out his life by what was left of his right leg," Tom Boswell wrote when Veeck retired four years ago. On the tombstone, Boswell said, the epitaph should read, "Cause of Death: Life."

Bill Veeck died Thursday, 71 years old. He lived them all.

Jeff Blatnick

Th   here was a half-moon gash on Jeff Blatnick's left wrist. He
      held the wrist out to a buddy. "If I get rabies," Blatnick said,
      "it's from the Greek." These things happen in Greco-
Roman wrestling, where strong men use all their tools, even the
dental ones, to grab hold of whatever they can. "But this isn't
anything. You should have seen what the Greek did to the Yugo."

Jeff Blatnick floated in the ether of joy. The Greek could have
bitten off his ear and it wouldn't have mattered now. Blatnick had
won an Olympic gold medal, and now he smiled as photographers
asked his father and mother to bend down, to put their faces
alongside their son's.

"Jeff, I'll bite your ear this way," said his mother, Angela.

The cauliflowered wrestler hugged her. "I've got bad enough
ears."

His father, Carl, whispered into a gnarled ear, "You're a great
guy."

Jeff Blatnick put his arms around his parents. "This is
unbelievable."

You can have Carl Lewis and his megabucks fantasies. You can
have Nelson Vails, who wins a silver medal in cycling and pro-
nounces himself available for American Express commercials. You
can admire their talents and respect their works. You can have a
hundred Carl Lewises. One Jeff Blatnick is a better deal.

Athletes know the electrical system of their bodies. Pain speaks
to them over the wire. "Get off me," a knee says, "or I'll lock up and
then we'll be in a fine mess." As intimately as mapmakers know

rivers and ridges, athletes know the rise and fall of muscle and bone. In 1982 Jeff Blatnick knew something was wrong in his neck.

There were lumps in his neck on the right side, above the clavicle. The other night, now an Olympic champion, he pulled down the collar of his warm-up jacket. "Here." His fingers touched a scar four inches long. The doctors began their work there.

Jeff Blatnick is 27 years old. He'd made the 1980 Olympic team. He was an AAU champion. He is a big man, now 236 pounds, who lost only four times in college wrestling. Then in the summer of 1982 doctors did surgery to find out about the lumps in his neck. What they found was cancer. They told him he had Hodgkin's disease, cancer of the lymph nodes.

They removed his spleen. They did biopsies on every organ they could reach. "Experimental," Blatnick said. They sent him home five days later, but they weren't done. They would shoot radioactive stuff through him. For two months, twice a day, they shot the killer rays through a body that had been an an athlete's beautiful creation.

Blatnick couldn't take a shower for two months. The water falling on his skin hurt too much. He had wrestled 300-pound Russians and maybe even Greeks who bite. But that summer, he couldn't take a shower because it hurt too much.

"Honestly, I never felt that sick," he said. "I treated it like I was going to training camp for two months. I'd been on the B team, where we trained just as much as the A team but didn't go to meets. I looked at this thing that way, as camp. I just had to do what they told me to do."

Three weeks after the splenectomy, Blatnick was in the gym. In the whirlpool. Stretching. Moving around. Alive. His older brother had been killed in a motorcycle accident three years before. He wept then, for his brother. But for himself, no tears. It was time to work. Go to camp. Cancer camp.

"Once the zipper effect was gone here . . ."

He drew a line from his stomach toward his navel. That's where the doctors opened a door to get at the spleen. The zippered scar is 13 inches long.

". . . then I still had some pain, but I could start doing things."

In the fall of 1982, Jeff Blatnick drove from his home in Niskayuna, New York, to a wrestling meet in North Dakota. He would try. Sometimes the thrill of victory is nothing next to the thrill of trying. But in North Dakota he heard a message from his body: "Jeff, big fella, we're not ready yet."

The next summer, ready, Blatnick finished third in the U.S. Nationals. "You always have doubts about making it back," he said. "But I always had the dream and I kept hold of that dream."

In these Olympics, he beat the mighty Yugoslavian, Refik Memisevic. For the gold medal he beat the giant Swede, Thomas Johansson. He threw Johansson down, and when Blatnick was announced as the winner, the 5,000 people in the arena stood in roaring ovation. American flags wig-wagged. Jeff Blatnick dropped to his knees, weeping, and he made the sign of the cross before kissing the wrestling mat.

"The cross was an offering of thanks," he said. "I've been given a lot of chances in this life and I wasn't going to let this pass without giving somebody thanks."

So many people had helped, he said. He wanted them to be as happy as he was. He said he dedicated his victory to his brother, five years dead. He wept, almost breaking down, during a television interview a minute after his match, and his father said he hadn't seen his son cry that way since his brother died.

"These were tears of joy," Jeff Blatnick said, "not of despair."

And then he stood for the medal presentation ceremony. They played the national anthem and Jeff Blatnick began to sing along, stumbling over the words until the end when you could be 50 feet away and hear him sing, ". . . and the home of the brave."

Bjorn Borg

October 16, 1986

The ghost of Bjorn Borg came through town selling shirts. Five times in a row, the flesh and blood Borg won Wimbledon. Then he walked. He said good-bye to fame. And he sailed with his teenage bride to his island off the coast of Sweden. Five years have passed since then, and now the ghost of Borg comes to town selling shirts.

You say the ghost of Borg because no one runs to the nearest store to buy a tennis shirt hawked by a Swede named, say, Sven Kierkegaard. But when it's Bjorn Borg trading on his legend, when it's Borg using the ghosts of Wimbledons past, you go to the store if only to see how happy the man is five years later.

So many athletes who have heard the cheering cannot live in the silence. They have been made to feel heroic. They were warriors rampant in great stadiums. And then, someone hits the switch, the lights go out, the party's over. It is a kind of death, abrupt, unchanging. The silence comes after everyone. But Borg was different. He sought the silence.

John McEnroe has said, "The day will come when Borg regrets quitting." Borg was 25 years old when he walked away. He won six French Opens and five Wimbledons. He made maybe $100 million. The only flaw: in 10 tries, he failed to win the U.S. Open, last in the summer of 1981.

In memory, Borg is broad shoulders and no hips. He has a longshoreman's rocking walk. He wears a headband around blond hair so long it reaches his back. His eyes are narrow-set and blue. There is the dirty stubble of a 5 o'clock beard. His footwork is so quick it seems supranatural. The two-fisted backhand returns everything. There is never a trace of emotion's fire on his face.

At 30, Borg has cut his hair short and it has grown brown out of the sun. There is still the dark stubble of beard, and the body, lean as ever, moves with a soft grace. He looks ready for McEnroe.

McEnroe is a romantic under that rage. He won the 1979 U.S. Open and came to the '80 Wimbledon final against Borg, the Swede's streak at four in a row then. Borg beat McEnroe in five sets. The fourth set, McEnroe's, went to a 34-point tiebreaker lasting 22 minutes. That day, McEnroe learned what Wimbledon was.

"You could definitely feel something in the air, more so than I've ever felt anywhere else," McEnroe said. "It was just the way it was really quiet. No one was saying a word. You could hear everything. That's when I knew this was the way tennis should be."

Few athletes can walk away from such enchantment when they're the best at what they do. Bobby Jones did at 28, Sandy Koufax at 30, Jim Brown and Rocky Marciano at 31. Some were hurting physically, some refused to be consumed by their games. Borg just wanted out of the circus.

Maybe a rock star suffers the attention of a McEnroe or a Navratilova. No baseball or basketball player does. The stars of tennis rank second only to soccer's in international celebrity. Borg, when he walked away, spoke of the suffocation of fame. He said he would never play the big ones again.

Yet the question persists: Bjorn, will you come back? The answer given at the shirt store, an answer so pat it carried the tone of a recorded speech: "I'm not coming back. If I miss anything, it's probably the U.S. Open, but I don't really miss anything. I did tennis and I did it well. I don't need to do it all over again."

McEnroe suggested regret. Borg's answer: "No, never. I am so happy for the decision I made."

Borg divorced his wife and sold his island. Now he lives in Stockholm with Jammike Bjorling, 20, the mother of his year-old son, Robin. This year for the first time since 1970 he spent a summer at home.

"We fixed up our house," he said, his voice cheery. "I enjoy the water. So we did water-skiing, fishing. We saw friends. I play soccer, too, and in ice hockey I get to play all the positions — except goalie, no goalie. All these things I could not do when I played tennis. There was no time for anything but travel, play tennis, eat and sleep."

Borg says he now plays tennis three hours a week with two four-man tournaments a year. He speaks warmly of Jimmy Connors and their wars of attrition. He says of McEnroe, "He was a different style than Connors, more aggressive, but exciting, too."

A legend at Wimbledon, Borg each summer is invited back as a guest. He never attends. He last was there when McEnroe beat him in the 1981 final. He said, "Why should I go? It doesn't give me a kick. It is tough for me to understand why players go to tournaments when they are not playing."

Borg shrugged. "I prefer to be out fishing."

Bob Knight

May 2, 1988

Bloomington, Indiana

Bob Knight's office seems to have been decorated by hurricane. Papers have come to rest in a hundred places. Clocks are upside down. Trophies tilt sideways. The coach's desk is buried under books and letters. A visitor, awestruck by the calamity, suggests the hiring of an arsonist as the only way to straighten out this mess.

"I'm offended," Knight says. "You should have seen it before we got it in order. Everything's organized in here now. Hell, no, it's not a mess, not now."

On second glance, he is right. Though the carpeting is all but out of sight under a covering of white envelopes, the envelopes are piled in a dozen neat stacks on the floor and on chairs brought in for the emergency. Cardboard boxes are lined up against a wall, as orderly as scared freshmen in Knight's presence for the first time. Knight picks up a clock, one of a dozen in the room with an Indiana basketball motif. "People spend days and days making up these things to send here," he says. "I must have got 75 or 100 clocks."

Knight is a big man, tall and thick, but unlike most big men he minimizes his size. His shoulders are rounded; his face has fine features (even a dimple), and he lowers his smallish head in conversation, bringing his dark eyes to bear on his subject, as if committed only to a battle of wits for which his physical bulk would be an advantage both unfair and, he is certain, unnecessary. He was a star player in high school (described by his coach as "volatile and egocentric"). On Ohio State's great teams of 1960 and '61, Knight was a restive reserve. And now on a May day in 1988, even with his middle-age bulk, Knight moves through his office with an athlete's easy grace, stepping over a pile of letters to reach under a chair where he picks up some posters.

Knight says, "You want to see something crazy, look at this." The six posters are each three feet long. Pasted to them are words of various type sizes and designs carefully clipped from newspapers and magazines. They are arranged in lopsided sentences as if done by a kidnaper demanding $1 million in ransom or else he'll let the air out of all the basketballs in Indiana.

"Read 'em," Knight says, and the boards turn out to be a high school coach's application for a job as one of Knight's assistant coaches. "I didn't hire him, but he got me to read his letter."

Knight loves it. He loves it all. All he wants is to be loved. If not loved, respected. He wants to be Ted Williams, whose only dream was for people to see him walking down the street and say, "There goes the greatest hitter who ever lived." Knight wants people to have an idea about him, too. "I want people to say I worked at it and I was an honest son of a bitch."

Obscenity is the defeat of language. But Robert Montgomery Knight, like Ted Williams, prefers an obscenity to a nicety any day. So masterly is Knight's command of epithet and expletive that the naughty words often do work which seems beyond their defeatist's reach. A recruit once promised Knight he would be shorn of long hair and show up at Indiana with a crew cut. "That son of a bitch is coachable," Knight said, and the sentence fairly vibrated with battlefield bravado. Obscenity is locker room talk, foxhole talk. By such macho posturing, the athlete and the soldier say they're going to win. This is savage if unwitting irony, for they deny the idea of defeat by stealing and converting to their own uses the language of defeat, which is obscenity.

Winston Churchill harnessed obscenity to his own disparate purposes. (The great man favored short Anglo-Saxon oaths "mostly beginning," he said, "with the earlier letters of the alphabet.") So does Bob Knight make words dirty-dance in praise as well as in damnation.

His father, Pat, a railroad freight agent, cursed in Sunday School. Knight said, "He was the most honest man I ever knew. He stood up in Sunday School class during the Korean War and right in the middle of some charitable discussion, he shouted — he couldn't hear well, so he talked loudly — 'If you ask me, I think we ought to let MacArthur go in and bomb the hell out of 'em.'"

Give 'em hell, even if it's in Sunday School. "Ted Williams is my idol," Knight says. "His singleness of purpose is what I liked. And another thing: he never tipped his cap."

Knight admires the barbed wire in a man. He reads Louis L'Amour's western novels full of sagebrush, pioneers and sidewinders both reptilian and human. For years Knight had one plaque on his office wall; it quoted George Patton on the need to worry about "loyal friends" who will do "their hypocritical goddamnedest to trip you, blacken you and break your spirit." Now a second plaque quotes Abraham Lincoln during the Civil War as saying he's going to do the job the right way even if at the end he has only one friend, himself. On a bookshelf sits a small Harry Truman sign, "The Buck Stops Here."

Defining another coach, Knight defined himself when he said, "He's an iconoclastic anachronism. He does what he believes in. Period. And he believes he's smart enough to do things his way, to figure out how to do things, and tough enough to get 'em done his way." Churchill once joked in definition of his character, "Megalomania is the only form of sanity."

A longtime friend and fishing buddy of Knight's, a newspaperman named John Flynn, said, "Calling Bob Knight 'Bobby' is like calling George Patton 'Georgie.' It doesn't fit. Bob is the meanest sumbitch on two wheels. And remember. Under that surface veneer of meanness lies a really thick layer of more meanness." The coach once placed a Tampon in a player's locker; another time he grabbed a player's testicles to make sure, he said, the player had them. "Knight is a despicable human being," says Louisiana State coach Dale Brown.

Knight also is a sentimentalist. John Flynn owned a weekly newspaper. When the newspaper ran into financial trouble, Knight offered to write a column if it would help raise circulation. Later Knight drove 100 miles to speak at a dinner raising money for his friend's failing enterprise; he did it for free when $5,000 was his normal fee. About Dale Brown, Knight sneers. "Is he sane?"

Any man so fierce as both a friend and an enemy lives according to absolutes. Knight makes judgments quickly and acts on them. That's one thing if you're an English teacher behind ivy-covered walls; no one notices. If you're Bob Knight acting on your best judgment and that best judgment says, "Throw the son of a bitch in the garbage can," then people are going to notice.

Not that Knight much cares. The man he tossed in the garbage can, an LSU fan, had called him an asshole one too many times. He had it coming, Knight says; besides, he says, no one knows how many of those confrontations he has walked away from. "There's a thousand assholes out there who have called me an asshole and got away with it," Knight said. "But not that asshole."

People have come to think Bob Knight is trouble. He once kicked a chair in Madison Square Garden. He jerked a player into the huddle by his shirt front. He was arrested in Puerto Rico for pushing a policeman. There was the LSU fan in the garbage can. Knight threw a chair across the floor during a game in '85. Two years later he caused the forfeiture of a game against the Russians. Knight fired a shot from a starting-gun blank pistol over a reporter's head after not speaking to the man for a year; his idea of a joke, just as he thought it great fun to put his hands around a TV reporter's throat and take the man to the edge of a tall building where he asked onlookers thumbs-up or thumbs-down while the TV guy was bent backwards over a balcony railing. The list reached absurdist lengths in 1988 when Knight said on national television, "If rape is inevitable, relax and enjoy it."

Knight has insulted coaches, newspaper reporters, women, referees, gamblers, players, boosters and his own fans, who one night chanted at a referee, "Bullshit," until Knight, the Amy Vanderbilt of profanity etiquette, took up the public address microphone and told them, "We don't do that crap here."

I once asked Knight if he were as sumbitchin' mean as John Flynn, his buddy, would have us believe.

"Do you really think I'm mean?" Knight asked.

"In the top five."

As Knight laughed, I reminded him of a team meeting he had called. This was his story: "I said to the team, 'Everybody who is satisfied that Tommy is doing everything he can to be a contributing part of this team and is putting out like everybody else, raise your hand.'

"Not a single hand went up. So I said, 'Now, everybody who is fed to hell up with Tommy's sitting on his ass and generally acting like a shit, raise your hand.'

"Eleven hands went up."

I said, "Let me play the devil's advocate, Bob, and say that was a mean thing to do to a kid, humiliating him in front of his peers. Why didn't you do that in your office, alone? Why is it necessary to be that mean?"

"Hey, those 11 kids didn't raise their hands because I wanted them to raise their hands. I do it that way. Is that mean? Is that intelligent? Is that an insight into what will work best? . . . I did it because I thought it was the absolute best way to prove a point."

Knight's barbed-wire philosophy: "I believe 'no' is the most important word in the English language. No, I won't. No, I'm not going to. No, I refuse to. But I don't think many people can say no to a lot of things. They can't say no to excess in alcohol, sex and smoking and eating. They can't say no to the temptation to cheat in recruiting or to hedge on expense accounts. . . .

"No, I'm not going back to Puerto Rico and pay any goddamn $500 fine because I don't think it's right. I'm willing to take stands on things where other people aren't. I am, I guess, a crusader." (For a TV spot against drinking and driving, Knight simply ordered people to quit drinking. "Nobody's ever died drinking too many milkshakes.")

And Knight said, "There are lots of times, too, when I feel like a lone ship on a stormy sea and I don't have any sail."

In 1979 friends were worried about Knight. His Ohio State coach, Fred Taylor, said, "Bobby is driven by a force greater than any coach I've ever known. Nobody could keep that pace without it reflecting in his face and emotions."

Edwin Cady, Indiana's faculty representative when the school hired Knight, said, "Bobby has shown a certain immaturity throughout his entire Indiana career. He is in a race now between immaturity and disaster."

"The only hope I have," said Robert Byrnes, a Knight devotee and an Indiana professor of eastern European history for 22 years at the time, "is that someone, perhaps a Fred Taylor, can tell Bobby, 'You can be intense and demanding, and you can do it without the vile, unspeakable language and without the rude and barbaric behavior.' I just hope it can be done before somebody, or something, drives Bobby out of the job."

Byrnes, for his own instruction, often came to Knight's basketball practices. "Bobby is the greatest teacher I have ever seen. If he were a history professor, he'd put us all to shame. He has this intensity, along with a really first-rate mind that just happens to have turned to basketball. I come away from his practices — I'm almost embarrassed to use this word — inspired."

Indiana's practices are lessons in iron discipline. "Discipline is doing what you have to do, and doing it all the time," Knight says. At practice one day, he said to a player, "If you don't know the answer to this question, John, I'm going to kick your ass." The player said, "Shot fake," and Knight slapped hands with him softly. . . . Indiana's practice court had a white line in a semicircle 16 feet from the hoop. Only one offensive man was allowed inside the lines, keeping the area free for cutters. . . . In a two-man passing drill, the catcher called out names of both the player passing to him and the player to whom he passed. . . . "Next year," Knight said, "we're going to try something from the military. They used flashing targets to test gunners' recognition of aircraft types. We'll do things such as flash names, like Jones or Brown or White, and have the player pick out instantaneously which is the best shooter and ought to get the ball on the break." And then, with players flying upcourt, Knight shouted from the far end, "John, why did Kitchel get that shot?" John answered, "Shot fake." Knight nodded, pleased, and John took the silence as an ovation.

Cady: "If intercollegiate athletics can't keep Bobby Knight in it, for his integrity of purpose, it probably doesn't have much future. It is terribly important for all who care about intercollegiate athletics to save the Bobby Knights of the world. Let the crooks go. I can tolerate Bobby's extracurricular shenanigans much easier than I can tolerate cheating."

Among the hurricane-strewn debris in Knight's office this week in May of 1988 there is a plaque given to Knight by his former players as thanks for basketball lessons that served them well in life. Steve Downing, the center on Knight's first Indiana team and now an assistant coach, said, "I love Coach Knight because he pushed me to limits I never thought I could reach. He was hard, but they were the two most important years of my life. Once you play for him, you can do anything." Said St. John's guard Chris Mullin, who played for Knight on the 1984 Olympic gold-medal team: "If you turn down Coach Knight's volume, the things he says are 100 percent worthwhile." Georgia guard Vern Fleming: "We paid the price — we heard some words from Coach Knight that we may not be used to hearing — and we did what we set out to do."

Bob Knight is . . . what?

A raging martinet.

An inspiring teacher.

A vulgar bully.

"He's Lombardi, only in basketball," said Gerry Gimelstob, once a Knight assistant.

He is a coach who changed his game forever. Under Knight's orders, you play man-to-man defense with not an inch given. You play an offense which gets everyone the shots he can make. You play both ends of the court as if it were the most important work you'll do in this lifetime. You play as if you want to win as badly as your coach wants to win.

"Your opponent is yourself," he says, "your opponent is your potential. The whole thing to me centers around the orchestration of the game; how well are we playing? To me, as a coach, the whole incentive is the beauty you see in a game where you've played well. I really believe that if you see that beauty, you're going to win the league and you're going to win championships."

You hear Knight, in a locker room talk, tell his players . . .

"See, boys, basketball should be your favorite class. Because what basketball has done for teams here in the past is taught those kids how to compete. That's a great thing to learn. I guarantee you we've had players who have sat in the classroom with people who had 3.7 cums, who they no way should have been able to compete with after college, and have gone on and done much better than those kids did. Why? Because they knew how to compete. They know how to stay after something. They knew how to get knocked down and get up."

Knight is himself an insatiable student. The library in his home-town, Orrville, Ohio, used to put up a list of the 10 kids who read the most books that week. "It was always me and nine girls," Knight said. He quotes the Chinese warrior Sun-Tzu ("The good fighters first put themselves beyond the possibility of defeat and then wait for the opportunity of defeating the enemy"). The first time he ever spoke to Ted Williams, Williams conducted a pop quiz on fishing. "He called me and said, 'What length rod did you use on those rivers in Montana? What weight line? What kind of leader did you use? How big are the flies?' I know what this is. I got to answer these questions correctly or he's going to hang up the telephone." The student aced the pop quiz.

Knight, on the best coaches: "In no particular order, Lombardi gave a meaning to playing as well as you can by demanding of yourself that you play as well as you can. . . . Paul Brown brought a quality of organization to sports leadership and coaching that had never been there before. . . . Red Auerbach brought a psychology of approach, an 'inner arrogance.' . . . In college basketball, three people stand out: Clair Bee, Pete Newell and Henry Iba. There've been a lot of great coaches and they all have benefitted in some degree from what those three figured out."

On Col. Earl Blaik, who made West Point football the standard of 1940s excellence: "Pete Dawkins, the year he won the Heisman Trophy, had an injured Achilles. They got him going up on a 2 x 4 and he can't get up on it. Col. Blaik's behind him saying, 'Get up, Pete, get up on it, Pete, get up, Pete, Pete, get up.' And Pete said, 'Goddamn it, Colonel, I can't get up on it.' Well, you could hear a pin drop. Everybody had visions Pete would never run another play for Army. And Col. Blaik just turned and walked away. He knew he had pushed Dawkins to the limit."

On basketball in Indiana: "You can drive along and see the buckets on the barns and the goals in the backyards in dirt. I'll drive through a town. It could be any town. And I'll say, 'I bet in the next mile I can see 15 basketball goals.' I'll count the goals . . . "

Now this week in May of 1988, I am with Knight in the coaches' locker room by the Assembly Hall basketball court. This week the rape remark has given everyone an excuse to reprint the list of what one newspaper called Knightmares. "Out of context, it looks like the diary of a madman," I say, "but I know there are good reasons and explanations for all of it, some of which you've admitted is your fault."

I have the floor. "At bottom, that's what I admire about you. At bottom I think you're serving the truth. Now, the truth as I see it may be different from the truth as you see it. But truth is what you're serving. That's why it's impossible for you, I think, to tailor your behavior to fit any media image of Bob Knight. The image isn't the real Bob Knight. It's only a suggestion with no depth. If you're just Bob Knight, Ohio State grad, trying to explain stress, then you say what you believe in the context of your answer; you don't say what's politically expedient for this 'image' Knight. I may think what you said was dumb. But I admire you for being honest. I don't think you're trying to fool anybody with mirrors. You're not trying to be anything but what you are. And most of the time you're Bob Knight, a really smart guy.

"Whereas, if you were worried about being cast as a madman, none of these 'incidents' would happen. Maybe you'd even be cast as a saint, like John Wooden. He let cheating go on at his place forever but knew how to manipulate image. I'd rather have Bob Knight making a mistake now and then. To do anything else would be to live a life that is false to what you are. You'd be selling out your most important deal. Integrity."

Knight says, "I either have to be something I'm not, to appease all this bullshit. Or I gotta try and muddle along being what I am, hoping there'll be some people that understand what the hell I am."

Ted Williams understands. Someone once asked the greatest hitter who ever lived if there are people in other sports whom he admires. Williams said, "Bobby Knight. I love his intensity, I love his discipline, I love his devotion. He's just one hell of a guy."

Joe Louis

April 17, 1981

Las Vegas

J oe Louis lies in state today. Caesar's Palace built a boxing ring and the casket is in the ring. The ring ropes are red, white and blue. The ring posts are covered with black cloth.

To see Joe Louis, you walk up the six ring steps, past flowers in the shape of a crown (sent by Redd Foxx) and past flowers in the shape of a boxing glove (from Leon Spinks). Then you look over the top rope of the ring into the casket.

Opera music is playing in the Sports Pavilion, a warehouse of a place with sheet metal walls. The walls are covered with black curtains 20 feet high.

Next to the boxing ring, Caesar's has propped up four trees, each maybe 10 feet tall.

At 10:38 this morning, a man with a television camera on his shoulder crawled through the ring ropes and walked to the corner of Joe Louis's casket. He was looking for an angle. He sighted through his lens. No, not quite. A little to the right. There. Now he had Joe Louis's face in the frame, just right so the film would show a mourner and the champ in one shot.

When you thought the Joe Louis story could get no sadder, they put him dead in a boxing ring in a casino's tin warehouse.

In a touch of kindly grace, President Reagan has said Louis can be buried in Arlington National Cemetery, a hero's place. There the great old champion at last will be out of reach of the men who spin roulette wheels.

"It was a messy scene this morning when Caesar's people tried to talk Martha (Louis, the widow) out of the Arlington burial," said a member of the family. "I guess they thought it would steal their thunder. If Caesar's had its way, they'd stuff and mount Joe and stand him in the lobby forever."

Not everyone in Joe Louis's family shares those cruel sentiments. Joseph L. Barrow Jr., the champion's son, never really knew his father except that he knew this: he loved him and he wished he could have helped him. If some of us, melancholy, see a gambling palace abusing the memory of Joe Louis, his son says that's our problem.

"Being at Caesar's doesn't bother me at all, because my father loved it here," said Barrow, 33, who uses his father's original name. "He enjoyed his job as a greeter, he enjoyed having people come up to him for autographs and he enjoyed being part of the public environment.

"The only thing that bothers me is when people impose their values on his environment. It may not be the life you like, or the life I like, but it was his life. He loved it. People who talk about him as a freak without dignity don't know Joe Louis. I hate to see people demean him for his life here when it clearly made him happy."

Martha Louis, not Caesar's, decided to have the services in the Sports Pavilion, according to Barrow. "My stepmother wanted it," he said. "And, of course, Caesar's would do anything for her and my father. Caesar's Palace has enough promotion and publicity. They don't need this."

Barrow worked the last four years in Washington as director of the marketing for the Department of Energy. He now is vice president for corporate marketing for Wood Brothers Home of Denver.

Barrow's parents were divorced shortly after his birth. He grew up with his mother in Chicago and saw his father only occasionally. Their relationship seems to have been limited to the father's insisting that the son get a college education and the son's saying, "Yes, sir." He became a banker upon graduation from the University of Denver.

We sat in a dark bar at Caesar's for an hour. Barrow remembered a car ride with his father. "I was about 3 years old. I asked, 'Is this going to be your last fight?'" His father, a burnt-out case at 36, said,

"Yeah." That must have been the Marciano fight, Joe Jr. said in the dark Wednesday, and he remembered being sad when his father lost to the younger man.

"If you ever fight, Punchy," the smiling champ often said to his son, called Punchy because he was a small baby, "remember that I've got a good right, and I'll use it on you."

Joe Louis Barrow Jr. never fought. He said he had only one wish about his father's life.

"I wish I had been older because with me a banker he'd damn sure have kept some of that money he made," the son said, bitterness on those words. (So bitter that I later made a note: "Joe defends his father's life in this pit because he loves him, not because he thinks life here is worthwhile. He would have changed it if he could. This is a city of victims, and Joe Louis was a victim. Joe Jr. knows it.")

The son is proud of the father, saying: Joe Louis was a hero when this country needed a hero; Joe Louis changed lives by showing that a poor black kid can make dreams real; Joe Louis "always smiled on the inside," and if he stumbled a lot in the last 30 years, "he still is a great man who is loved by millions of Americans and will be remembered forever."

Bill Murdock, 66, of Las Vegas wept as he looked over the red ring rope into Joe Louis's casket today. He wore coveralls, had a blue bandanna around his neck and carried a big straw hat. He had come from his job as a gardener.

"I knew Joe for 41 years," he said. "I traveled with him and worked with him all over the world. Of all the men who ever got in the ring, he was the greatest marvel. Of all the warriors and gladiators, he was the greatest. Above all, he was a great human being. If we had four billion people like Joe Louis, we would have a beautiful world. I loved him. God bless him."

April 18, 1981

Las Vegas

They came to a tin warehouse, but they left from a church. They came to say a sad good-bye to Joe Louis, but they left clapping hands in joy and waving to the champ.

Maybe two thousand in blue jeans and shorts and evening gowns and tuxedos came to a funeral service for a sick old man. They left from a celebration for a hero, a black man who rose from a cotton field, a hero who lifted a nation to his shoulders.

The night before, Muhammad Ali sat in a dark hotel room and spoke of death. "I wish people like Joe Louis and people I love didn't die before me," he said. He whispered in the dark. "I want to die before them. I don't think I could stand to see my son in a casket. Joe Louis, my, my. Whatever I said before, I didn't mean it, 'cause Joe Louis was the greatest. And now he's gone on to a better life. He has passed all the tests for him on earth to go to paradise."

More than once, Ali has said he didn't want to wind up the way Joe Louis did. Poor Joe. Poor, broke, sick Joe.

"I never said that, not that way anyhow. That's demeaning. Look at Joe's life. Everybody loved Joe. He would have been marked as evil if he was evil, but everybody loved Joe. From black folks to redneck Mississippi crackers, they loved him. They're all cryin'. That shows you. Howard Hughes dies, with all his billions, not a tear. Joe Louis, everybody cried."

Sammy Davis Jr. sang at the funeral services in the Sports Pavilion, a tin warehouse of a building behind the Caesar's Palace gambling casino. Frank Sinatra spoke. Ali and Larry Holmes were pallbearers. "Joe's biggest fight ended a few days ago," Sinatra said. "And I don't know how the refs voted yet, but I lay you 100 to 1 he gets a unanimous decision."

And then Jesse Jackson spoke of poor Joe.

Jesse Louis Jackson is a black preacher born four years after Joe Louis won the heavyweight championship he would keep for 11 years. The Rev. Jackson is director of Operation PUSH, once a lieutenant at the side of Martin Luther King.

Poor Joe, for so long a champion, the hero who sent Hitler's lackey Schmeling home on his knees, the hero who made dreams seem possible. Poor Joe, for so long a piece of tragedy.

Jesse Jackson stood in the middle of a boxing ring today, right behind Joe Louis's casket in the tin warehouse, and Jesse Jackson said there was no such thing as poor Joe.

"We don't identify with the 'poor Joe' stories," he said.

Jackson is Martin Luther King's heir at the pulpit, a preacher whose words become song, whose ideas take flight. He already had said what good things Joe meant to America's black people. "When we were vulnerable and the scent of the Depression was still in our clothes . . . when lynching mobs threatened our existence and we were defenseless without legal, political, economic or military protection, God built a fence around us and Joe was anointed and appointed the gatekeeper. What a gatekeeper! He was our Samson, he was our David who slew Goliath."

All champions, Jackson said, are not heroes. Heroes are born of necessity. "Joe is our hero because he responded when we needed him." Against the darkness of history that was called Hitler, Joe Louis was a star shining brightly when we most needed a light. "God sent Joe from the black race to represent the human race," Jackson said. "He was the answer to the sincere prayers of the disinherited and the dispossessed. With Joe Louis we had made it from the guttermost to the uttermost, from slaveship to championship. Joe made everybody somebody."

Across America there came children named Joseph and Josephine, Louis and Louise. There came a dance called the Joe Louis Shuffle. "When Joe fought Max Schmeling, what was at stake was the ego of a nation and the esteem of a race of people. In a way that politicians and potentates couldn't do, Joe made the lion to lay down with the lamb. He was snatching down the cotton curtain."

So don't tell Jesse Jackson about poor Joe.

There was nothing poor about Joe Louis.

"For the children of '37," Jackson said, his voice in full flight, rising and falling, now filling the tin warehouse, now a whisper pulling listeners forward, "who crowded around the radio, hanging from the trees in the fields and watching the newsreels, they don't understand 'poor Joe.'

"For those who danced in the streets when they heard the referee say 10 and the announcement of a new champ, they don't understand 'poor Joe.'

"For those who danced on tin-top roofs, who ran the streets beating cans with sticks, for those who rang church bells and fell to their knees to pray, and looked at their bosses and suppressed their joy because it was too dangerous to smile, they don't understand . . ."

Now Jackson, by the magic of his song, turned the pejorative into a royal name.

". . . poor Joe."

The preacher smiled. People wept.

"For little black children whose little chests expanded and busted their buttons from their raggedy shirts, they did not understand 'poor old Joe' stories measured out by the government's meanness.

"Something on the inside said we ought to be free, something on the outside said we can be free.

"Joe, we love your name. To all the witnesses gathered here, you all leave and tell the story. Turn out some more editions — Extra! Extra! — the way they used to do.

"Tell the people when you leave here, that Joe Louis is still in the center of the ring without challenger or peer.

"Extra! Extra! Tell them when you leave this place that Joe Louis is too high to reach now. Extra! Extra! Read all about it! The pearl of the black race, the treasure of the human race. You're still the champ, 'poor Joe.'"

Puffing up his chest, Jackson said, "We all feel bigger today because Joe came this way. He was in the slum, but the slum was not in him. Ghetto boy to man, Alabama sharecropper to champion. Let's give Joe a big handclap. This is a celebration. Let's hear it for the champ. Let's hear it for the champ!"

And it was heard, hands clapping in the tin warehouse of a church, and then the preacher said, "Express yourselves, be glad. He lifted us up when we were down. He made our enemies leave us alone. He made us feel good about ourselves. Wave to Joe now. Give the champion a big wave."

Two thousand people stood, their arms overhead, swaying their arms slowly from side to side, tears touching their smiles.

William Andrews

October 12, 1986

You're William Andrews who went through the pain. You're William Andrews who was a great running back for the Atlanta Falcons on the summer day your knee came apart. Now you're back, two years later, you're back when you don't need the money. They'll pay the $8 million even if you never play again. You're William Andrews who said you made it back because you love the game. And now, five weeks into it, you say you wonder. You're not playing much. "Why spend two years of your life in rehabilitation just to come back and sit?" you say. You say, "There are times when I wonder what I did to deserve this."

You're William Andrews and you're wrong on this one. You're an old warhorse, proud of it, and you want to run in battle. But you're not ready. You're not fast enough outside, not quick enough inside. You want to be a star again, the William Andrews who could do it all. It is easy for us, who didn't feel the pain, to say you want too much too soon. You took the risks, you paid the price, it was your knee coming apart. Now, after two years of working through the pain, you want it all back.

And that part of it is wonderful, even inspiring, for there is the fire that made William Andrews what he was and what he is yet. No one ever doubted you. They'll hear you now and say William would give you his heart to win. They'll say, yes, here is the absolute proof of who William Andrews is: he doesn't want to come back and sit. Use it or lose it, you say. "Once it's sitting on a shelf, it loses its punch."

Professional football teams are not welfare agencies duty bound to

55

help the halt and the lame. They would turn away a saint/quarterback if he couldn't throw the thing down and out. You're William Andrews and maybe the Falcons gave you a longer look than they'd give a stranger off the waiver wire. They wanted you to make it back. But they did nothing out of charity. You earned a job. You're William Andrews and two years ago you couldn't walk. For six months you couldn't so much as wiggle your toes. But now you run, you block, you catch passes, you play on special teams.

Not that you like special teams. Would a Payton, you wonder, take a job on the kickoff return team? Would a Riggins? Did Franco Harris ever face the mad bombers on kickoff coverage?

"I've never played special teams," you said. "Never . . . not until this year."

Maybe it embarrasses you. But there you are, a blocker at the 20-yard line, William Andrews doing gruntwork when once you were a shining star. You may think such work is beneath you. It isn't. Wherever you are, at H-back or on the sidelines, just seeing your number, 31, on a Sunday makes these Falcons more than they are. For if you no longer are the football player who moved near Payton's level, you still are the William Andrews who has scalded malingerers, who has stroked scared kids, who can by your credentials and manner make a team better just by being there.

Nothing becomes a man more than his acceptance of who he is. Rage against the night. Scream at the devils who would diminish you. Do all that or you'll never find out who you are. But then, at peace, a man ought to be the best at what he is. You're William Andrews and you want the ball and you say your talents are not being used. You're right to want more than you have now, but you're wrong in saying, "There are times when I wonder what I did to deserve this."

You aren't being punished. Your coach, Dan Henning, wants to win. He would suit up Lucifer if the prince of darkness could get open deep. It's the coach's judgment that you haven't made it all the way back. He sees strength, wisdom, courage. He doesn't see speed. He sees Gerald Riggs and Cliff Austin as better running backs.

Two years ago, the suggestion of Riggs and Austin as the better backs would have been laughable. But then came one bad step in practice, no one even hitting you. You're William Andrews and it all went away on one bad step in August of 1984.

Ligaments at the left knee were stretched, like taffy pulled until it is translucent. In a heartbeat, the ligaments were torn in two. Bones slid sideways. Springsteen sings of a knife all edgy and dull cutting a six-inch valley through the middle of his soul. You're William Andrews and the terrible sliding bones at your knee joint sawed through the muscle there, crude and cruel, jerking it apart as a jackal tears at carrion.

Two weeks later, in a cast from your thigh to your toes, you said of the moment it happened, "It was everything I could do to hold my head up. . . . All I could think about was the pain."

Doctors have put together knees damaged worse than yours. But when the parts slid loose in there, setting off a mean war in a tiny room, something came down hard against the peroneal nerve. The nerve runs 20 inches from the knee toward the foot. It was six months before that nerve could transmit any message to your foot, six months before you could as much as wiggle your toes. "A flicker of movement," your doctor said in December of 1984, and he was thrilled.

"My leg's asleep," you cried out that day on the practice field, the leg asleep because the nerve was injured. Even as pain flamed in the knee, the leg slept, numb.

You're William Andrews who knew the pain. General manager Tom Braatz once was asked if you'd make it back. He said, "That's a God question." You said that when you saw your toes flicker, you had no doubts. The pain was a small price to pay if it bought you another day playing football.

"Whatever comes down the pike, I can accept it," you said this summer. You just wanted to be back. "Anything else is icing on the cake."

But now, five weeks into it, you're anxious and that's good. The great ones have no patience. They make things happen in a hurry. You're William Andrews and it's good to see the fire at full flame in you. But there's no rush. Two years gone are not replaced in five weeks. By carrying your 31 to where we can see it, you've done a small miracle. The big one can wait.

Sammy Boulmetis

April 12, 1981

Laurel, Maryland

Not far from the Laurel race track, there is a night club of the urban cowboy persuasion.

Paul Nicolo chose it as the place in which he would corrupt his best buddy, Sammy Boulmetis. They are an odd couple. Both are jockeys, but Nicolo is a street-tough kid from Boston and Boulmetis is the boy next-door who at 24 still won't use profanity in front of his parents. Nicolo said no one ought to be that nice, and so a month ago he watched happily as the boy next-door, after an unprecedented two beers, paid $2 to ride the night club's mechanical bull.

"I can bust this bull's buns," Sammy Boulmetis said loudly, putting down his beer and taking a hard look at the saddled robot.

"Cut the crap and get to it," Nicolo said.

The race track has a lot of folks called common, meaning they're lowdown, but the kid from Boston knew Boulmetis was uncommon and he loved him for it. Only Sammy could get away with teasing Nicolo about the chaps he wore for morning workouts; "tah-tah chaps," Sammy said, as if speaking to a British dandy and not a Boston tough. Now, because Nicolo would leave Maryland soon, moving his tack to Kentucky for the spring, this might be his last night out with Sammy for a while.

"You gonna ride or not?" Nicolo said.

The bull needed only five seconds to toss Boulmetis on his ear. Nicolo later would say it was the funniest thing he had ever seen when Sammy, staggering up, looked at the bull and said, "I've got him now."

59

The second time around, Boulmetis rode the hair off that bull. And he said to Nicolo, "Your turn."

"Nope," Nicolo said. "I get paid to ride. I don't pay to ride."

* * * * *

Sammy Boulmetis was paid $35 for the ride that broke his back three weeks ago.

The son of a rider, a rider himself seven years and better each year, Boulmetis worked for the $35 as a substitute rider on a filly named Val Des Portes in the ninth race at Pimlico on March 22. The jockey who had ridden the filly in her only other race, Ken Black, had to ride for another trainer in the ninth. Boulmetis worked the filly one morning two weeks earlier and the owner liked the courteous, clean-cut kid. So Boulmetis's agent, Bobby Vaughan, got the assignment for his client.

As the field turned into the stretch, Val Des Portes was far behind. The book on Boulmetis is that he sits still on a horse, keeps out of trouble and finishes strongly. Even with the filly out of it, Boulmetis did an honest day's work. He passed Noble Jade, the horse Ken Black rode, and was running next to last when, with a report like a gunshot, Val Des Portes' right foreleg shattered.

Had there been warning, it might have been different. A jockey knows the signals of pain from a horse, the half-steps of indecision that come in an animal bred both for running and courage. Given warning, a rider can pull his horse's head up to slow down.

That's why the Jockeys Guild, the riders' union, has campaigned for strict enforcement of medication rules. Because tracks all over America run day and night nearly every day of the year, the demand for horses increases annually. To keep horses running, some horsemen have sent horses to the races so drugged up that their brains could not receive warning signals of pain from their legs.

In the old days, unscrupulous trainers "nerved" their horses, which is to say they took a knife and cut the foreleg nerves that deliver the messages of pain. Now they use laser beams and drugs.

By all accounts Val Des Portes was a sound horse, making only her second start. She was a victim not of man, but of her breed. Thoroughbreds are 1,000-pound animals running 30 miles per hour on legs half the thickness of Pete Rose's forearm. As all that force came down on the filly's left hoof, the leg exploded.

The horse went down. With no warning of danger, Sammy Boulmetis was perched atop the filly's shoulders, pushing her to work harder. He might have sat back and coasted home for the standard $35 a rider gets for running out of the money. But Boulmetis did honest work, and so he balanced himself over the filly's neck as if this nondescript ninth race were the Kentucky Derby. Always vulnerable, jockeys are never in more danger than when driving their horses to a better effort.

Race trackers talk of spills. A jockey doesn't fall; he doesn't have an accident. He takes a spill. It sounds dainty, almost harmless. A spill. The half-ton animal falls forward and the 100-pound kewpie doll of a man is spilled off its back. These brave little men are spilled so often they don't keep count. Three weeks earlier, Sammy Boulmetis had X-rays taken of his shoulder after a spill at Bowie. The shoulder still has two pins in it from a spill in '78.

This time, in a meaningless race that would earn him $35, Boulmetis was thrown violently against the ground.

Maybe he broke his back on impact, or maybe it was broken when Ken Black's horse, coming up from behind, stepped on him.

* * * * *

The first time he saw the X-ray picture of his son's spine, the old rider said he let his eyes go shut.

Sammy Boulmetis's spine was broken in two. The top piece ran straight and true to about waist level. The piece in the pelvic region was twisted at an odd angle with the broken-off end pulled an inch and a half away from the rest of the spine. Jockeys see a lot of X-rays, but Sam Boulmetis Sr. said he had never seen one this bad. The picture showed a snowstorm of bone fragments along the broken twig of a spine.

A printer's devil in Baltimore after World War II, the elder Boulmetis took a job at the Laurel race track because everyone kept telling him he was little enough to be a jockey. For eight months, at $50 a month, he mucked stalls and hot-walked horses, occasionally wangling his way on top a horse for a morning workout.

He won his first race May 10, 1949. He won nearly 2,700 more before he retired in 1966, a Hall of Fame rider.

Only 37 years old then, he said he quit because he had four children from 6 to 13 and he wanted to go out on top.

Wise guys at the track didn't buy it. They said he no longer was the daring gambler of his youth, that he preferred safety to risk. Given a choice of taking the outside or flying into a closing hole on the rail, the wise guys said Boulmetis always took the long way. Any horse Boulmetis rode would have to be much the best to win, they said.

Jockeys don't admit fear because to admit it is to betray the hero's code of the bravest little men in sports. "You don't think about going into a hole — you just go," Sam Boulmetis Sr. said. "You're there before you realize there is a hole. It's reflexes. What happened to me was reflexes. That, and competitive desire. I could feel it wasn't the same. Before, if I got beat, I was annoyed. Later, I wasn't."

It wasn't fear, he said. Maybe 20 times in 20,000 races in his 17 years, Boulmetis went down with a horse. He was never hurt seriously, just broken arms and legs and the collarbone a few times.

"Being scared? No. Getting hurt? No. I didn't have that fear. It was just certain things I wanted for my family. And I had a good job waiting as a patrol judge."

Now a state racing steward in New Jersey, Boulmetis, 51, was putting sealer on a new kitchen floor at home when the phone rang just after 5 o'clock March 22.

Four hours later, in Baltimore's Sinai Hospital, he looked at an X-ray that made him close his eyes against its story.

* * * * *

Julie Snellings quit her race track job in Florida and drove two days to get to Sinai Hospital. She believed she knew what Sammy Boulmetis wanted to hear. Only she knew.

Julie's sister, Cyd, is Sammy's fiancee. The rider's parents stayed at the hospital all day every day. Paul Nicolo was there. So was Bill Passmore, a jockey who at age 48 had ridden with Sam Boulmetis Sr. and later taken Sammy as a race track son. Two years ago, Passmore broke his back, cracking two vertebrae in about the same place Boulmetis did. Passmore had seen a lot of X-rays, including his own, but Sammy's pictures caused a chill to pass across his shoulders.

They all cared, but Julie Snellings drove two days because only she knew what Sammy Boulmetis had to hear. Only she was in a wheelchair.

For six months in 1977, Julie Snellings may have been the best woman jockey ever. She won 46 races on the Maryland-New Jersey circuit. Her agent, Chick Lang Jr., said Snellings looked like the woman who would make it big because she had built credibility without going to bed with trainers. She came from a race track family; her mother was a trainer for 25 years and her father, Aubrey, was a top rider in the 1950s until he broke his leg in a spill at Charles Town. Eighteen years ago, when Julie Snellings was 5, her father committed suicide.

Always a strong kid behind soft brown eyes and a smile that could melt a steward's cold cold heart, Snellings wrote a letter in July of 1977 to an old boy friend, the jockey Jackie Fires, who had been paralyzed in a spill at River Downs.

"You're the toughest guy I ever met," Snellings wrote. She said it took her a month to find the right words. In that month she tried to put herself in Jackie Fires's place. She would hold her legs motionless and try to get out of bed. Before she wrote anything, she wanted to know how it felt to be paralyzed. Then she wrote to Fires, "If anybody can do it, you can."

Her spill happened the next month at Delaware Park when a careless rider cut in front of her horse and tripped it.

As Sammy Boulmetis would be a substitute rider four years later, so was Julie Snellings a substitute on her last mount. She didn't want to ride Roc Ruler, because she already had made six rides on a 100-degree day, including one for the nation's leading trainer at the time, King Leatherbury. Working for Leatherbury, she said, was the biggest thrill of her life. But when Roc Ruler's trainer begged her to help him, she did. A new rider needs friends.

It was a race for 2-year-old maidens. No rider likes such a race because 2-year-olds are unpredictable and often unmanageable. If they don't pin you screaming against the gate, they may toss you over the rail. It is all a rider can do to keep these babies going straight. Julie Snellings sensed she was in trouble as soon as a horse passed her on the outside. She knew the jockey as a punk with no brains.

She feared he would cut back in front of her too soon. She tried to take back her horse, to slow down. It was too late. Her horse's reaching front legs clipped the heels of the punk's horse.

Catapulted from the saddle, Snellings landed on the back of her neck. She broke the fifth, sixth and seventh thoracic vertebrae. The spinal cord was severed.

Doctors were direct. They told her immediately she would never walk again. She hated them for not lying to her. All she wanted was some kind of encouragement, even false hope. Without hope, she told them to let her die. Pull the plugs, get these tubes out of my throat. Kill me, she said. When a nurse said, "Young lady, you better get used to it, you're never gonna walk," Snellings grabbed a pitcher of water at her bedside and threw it in the nurse's face.

One day Jackie Fires called.

"Remember the letter you wrote to me?" he said. "I put a return address on it and it's coming back to you."

* * * * *

So four years later, by now lighting the world again with her smile, Julie Snellings believed she knew what Sammy Boulmetis needed to hear. Only Julie Snellings, of all the people who loved Sammy, really knew what he needed. Her sister was engaged to him, but her sister wasn't a rider and her sister wasn't in a wheelchair. Only four months before Boulmetis's spill, Snellings watched him sneak her four years' worth of medical reports out of the house. He sat in his car for three hours, she said, reading about her physical and emotional problems.

Boulmetis often pushed Snellings in her wheelchair, teasing her by suddenly tilting the chair up, and Julie, laughing, would say, "One of these days, just wait, when I'm walking and you're in this thing, I'll scare the hell out of you."

Snellings shared with Boulmetis an intimacy of dreams and fears. She would know what to say, and he would listen.

She sneaked into his hospital room after the rider's parents had left the building. She had to sneak in because the parents were worried that seeing Snellings in her wheelchair would hurt their son.

And then the rider in the wheelchair said to the rider in bed, "There are a lot of people crying outside this room, because they think you're not going to make it. But I'm not crying, and do you know why? Because you're going to walk out of here. As low in your back as the break is, the spinal cord can't be severed."

"Julie, they told me it was," Boulmetis said. "But, Julie, I've got this tingling in my leg. Did you have that?"

"Sammy, listen to me. That's good. If your leg is tingling, the spinal cord isn't severed."

"Really?"

"I wouldn't be telling you if it wasn't so."

* * * * *

Racing killed her father by suicide and put her baby sister in a wheelchair by a spill.

But Cyd Snellings wasn't worried when she met the jockey Sammy Boulmetis. She is 24, a race tracker, working at the mutuel windows some, in the photo department some, and she wasn't worried about falling in love with a jockey. With his shoulder ripped up in a spill that summer of '78, Boulmetis had his arm bandaged for their first date. No big deal. Comes with the territory.

This past Christmas Boulmetis gave Cyd Snellings an engagement ring. The boy next-door and the tiny girl with the China doll beauty are building a home in Baltimore. Something worse than a ripped-up shoulder can't happen to Sammy, Cyd thought. It happened to her sister. That was a guarantee against it happening again to anyone close to her.

At Sinai Hospital about 6 o'clock on March 22, a doctor told Cyd Snellings that her man had the worst broken back he had ever seen. "I hate to be blunt," the doctor said, "but Sammy probably will be paralyzed from the waist down forever." Everybody was crying in the

65

hallway, Cyd Snellings said, and then she screamed. "No, no, this can't be happening, this doesn't happen twice in a lifetime, I have to see Sam."

She ran into his room, pulling away from doctors, and the first thing Sammy Boulmetis said to his fiance was, "Now I'll be able to keep Julie company."

"Oh, God, Sammy, don't say that."

They had given him medication against the pain. "I love you bad, Cyd."

"I love you, too."

"Just be strong for me," he said.

* * * * *

Sammy Boulmetis traded in his black Riviera for a silver Peugeot diesel because the black car showed all the race track dirt. Next to riding, he loves working on that car the most, tuning it up, making oil changes. Most race trackers' cars look like a horse slept in the front seat. Not Sammy Boulmetis's Peugeot. "It's the world's cleanest race tracker's car," Bill Passmore said. The car is just like the rider, Passmore said: clean, bright, handsome, economical.

His agent, Bobby Vaughan, said Boulmetis is "the greatest kid you could ever imagine. You want to know about Sammy? The horse he took the spill on, they called it by a nickname, Pickles. The first thing Sammy said to me when he came out of the sedative was he winked and said, 'Robert, how's Pickles?'"

His peer/father confessor, Passmore: "He's a super fella, a real stand-up fella who never said a bad word about anybody and if he heard you say something bad about anybody, he'd stand up for them."

Paul Nicolo, his buddy, went to Boulmetis's hospital room in Baltimore. Everyone was quiet, worn down by melancholy.

"Sam, does this mean you can't do my oil change?" Nicolo said.

* * * * *

On the first Sunday after Boulmetis's spill, doctors at Thomas Jefferson University Hospital in Philadelphia gave the rider's family good news.

The spinal cord, as Julie Snellings had said, was in fact not severed. The break in the spine occurred below the cord and affected only a bunching of nerves known as "the horse's tail." The nerves were bruised badly, but Boulmetis did have feeling in three spots down his right leg and high on his left thigh.

Doctors would do surgery the next Thursday, April 2, in an attempt to realign the pieces of his spine. The injury was "a bad fracture dislocation of the lumbar spine, a relatively common injury in high velocity car crashes," said Dr. Jewell L. Osterholm, chairman of the department of neurosurgery at Jefferson and a project director of the Regional Spinal Cord Injury Center of Delaware Valley, one of only 14 such specialized centers in the U.S.

"The prognosis," Osterholm said before the surgery, "is better than with a cord injury. There is some possibility to recoup use of some muscles."

* * * * *

Paul Nicolo, on hearing the news in Baltimore, delayed for a day his move to Kentucky's Keeneland Race Course. He would celebrate.

He put on his tah-tah chaps.

He went to the urban cowboy place.

"I'm gonna ride that damned bull for Sammy," he said.

The tough kid who doesn't pay to ride paid this time. Nicolo rode the hair off that thing, going around five times, stopping only when blisters came up on his hold hand.

* * * * *

To prepare Boulmetis for surgery, the Philadelphia doctors first put him in traction for five days.

They drilled four holes in his skull to attach a metal ring. From pins through his knees, they hung bags of sand.

Sam Boulmetis Sr. saw a new X-ray picture. This time he kept his eyes open. Now he could see hope. Slowly, the pieces of the spine were moving toward each other.

The doctors finished the work Thursday when they inserted two steel rods along the spine, clamped them and a metal plate together next to the spine and grafted bone from the hip to the point of the break — all done to stabilize the spine, once shattered into snow-storm fragments but now a pretty X-ray picture of the orthopedic surgery work done by Dr. Jerome M. Cotler, Osterholm's partner in the Jefferson acute care department.

The first night at Sinai Hospital in Baltimore, Sam Boulmetis Sr. thought his son would be yet another of the dozens of brave little riders he has seen go from the track into wheelchairs. One of them, Ron Turcotte, who rode the great Secretariat, called the hospital the other day. Another, Julie Snellings, is writing Sammy Boulmetis a letter just as she wrote Jackie Fires a letter four years ago.

Now the old rider thinks his son, by using braces, will walk again.

"The good news," the elder Boulmetis said, "is that a lot of Sammy's nerves were not damaged. The doctors are very optimistic he will get more feeling back in his legs. There is even a little bit of movement in the right leg. In the left leg, he doesn't have any movement, but when they asked him to move it, you could see the thigh muscles trying to move. That's a good sign because he couldn't do that before.

"There was lots of pressure on the nerves and they were badly bruised, so it will take a long time, maybe a year, for the nerves to be okay. But the doctors right now feel Sammy has an excellent chance of walking with braces."

Dr. Osterholm wouldn't go that far in talking to a newspaperman. "The injury is to the cauda equina — the horse's tail — and those nerves have the potential for recovery. The patient is recovering, improving all the time in terms of sensation. The prognosis is reasonably favorable, but this was a very severe injury and I am hesitant to say how much will return."

Next week Sammy Boulmetis will be fitted with a "tortoise shell," a molded, removable plastic vest used for support in place of the maddening body casts so many riders have endured. As soon as he gets the shell, Boulmetis will go downstairs at Jefferson to the rehabilitation center.

"He can't wait to get started," his father said. "And as soon as he can sit up, Sammy wants to see everybody who wants to see him." He didn't want to talk yet, while on his back, but Boulmetis told his father to tell the newspapers to thank the Sinai hospital people and the Jefferson spinal cord unit.

"Some of our prayers have been answered," the father said.

* * * * *

Because Sammy Boulmetis is allergic to plants, the family has asked that no one send flowers to the hospital.

Paul Nicolo knows that, but he intends to ignore the family's wishes the first Saturday in May when he is at Churchill Downs for the Kentucky Derby.

"I'm going to get a rose from the winning jockey," the tough kid said, "and send it to Sammy."

May 15, 1982

Washington, D.C.

When we last saw Sammy Boulmetis, he had been caught in the act of accepting too much help from his fiancee, Cyd Snellings.

"That glass!" said the redhead Maggie, a physical therapist. Cyd Snellings held a milkshake glass so Boulmetis could sip from its straw. Maggie said, "What are you doing holding that for Sam?"

Snellings' silence said, yes, she was guilty of the dark deed.

"Sam holds his own glass," Maggie said.

We were in a Philadelphia hospital last April, a month after Boulmetis broke his back in a spill at Pimlico. Doctors twice operated on the jockey, 24, and put his lower spine back together with stuff that sounds like an all-star lineup from Tru-Value: springs and rods, clamps, screws and staples.

Boulmetis said, "The X-rays look like a junkyard."

In Room 911 of Thomas Jefferson University Hospital that day a year ago, Boulmetis also said, "I've got no complaints." Had his crushed vertebra been the next one up the spine, he likely would have been a quadriplegic.

"Right now, I have feeling that is almost normal in my right leg down to the knee. And on the inside of my right calf, I have some sensation. In the left leg, I could flicker a muscle until about a week ago but then I had some kind of little infection and the leg blew up. I haven't been able to flicker the muscle since."

Boulmetis doesn't remember his spill.

"All I remember is going up on the filly's ears," he said. "I remember being kind of sideways, being up on her head."

Cyd Snellings said, "You weren't on her head for long."

Who's to know what to tell someone with a broken back, but doctors made a mistake telling Sammy Boulmetis he might never sit up again. He held his own milkshake that day last April when he seemed so frail, seemed forever flattened against the bed. Now he can walk.

"I'm doing a lot better," he said. "Even some pain is going away."

Boulmetis wears molded plastic braces on his legs, under his jeans, and he walks with hand crutches, swinging his legs along. The other day his brother, Jimmy, needed someone to drive a horse van 100 miles. Sammy Boulmetis did it. He has enough control of his right leg, where feeling has returned down to the knee, to drive an automatic transmission vehicle.

"I guess the doctors paint as black a picture as they can," Boulmetis said. "Then if anything better happens, it's gravy. Now I only use my wheelchair in the house. I'm small enough and light enough they could make these plastic braces that are molded right next to the skin. I have these Canadian crutches, up over my forearms, and I swing through the gate."

He wore a molded body vest until November. In December he learned to use the crutches. To walk.

"It's unbelievable, the things he's doing," said his father, Sam Boulmetis Sr., and his mother said, "He just keeps getting stronger. It's wonderful."

"I've been lucky," Boulmetis said. "This first year has been depressing sometimes, that's true. But I don't get upset much about anything ever."

At times this first year with all the hardware in his back, Boulmetis said the pain was terrible. "It's like spasms," he said. "And phantom pain, like amputees who still feel their feet. I go through all that. You know Ron Turcotte, right?"

Turcotte, who rode Secretariat, is another of the 40 jockeys now paralyzed.

"I read an article where Ron said his pain felt like barbed wire around his chest and somebody was twisting it."

Boulmetis tried everything against the pain, including acupuncture. "The only treatment I get now is acupuncture once a week. I'm a believer. I couldn't sit up 10-15 minutes because of pain. I've been able, with acupuncture, to cut down my pain medication."

This summer Boulmetis will attend a race track official's school in New York. He figures his future is around racing. He's also buying a condominium in Cherry Hill, New Jersey. He's getting married at the end of the summer.

"Regrets?" Boulmetis said in Room 911 a month after his accident. "You kidding me? I loved riding. I enjoyed the life. If I didn't, I wouldn't have been out there. I had a good time, I met nice people, I rode nice horses, I had a great experience. I have no room for regrets."

Ben Hogan

April 10, 1986

Augusta, Georgia

Hogan. Ben Hogan. It was 1967, all those Aprils ago, when Hogan shot 66 at the Masters the third day. His 30 on the back nine tied the record. It left him two shots out of the lead. He last had won a major tournament in 1953, the year he bestrode the golf world, winner at Augusta and in our Open and in the only British Open he ever played. Now, this day in 1967, he was 54 years old. His knee — which knee? the left? — was no good and at every step there was an old man's hitch. He walked on.

You remember the first one best. Your first Masters. You stood on the shoulder of the knoll rising to the clubhouse veranda. Homework told you this had been an indigo plantation a hundred years before Bobby Jones saw a golf course in this land. You even read a piece by Bobby Jones, his advice and admonitions to the patrons of Augusta National Golf Club. They were asked, in a gentle way, to behave and take glad notice of the golfers' good work.

You stood under the trees by the clubhouse. A little sign of identification was tacked to each tree. Good. You wanted to put such information in your story so the folks back home would know you knew what kind of trees they had at Augusta National. You asked a native about the purple stuff on the tree branches. Wisteria? Thank you. Those trees down the entrance lane? Magnolias. Thanks again. Magnolia Lane. Perfect.

Maybe in time you would think of Magnolia Lane as gateway to the 19th century, but your first time, all dreamy, you saw the magnolias only as part of the beauty that was Bobby Jones's place. This was a cathedral, the architect a saint. What you wanted most, coming to Augusta a first time, was to walk the same ground as Hogan. The old man's time was gone, but you didn't care. You knew the importance of Hogan was not today but always.

To see Hogan practice, you arose at dawn. You knew he was little, but not that little. Only his hands seemed the stuff of legend, thick and rough, as if hewn from rock. Every shot with every club flew two yards left of the target and then fell two yards right, a fade two decades in the making, the ball dropping in the caddy's shadow.

So much to see at Augusta. Sarazen's plus-fours. The double eagle, Gene, did you have any idea? The azaleas and dogwood, Rae's Creek, young men walking in the dream of their life, Nicklaus and Palmer, the ones who will be great and those who know what it's like, all of them coming to Amen Corner knowing, if they love this game and this place, that Hogan did it there in 1967. He was even par at the turn. He birdied the next four holes.

Hogan hit a 7-iron to seven feet at the 10th. A 6-iron to one foot at the 11th. Another 6-iron to the 12th, that one 15 feet away. He reached the par-5 13th with a 4-wood second shot, using two putts from 15 feet. Your first time at Augusta, you didn't see any of it. You saw only the scoreboard. And someone said, *We better get out there.* By the time you saw Hogan, he was making pars — until the 18th.

The 18th fairway is a long, wide, ascending aisle in the Jones cathedral. From both sides, as Hogan limped uphill, came the sound of hands clapping. No shouts, no whistles. Hands clapping. Rainfall dancing on a tin roof. Hogan had put a 5-iron second shot on the green, maybe 25 away, above the hole. You saw the little man in the white cap standing over the putt that day. You see him still.

The yips had him bad. For a player of Hogan's dignity, it became an act of courage to draw back the putter when that action might provoke a spastic jab at the ball. Yet he had made five birdie putts that day, and now he stood over a sixth in nine holes. He would say, "I apologize to everyone for taking so long to putt. I still freeze some, but I'm trying. I can hear people in the gallery saying why doesn't that man go ahead and putt. I wish I knew the answer."

On the 18th, you wanted him to make the putt. You wanted it for him. One last putt, a man telling us again what he had been. And then, with the cathedral gone silent, Hogan stood over the long downhill putt. Standing. Standing. And then, somehow, he moved the putter back. Just a touch, really. And down the hill it came. Slowly. Gently. It dropped from our sight then. Somehow Hogan had made the thing. Made it for his 30, made it for his 66.

He took the warmth of the people and thanked them by lifting high his flat white cap. His shadow fell long on the green for it was late in the day. You saw all this, and you were glad, and you hoped the old man, a hard man, liked it as much as you did. You followed him into the clubhouse. He told reporters he didn't expect to win the next day (he shot an aching 77 to finish 10th). But what he said didn't matter, anyway.

The moment mattered, Hogan again Hogan.

"There's a lot of fellas that have got to fall dead for me to win," he said, the words spoken kindly to reporters kneeling at his feet. "But I don't mind telling you, I'll play just as hard as I've ever played in my life."

Hogan loved it. He sat on a padded bench in the clubhouse. His back was to a sunlit window with lacy curtains. He was balding, his hair gray and white at the fringes. His face was a Texas rancher's shaped by wind across flat land and sun without rain. But the sunlight this day came through white lace curtains to touch Hogan, the sunlight golden and soft, a halo's softness. You remember Hogan with the sun soft on his face one more time.

Dan Jansen

February 15, 1988

Calgary, Canada

ornings at dawn, the Jansens skated free, gliding as if on
air. They piled in the car and went to the rink. They grew
up on the ice, all the Jansens, the father, the mother,
their nine children. The ice made them one: one language, one
idea, one dream. To make a living, Harry Jansen worked as a
policeman. To live, he went to the ice and took his children with
him.

The youngest, Dan, turned out to be the best. All the good
speedskaters come out of the Jansens' town, West Allis, Wisconsin,
where the ice glows golden in the dawn. One of the Jansen girls,
Jane, made the dreamy circles of those mornings until she learned
she wasn't fast enough. She married a fireman down the street.
They had three daughters, the oldest now 4 years old.

Maybe the little one is on skates by now. Dan was on the ice at
that age, his sister Jane there with him. She was five years older, and
she made the baby brother hers. Midwest stock all of them,
scrubbed-clean church folks, a model of the extended family —
"Solid as the day is long," said a Milwaukee journalist who has
known them 10 years — the Jansens seemed touched by life's sweet
hand.

The cancer changed that. Jane's leukemia was diagnosed a winter
ago, early in 1987. The prognosis was melancholy. Chemotherapy
helped, but not enough. Without a bone-marrow transplant, necessarily from a family member, her time was short. There were two
matches of marrow, her sister Joanne and her baby brother Dan. It
was Jane's decision to ask Joanne for help. She didn't want to do

anything to interrupt Dan's skating.

By then, Dan Jansen had been to an Olympics, '84 at Sarajevo, where he finished fourth, a tick of the clock from a medal. He twice had been the U.S. speedskater of the year, '85 and '86. He twice won the World Cup championship, meaning he'd beaten the Russians and Germans and Dutch over the length of a season, the truest test of a skater. Only a week ago, in Milwaukee, he won at 500 meters in the world championship.

What he wanted, because even 22 is on the cusp of old age in speedskating, was one last shot at the Olympics. He wanted to move onto the ice at Calgary. All those dawns in the Wisconsin freezer, all his dreams, so much of his family's life — all for this moment, Calgary, where he could skate free on the ice, floating.

The marrow transplant helped Jane. Her summer was difficult, but she seemed to be beating the cancer. Dan said in the fall, "To see her fighting so hard, I figure I can work hard, too. I'm doing it for me and for her. I'm dedicating the season to her."

On Dec. 11, Jane Jansen Beres was readmitted to West Allis Memorial Hospital. On that day, in the Olympic Trials, her baby brother skated poorly, beaten by a lesser teammate. Dan said he thought about Jane. He couldn't help it. But it wasn't the reason he lost, he said. He was just outskated.

This time Jane didn't come home from the hospital. Before Dan left West Allis for Calgary a week ago, he stopped to see her. "It really hurt to leave her," he said here this week. "It makes all this seem unimportant." He tried to be brave. He thought he needed to be brave for her. He couldn't quit. Might she then quit? So when he said it hurt to leave her, Dan Jansen added, "She's with me spiritually."

The first phone call from the hospital came at 6 in the morning here Sunday. His brother, Mike, also an Olympic skater in '84, was on the line from Jane's room. Later Dan would tell reporters that he spoke to Jane and while she said nothing, he knew she understood what he said. Mike gave her a kiss for Dan.

The second call, an hour later, reported that Jane had died. In seven hours, her baby brother was to skate in the Olympics of his dreams. He'd made up his mind to skate whatever happened back home. "She wanted it that way," he said later. No, he had told reporters, he would make no speech about his sister if he won a medal. "She's my sister. We don't need any speeches."

He was on the ice this sad night for nine seconds, 10 maybe, before he fell. Entering the first turn, not a quarter of the way through his 500 meters, Dan Jansen's left skate slid under him. He fell on his left side. He spun across the track into the next man's lane. He came to a stop against the oval's padded wall.

It was over. After he rose, slowly, bent by the burden, Jansen began to move again on the ice. Not skating, only gliding, slowly, slowly, first with his hands on his knees, a man empty. He pressed his hands against his face. He let his head fall back. He glided, his right skate held above the ice, glided slowly, as if floating on air.

February 19, 1988

Calgary, Canada

For no good reason and for every good reason, Dan Jansen fell again. He caught an edge. He caught an edge the day he would go home for his sister's funeral.

When speedskaters fall, it's usually because they put a skate down wrong on the unforgiving ice.

They say they caught an edge. That means the skate's blade sliced into the ice at an odd angle and wouldn't straighten up.

The moment's dispute with physics most often is won by the skater, whose strength and balance and skill brings the blade back to its good work. He does it so smoothly no one sees it done.

Only when the skater pushes the blade too far over, only when the blade creates a gash with sides so steep as to trap the steel in there — we're talking hundredths of an inch here, the tiniest of scratches in the mirror of ice — only at this inexplicable moment does the skater go down.

Flying now.

Fallen then.

Flying, Dan Jansen had a chance to win an Olympic gold medal. This wasn't his best event. This was the 1,000 meters. In his best event, the 500, he had fallen four days earlier, a Sunday, the Sunday afternoon of his sister Jane's death, the older sister by five years who thought of him as her baby. They skated together, they played together, they were friends. They were of one heart.

Flying at 200 meters this night, flying at 600, Dan Jansen was the fastest man on ice with 400 meters to go, faster than the man who later would win the gold medal, Nikolai Guliaev.

Flying around the turn and now on the straight backside, Jansen had just under 200 meters to go, another 13 or 14 seconds. He had made it around three turns already. He had fallen in the first turn Sunday. Down the backside, he said, he felt very strong. Some experts believed he must have been tired to fall on the straight backside. No one falls on the straight unless they have a cramp or lose rhythm or lose concentration, usually symptoms of exhaustion. Jansen insisted he felt really good.

And then he fell.

He said he caught the right edge of his blade and couldn't roll it back to perpendicular. It happens to all skaters, he said. But it doesn't happen often in a race. Until Sunday, the day his sister died, Jansen hadn't fallen in a race all season. He couldn't remember ever falling in a straight.

"It happens to everybody," he said. "You put it down and it catches too much, you can't roll your blade over."

He hadn't forgotten Sunday, hadn't forgotten the fall in the first turn. He said so at a press conference after this melancholy 1,000. He also said he had put that fall behind him. A brave thing to say. He has to say it. But an Olympic speedskater doesn't forget falling in his best event. And a man doesn't forget his sister. He may, if she's in his heart, think of her with 200 meters to go, 14 more seconds to go, a gold medal possible. He may, even feeling strong, lose concentration.

And then he fell. He caught an edge. He moved too much weight to the outside of the blade. He may have made the same mistake a thousand times. Only this time, for no good reason, he couldn't get the skate up straight. For every good reason, Dan Jansen was not the same man he'd been before Sunday. On this day he couldn't do what he'd always done before Sunday.

Flying then.

Fallen now.

He went down on his right side. He slid for three seconds, maybe four, an eternity, spinning slowly, coming to rest, again, against the oval's padded wall, now in a sitting position. The man skating with him glided silently away around the last turn. Silence. Silence everywhere. Watching Jansen there on the ice. Watching him drop his head into his hands. Feeling his emptiness. An emptiness beyond pain. He would say later he didn't remember anything at that moment. The world champion a week ago, empty now, saying sadly, "I didn't even finish the race."

If Jane had asked him to stop skating and be with her, Dan Jansen said, he'd have spent the year with her. She said skate, and he skated. He fell twice in these Olympics, and this night he put his face in his fiancee's shoulder, and he went home this night to be at his sister's funeral.

He'll be all right in time. It was a relief, he said, to get this week's racing done. It wasn't important that he win anything. "I did what I could," he said, and what he did was wonderful. He skated for Jane.

April 22, 1988

Some letters come addressed with only his name.

"Dan Jansen."

The mailman knows where to deliver the letters.

He knows because in February of this year, on an icy oval in Canada, Dan Jansen fell into our hearts to stay.

The letters keep coming, even now, the bags smaller but still coming, letters by the thousands.

He answers them as best he can, but every time he feels he has made a dent in the pile, more letters come. Letters addressed to him in Calgary, addressed to ABC-TV, addressed simply with his name, as if he belongs to the world and the mailman will find him.

Some people want to tell Dan Jansen how it felt when a friend or relative died. They want him to know he is not alone. People send money for leukemia research. Others send money to the small children of Dan Jansen's sister, Jane Beres, who died the morning Jansen would skate in the Olympics.

She was his older sister, a speedskater before him, one of nine children, all skaters, all skating in the golden chill of winter mornings in Wisconsin.

His sister was a thousand miles away, in a hospital, dying of leukemia, when Dan Jansen went to Calgary for the Olympics. She wanted him to go skate. He was part of her, and she wanted him to go skate. It would help them both.

"The week before, I'd won the World Championships," Jansen said. "When I went to Calgary, I *knew* I'd win."

This was over breakfast yesterday morning, Jansen passing through Atlanta on promotional business. As he spoke . . . *I knew I'd win* . . . his face changed. Just for part of a second, a cold shadow of iron will moved across Dan Jansen's little boy face.

The telephone rang at 6 o'clock the morning of the race he knew he'd win. His sister was on the line, unable to speak by then. He spoke to her one last time. After all the years, the golden mornings on the ice, big sister and her kid brother, it would end with him speaking into a silent phone.

That night at the speedskating oval, Jansen came onto the ice slowly, moving slowly in icy circles. His family later would tell him they had never see him so pale. A reporter's memory of that moment is that Jansen seemed empty, circling to nowhere, a man lost with no destination in mind.

Barely 10 seconds into the 500-meter race which he once *knew* he would win, Jansen fell. The next time on the ice, for the 1,000-meter race, Jansen skated through 800 meters faster than any man would that night. Then he fell again, again sliding across the ice, helpless against momentum when only a second before momentum had been his ally.

Jansen went for two helpings at the breakfast buffet on this bright morning two months after those dark days. He said, yes, he had been empty the night of the 500. He spent that day "mostly crying," and he came to the oval eager to put his body into motion, anything to stop thinking about it. But on the ice he felt out of joint, not awkward really, but just not in synch, not the Dan Jansen he needed to be.

Four nights later for the 1,000, he felt good. He felt very strong, he said, even after the burning 800 meters. Usually a skater comes around the next-to-last turn struggling against exhaustion to maintain the deep lean essential to speed. Not Jansen.

"I felt strong," he said that night, and he said it again at breakfast two months later, adding, "Not to say I'd have won the gold, but I would have won a medal." He let his eyes fall closed a second. "I still can't believe it."

From Calgary, Jansen flew to Norway and Germany for the last two meets of the World Cup season. He won one race and won a season-long Cup championship. It was good to get away — "When I look back on the whole Calgary ordeal, it's a blur" — because it gave him breathing room, no reporters asking how he felt, no one telling him how brave he had been when he knew who the brave person had been.

Maybe there is another Olympics for Dan Jansen. He wants to enroll at the University of Calgary, the Olympic oval on its campus, his fiancee a skater there. He'll take it a year at a time, and if he can find a sponsor he may keep at it until the '92 Olympics.

Back home in West Allis, Wisconsin, Dan Jansen took his sister's little girl to a skating rink. Her name is Susie, and she is 4 years old. It was her first time on skates, just as Jansen had been 4 when he first tried to stand up on the wiggly things. Smiling at breakfast two months after Calgary, ol' Uncle Dan said of Susie, "She did good."

Dave Bresnahan

September 5, 1987

Since the potato, Dave Bresnahan has been famous. "I need an agent now more than when I played," said the man who threw the potato. It has been four days since he peeled the potato and threw it into left field. "I've slept 10 hours in four days. We've been laughin' our hind ends off."

On Monday in Williamsport, Pennsylvania, Bresnahan rose from his catching crouch, threw the potato past third base, reacted in disgust and then (a glum look pasted on) watched as the runner trotted home — whereupon the triumphant Bresnahan tagged him out with the baseball hidden in his glove.

This was in pro ball, the Class AA Eastern League. Bresnahan is (was) a backup catcher hitting .149 with no home runs and six runs batted in for the last-place Williamsport Bills, a Cleveland farm team which was 27 games out of first place when Bresnahan did it.

The story begins in the company of a few beers two weeks ago. "What about a potato?" Bresnahan heard himself say to the guys. He had read about an old-timer tricking a runner that way. "So we got out a rule book. You know what? There's nothing in there about potatoes."

At 25, a fourth-year pro, Bresnahan is a college graduate with a real estate license. He likely made $300 a week at Williamsport. As one of the club elders, his word carried weight; and the more beer that went down, the more perfect the potato caper seemed.

Bresnahan went to the Weis grocery store. "All the potatoes were in sacks. I only needed one or two. So I fit a couple through the holes. I told the produce man I didn't need a big one like a football.

83

One like a baseball. Nice and round."

Two potatoes cost 15 cents.

"I peeled one, to make it round and white, and went out in the yard to test-throw it, to see if it'd flutter or what. It was slippery, but it worked good. I was ready."

Bresnahan's teammates knew about his half-baked potato scheme. He kept the potato in a spare glove in the dugout — until the right time.

"When a man got to third, I turned to the ump and said, 'My glove's broke.' I went to get the spare glove. Then I called for a slider low and away. We didn't want the guy to hit the pitch, or I'd be standing there with a potato in my hand."

On the pitch, Bresnahan transferred the potato from the glove to his throwing hand.

"I threw the potato right at the runner. My third baseman, Rob Swain, did a good job of not catching the potato. If he'd caught it, I think we'd have picked the runner off. But Rob let it go all the way into left field."

The runner trotted home.

Bresnahan was waiting.

He tagged him, the third out, and then rolled the ball to the pitcher's mound. Fine. Except for one thing. The umpire didn't say a word.

"The umpire didn't know whether to spit or wind his watch," Bresnahan said.

Finally, the umpire announced, "Safe," and, looking at Bresnahan, said, "You can't use two balls on one play."

Bresnahan had him there. "I didn't do *that*."

"Yes, you did," the umpire said. "You threw one into left field."

"That's not a ball, that's a potato," Bresnahan said.

At which point, Bresnahan said, the umpire became very upset. By then the third base umpire had retrieved the disguised missile. On reaching home plate with the evidence, the umpire said words perhaps never heard outside a GI mess hall. He said, "It's a %$#% potato."

Bresnahan argued the umpires' decision to give Reading the run. He said, "You can't give 'em a run on a wildly thrown potato. Can you? Look it up."

The next day, Williamsport let in customers for $1 a ticket if they brought a potato. Bresnahan autographed potatoes, signing them, "This spud's for you."

Bresnahan also was fined $50 by killjoy manager Orlando Gomez (who took Bresnahan out of the game after the fifth inning comedy). Then it got worse for Bresnahan. He was fired.

"The Cleveland farm director called me and was laughing," Bresnahan said. "He said, 'That was ingenious. What are you trying to do, get on the David Letterman show?' But then he said, 'We can't condone it. We have to make an example of you.'"

Before leaving Williamsport, Bresnahan bought two sacks of potatoes. He put them on Orlando Gomez's desk. He attached a note. It said, "Surely you don't expect me to pay the $50 fine now. However, I will oblige you by giving you 50 potatoes. This spud's for you."

Howard Cosell

June 13, 1988

New York

Howard Cosell is barefoot. Why, I don't know. But for two hours he is barefoot. Otherwise, he is dressed for dinner in slacks, shirt and a tie tossed around his neck. It is just after 4 o'clock in the afternoon and he has to record a radio show at 4:30. So the barefoot broadcaster pads into his kitchen and punches a button on a five-button telephone. With a trembling hand, he punches in a call to his assistant at ABC Radio. He wants the sports news. It is 4:19 now. The phone is ringing, but it is not ringing fast enough for Howard Cosell. And then it is not ringing at all.

"Son of A BITCH! Cut OFF! What the . . ." He holds a pen to take notes from his assistant, only he can't get her on the good-God-damn telephone. So he punches in the numbers again, sneaking a look at the clock over his kitchen stove. It's 4:22 and air time is 4:30 and Howard Cosell does not know the sports news upon which he will base his day's commentary. The phone is ringing. Cosell writes a name on a scrap of paper and says to me, "Don Chaney'll be the first thing Michelle tells me." Don Chaney had taken the Houston Rockets job the night before. "Come on, COME ON!" The telephone is very close to losing its job with Howard Cosell.

Now Michelle answers, and Cosell's voice slips to a kindly tone, almost a whisper of flirtation. "The sports news, Michelle, what has happened today in SportsWorld," Cosell says, and I write it that way, SportsWorld, because Cosell says it with a sardonic twist, as if speaking of a pretentious theme park for silly little fools.

Now Cosell scratches a name onto his notepad. "Larry Brown," he says into the phone. "How much money? Three-point-five. For how many years? Five." The tremor in Howard's hand makes it hard for him to write anything. It's no disease, he says; it runs in the family. He's 68 and healthy, still capable of astonishing, even breathtaking bursts of energy. He can whup any man in the room at talking. Michelle gives him Don Chaney's name. "Anything else?" Cosell says. It is 4:25, and he says into the phone, "Johnny Mac. Eighth. Who's first, Lendl? Wilander. Edberg. Where's Becker? Sixth. In-CRED-ible. SIXTH!"

By June of most years Cosell and his wife Emmy have skedaddled to the Hamptons for the summer. But this spring doctors told Mrs. Cosell she had lung cancer. They said it directly. She might not make it through the surgery. She wrote farewell letters to the children and told them to take care of their father; she said he had never paid a bill in his life, wouldn't know how to do it, and would wind up on the street if the children didn't take care of him. The week before the surgery, Cosell told me, "If Emmy doesn't make it, I don't know that I want to be around."

Happily, she made it and she is with the barefoot boy broadcaster this day in their 27th floor apartment on East 69th Street. The doctors said she couldn't go to the Hamptons just yet; she had to get stronger. She sits on a sofa with her back to the city skyline. "It's a miracle," she says. "Now I can even say the words. Lung cancer. Before, I couldn't say it. But now I'm going to be OK." And from his chair across the way Howard Cosell says softly, "A miracle."

It is 4:27 and now he has the sports news and now he is up from the kitchen table and he says, "Follow me." We go to his study at the back of the apartment where Cosell pulls on a headset and sits in an easy chair. The easy chair has a pillow on the seat, a pillow bearing the words, "O Lord, Give Me a Bastard With Talent." The pillow is a gift from George Steinbrenner. Cosell sits on the Steinbrenner pillow before a microphone wired directly to ABC Radio.

"Michelle," he says into the mike. "Michelle? Mi-CHELLE! Is this up? Michelle, are we up? Let's do it, MICHELLE! IS ANY-BODY THERE? Son of a BITCH! Is any-THING WORKING? Here, talk into this mike while I go try to raise them by telephone." And he hands the thing to me. I put on the headset. Doing Cosell, I say, "Mi-CHELLE!" And a tiny voice comes into the headset, "Who's there?"

"Hold on, I'll get Howard," I say, and now it's 4:29, and now Howard Cosell has the headset on, and now there is a transformation, the heartbeat turned up a notch, and I hear another voice, *that* voice, which is to voices what the Grand Canyon is to ditches. That voice is saying, "Hello again, everybody, this is Howard Cosell speaking of sports. Everyone in sports is a role model. We know that . . ."

Winging it, Cosell then ties Larry Brown, Don Chaney and John McEnroe into a news package and a two-minute commentary on their worth as role models for American society. He paints Brown as a glorified winner who is in truth a hypocrite if not a liar for pledging loyalty to Kansas only to go shopping for a better deal in the NBA; he sees Chaney as a man who has paid his dues and deserves a chance to make it big, and Cosell sees in the villified McEnroe a man of integrity who turned down a $1 million offer to play an exhibition in one of South Africa's segregated homelands.

"So who is the proper role model here?" Cosell asks his listeners.

I am impressed. In no more than 10 minutes, Cosell has scratched down three names on a notepad, divined a thread which connects them and ad-libbed a national two-minute broadcast. "Good job," I say as the barefoot one leans back in an easy chair.

"Not a bad notion, was it? SportsWorld, an American dreamland," he says.

"If you think so little of it, why do you still do these broadcasts?" I ask.

"Nobody else will tell the truth. Somebody has to do it." Cosell leans back in his easy chair.

There you have it, Don Quixote barefoot, the aging knight tilting at the windmills of SportsWorld. Cosell is right, of course; nobody else does it on the air. But then, why would we expect them to? There's only been and will only be one Howard Cosell. And Cosell is honest enough to say this, too, about his radio work: "Besides, they pay me (here a pause for mental long division) — they pay me $7,500 a week. Not bad."

Cosell for the last four years wrote a nationally syndicated sports column. He had a television talk show. Both were dropped this spring. A book by a former vice president of ABC-TV Sports, Jim Spence, charged that Cosell drank heavily and drank on the job. Doctors found lung cancer in Emmy Cosell. Not the springtime of any man's dreams. But neither was it what a television critic wrote in *Sports Illustrated*; Cosell's world was falling apart, the critic said.

"The only thing that mattered at all was Emmy," Cosell says. His world falling apart because of a sports column? Because of a TV show? Ludicrous. After what Cosell has done for 35 years in broadcasting? "In 35 years, I missed five shows total," he says. "Of course, all the others I did in a drunken stupor."

And he's off and running. Cosell is doing play-by-play. Even as he sits barefoot in his 27th floor apartment on June 13, 1988, he does play-by-play of the first Monday Night Football game broadcast by ABC-TV. I start to take notes of what he's saying, but I can't keep up. He gives the date (September something, 1970), the place (Cleveland), the Jets against the Browns, Joe Namath passing for 299 yards only to throw an interception which is returned by Billy Lawrence, "number 51 on your program, deciding it for Cleveland, the final score 31-21, but, of course, I don't remember any of it because I was in a drunken stupor at the time."

Of Spence, Cosell says, "Never been in a broadcast booth in his life. An errand boy for Roone Arledge. What am I supposed to do, sue him? It's sick. It's not worth my time."

If Cosell is the preeminent sports broadcaster of his time — no one can argue otherwise — I think he also is a genius who changed sports journalism forever. His influence as a brilliant thinker on the ethics of sports touched newspaper reporters as well, for alone in our profession Cosell made his voice heard outside arenas and ballparks. He can not abide the idea that sports is holy, that athletes are paragons and role models, that winning is all-important and that fans have license to be brainless punks. Such a sermon deserves wide hearing.

Cosell also was showman, pomposity, philosopher, bore, pioneer, crusader and in his least appealing moments a mean bully trying to impose himself on a world he saw as an enemy. At the World Series in 1977 idiots below the ABC broadcasting booth chanted an obscenity at Cosell and threw a pair of pliers at him. In Baltimore, angry football fans cursed Cosell as he left the stadium with Mrs. Cosell on his arm. They put their heft to Cosell's limousine and rocked it to and fro. In Denver a bar sold bricks which customers threw at Cosell's image on a television set.

To those who say he brought it on himself, the answer is yes, he did; he brought it on himself if you figure that a man telling the truth as he sees it deserves to be punished for it. He was like no other broadcaster in an industry built on pandering to the fans' emotional attachment to their favorite teams; that is, he was critical of SportsWorld. He had a high fast ball and he didn't mind brushing big hitters off the plate. Though television is more show-biz than it is journalism, viewers went away from Cosell's work with a memory of not only his style but his substance. And the only measure we need of Cosell's substance was provided during the long and melancholy exile of Muhammad Ali, convicted of refusing the draft and then illegally railroaded out of the heavyweight championship by hyperpatriotic fools. Ali's only defender at any level of the national media: Howard Cosell tilting at the windmills of injustice as he saw them.

Cosell. The name is enough. Everyone, even an errand boy, has an opinion on Cosell. I want to put one or two more brushstrokes on the portrait.

Las Vegas, 1979. We join Howard in mid-narrative, which is where he usually is. "Being brought up the way I was, there was a time I *lived* for the Brooklyn Dodgers. After the delivery of our first born, Emmy the first night out sat on the hard seats of Ebbets Field."

Emmy Cosell, across the room this night a decade ago, graceful in a black evening gown and reading a book against the noise of her man, only smiled at Howard's memoir. "My treat," she said, and she said it sweetly, as if sitting on a hard seat wasn't really what she wanted to be doing straight out of a maternity ward. But what's a girl to do when her man is a maniac Bum worshiper and she wants to be with him?

Cosell puffed on a cigar. Soon he and Emmy would go to dinner with Barron Hilton, the hotel guy. It can be fun to be in Cosell's presence. You need not stand at a distance guarding against sudden bursts of bombast or even a hurricane of hyperbole. Cosell is passionate, yes. If, like Muhammad Ali, he sometimes imitates himself, we forgive that, for a Cosellian impression of Cosell is still — *alive.* And on this evening with Emmy near, Cosell was a gentle man, his voice turned down, never never interrupting his wife.

"Emmy, on the first night out, watched Luis Olmo hit two home runs," Cosell said.

"The baby was Jill," Mrs. Cosell said in the interest of supplying perpsective to her guy's report. "Now we have three grandchildren."

Early in 1979 Cosell began work on a new contract worth a reported $6 million for four years. Johnny Carson's deal, worth more money, calls for him to work 100 nights a year; Cosell will do twice that. "They want me on everything. The Kentucky Derby, Preakness, all our tennis, all championship fights, the baseball and, of course, the fulcrum which is Monday Night Football."

"Boooo," Emmy Cosell said.

A boo for MNF?

Louder: "Boooooo. I don't like it. The hassles. The crowds. I go with Howard to every one. I can't stand it. The crowds, people clawing at Howard."

Then in the fall of 1984 it was over for Cosell at ABC-TV. His contract was up, and he said he wanted out. On the steps of the ABC building in New York one lovely September day, Cosell raised his face to a warming sun. He was done. Done with Monday nights. Done with the poor Giffer, done with the Danderoo. Done and glad of it because, he said, "If you do anything long enough, if you have a brain in your head, it becomes a terrible bore." Done with the little things in life, Cosell stood in the warm sun and said that what he really wanted on such a day was to spend it with his sweetheart: "I'm tempted to go to the airport and get a charter to the Hamptons to be with Emmy. I miss her."

He loved the work, and he lusted for fame and money (as protection, he said, against the economic and anti-Semitic wars his father had lost). But near the end, Emmy wanted him off the mad merry-go-round. She saw her guy exhuasted; she saw him hounded by critics. So in 1984 he told ABC he was done. "Free at last, free at last," Cosell shouted on the steps of the ABC building that warm day.

Later, in his office, I asked him, "Free at last. Is that good?"

Cosell said, "It's good if you're 64 and your father died alone at 65 in a Charlotte hospital."

He said it so softly I barely heard it. I asked, "Do you think about death?"

"Sure," he said, falling silent. The conversation moved to other, more comfortable paths, back to the start when he literally was not Howard Cosell.

World War II had just ended when he first scratched at radio work. He was a lawyer with a Phi Beta Kappa key. But he liked the drama of games, and he carried a 45-pound tape recorder strapped to his stooped back to do interviews.

"A whole generation thinks I was born rich," said Cosell, the son of Isadore Martin Cohen, an auditor who traveled for a clothing company. The family's Polish name was Kassell. The immigration people made it Cohen, and Isadore always wanted the family name returned. His son, Howard, did it for his father.

"A whole generation thinks I always had it made," Cosell said. "The truth is, nobody ever worked harder and longer hours than I did."

Cosell was working when the news of his father's death came. "Emmy was out in Maplewood, New Jersey, at her parents' home with our two girls, and I was with Dick Groat and Don Hoak, trying to make a name for myself, interviewing them for radio."

Cosell said he still felt guilty about not being in Charlotte when his father died. He began a sentence, "That's why I am so determined . . ."

He stopped. "When I made up my mind if . . ."

He stopped again. "If, God forbid, Emmy should go first, I want to be there with her. And if I go first, which is more likely, I want to know that Emmy's there. And we're agreed on that."

Four years after saying those words, Howard Cosell stood barefoot in his New York apartment. It was June 13, 1988, a Monday afternoon. Right after the surgery, the doctors ordered Emmy to stay in the apartment. Now she had clearance to get up and go. Now, stronger every day, she could travel. So Emmy and her barefoot boy would go to the Hamptons on the weekend. The grandchildren would be there.

Rosie Ruiz

April 26, 1980

Dear Rosie,

Two Washington men want to make a deal with you. Henry Buchanan wrote to us the other day saying he'll put up $100,000 that is yours if you beat him in a marathon. Alex Fraser called to say he'll put up $10,000 if you come within five minutes of your time in Boston.

Buchanan, a certified public accountant, has run four marathons, his best time two hours and 58 minutes. He ran Monday in Boston in three hours and two minutes. He said you can pick the marathon, preferably in May for "Rosie's benefit. I don't want her to think I want 10 or 12 weeks to improve my condition."

He will put the money in escrow, Rosie. You beat him, it's yours. Lose, and you must permit "qualified and recognized officials of the Boston marathon to make a binding judgment on whether or not she was the women's winner."

"My motivation," Buchanan wrote, "is for other marathoners, both men and women, but especially for the girl who finished second (Jacqueline Gareau of Montreal). That's a disgrace. For these world-class runners, this year's Boston Marathon is their Olympics."

Fraser said, "I will offer $10,000 to the charity of her choice, the American Cancer Fund, the Heart Fund, whatever. I will put the money on deposit. I will give $10,000 if she comes to Washington in the next six months and runs a marathon within five minutes of the time she ostensibly ran at Boston."

Fraser, an oil investor, is interested in establishing the truth, Rosie, just as you say you are. He wants everyone to know the answer.

Did you or didn't you?

Did Runnin' Rosie run 26 miles, 385 yards and win the Boston Marathon?

Or did you take a taxi 24 miles, 385 yards and then slip into the race?

"I don't like people who bend the rules as much as she did," Fraser said, adding quickly, "if she did, in fact, bend them. On the other hand, if she really ran the race, she ought to get credit for it.

"Otherwise, she'll forever be like the guy who ran the football the wrong way (Roy Riegels) or Wrong Way Corrigan who intended to fly to South Dakota and wound up in Ireland."

What Fraser is saying, Rosie, is that you'll forever be remembered as the Boston Straggler unless you do something to stop it. That's why he is putting up the $10,000. He's serious.

So are you serious, Rosie. You insist you ran the whole way, just as you insist you ran every step of the 26 miles, 385 yards in New York to qualify for Boston. You have offered to take a lie detector test. You have cried in front of television cameras when asked questions such as, "What's the scenery along the Boston route?"

There was "beautiful countryside," you said.

"There were roads winding in and out," you said.

And still people don't believe you, Rosie.

New York invalidated your time of two hours, 56 minutes yesterday. They said you didn't run the entire route. They said you took the subway to the finish line. And they didn't even ask you about the scenery in Manhattan. You could have told them there were a lot of cars and tall buildings.

The Boston people are investigating your finish time of 2:31:56. They have talked to witnesses who said you entered the course with about two miles to go.

Other runners are just as serious about things are you are. These runners are outraged at the thought of a fraud. For one thing, they don't like your advisor, Steve Marek. They don't understand why anyone would run a marathon wearing a Superman costume. Steve does that. So when he showed up as your advisor, right away other runners said that if Marek had anything to do with it, it was a disgrace for sure.

Everybody is serious about this, Rosie.

Too serious.

It could have been fun.

Think of it, Rosie.

Instead of crying on national TV, you could have written a book. *Shortcuts to Fame* would have been a nice title. The book would start on Chapter 24.

As Bill Rodgers has done, you could have become rich by selling stuff with your name on it.

Rosie Ruiz shoes: They're so comfortable that when the marathon is over, your feet feel like they've only gone a mile or two. These shoes leave no tracks.

Rosie Ruiz shirts and shorts: Science brought us Day-Glo so that Ray Charles could see us coming from a mile away, but it took Runnin' Rosie to invent Day-Fade, the fabric that makes you invisible. Dogs can't bite what dogs can't see.

Rosie Ruiz deodorant: Splash it on and you smell like someone who just finished a marathon.

Rosie Ruiz doll: Wind it up and it takes the subway.

Soon enough all of America would be on the Rosie Ruiz diet. You get so thin you disappear. We would see you on an American Express commercial saying, "Don't go to Boston without it." And the card has no name on it.

You might be interested, Rosie, in one man's theory about New York and Boston. He thinks you were just having fun and got carried away. Wayne Welch is a Washington bureaucrat who dropped out of the Boston race after 18 miles.

"I suspect Rosie didn't intend to win Boston," said Welch, who based his suspicions on a photographer's report that she had ridden with you on the subway to the New York finish line.

"It was probably innocent. Rosie took the subway to the finish line and walked up behind the chutes for the runners. She had a bad ankle. She probably said, 'Can you give me some help?' And someone else said, 'Injured runner here.'"

Runners in New York wore computer-coded labels on their racing numbers. Racing officials took these labels as runners crossed the finish line. Welch theorizes, Rosie, that someone simply took your label by mistake and you wound up with that 2:56:29 clocking even though you'd spent most of the time riding underground, not running on the ground.

"People around her office must have been congratulating her for weeks," Welch said, "and she probably liked it, so she figured she'd do it again at Boston. She was 23rd in New York and maybe she wanted to be fifth or sixth in Boston.

"But being ignorant of running — she just doesn't have the skin tone or the muscle tone of a runner — she didn't know what a good time would be and she jumped into the race too soon. She came flopping in like a wounded duck. You could see she wasn't a runner."

What you ought to do, Rosie, is laugh about all this. Get Buchanan's $100,000 and Fraser's $10,000 and put on your own marathon. The winner's trophy could be a subway token.

Willie Pastrano

November 23, 1980

New Orleans

The old fighter is talking.

"I look at ordinary people in their suits, them with no scars on their face, and I'm different from these people."

Willie Pastrano is the old fighter, once a world champion, the light heavyweight champion for two years in the early 1960s. Though lit by the thin winter sun of a late New Orleans afternoon, the old fighter's face belongs to darkness.

"I don't fit in with them people. I'm where everybody's got scar tissue on their eyes and got noses like saddles. I go to these old-timers' conventions, old fighters like me, and I see the scar tissue and all them flat noses. They're beautiful. Galento, may he rest in peace. Giardello, LaMotta, Carmen Basilio. What a sweetheart Basilio is. They talk like me, like they got rocks in their throats. Beautiful."

This is Willie Pastrano, who once sat at tea with the Queen of England. Willie Pastrano, who knew a man who sawed people into pieces for disposal. Willie Pastrano, who made $100,000 in his last fight and a year later robbed houses and yachts, "sneaking in like a . . . dog," to buy the heroin he needed with his daily breakfast of gin and vodka, razor-blade soup.

"I was," Willie Pastrano said, "the living dead."

He quit talking.

The old fighter made the sign of the cross.

In a deserted firehouse with a threadbare ring, Willie Pastrano works as the boxing coach of the New Orleans Recreation Department. At the Superdome, a $4.80 cab ride away, Sugar Ray Leonard gets $7 million this week and Roberto Duran $10 million. Willie Pastrano, for his week's work, will clear $69.50.

He's broke, yes. "But look," he said, "I've had money, I've been rich." He'd rather be what he is now. Happy. He's happy to be alive. He is 45 years old, and sharpies will tell it was 8-5 against Willie Pastrano ever getting so old. Heroin addicts don't win many times.

"Just saying 'heroin' makes me feel like I taste it in the back of my mouth," Pastrano said. "I go to the doctor's office and see a syringe, it makes me sick to my stomach. You never really kick it. You always got the yen. You always got to fight. I'm the champ at fighting the junk."

At 190 pounds Willie Pastrano is only 15 pounds over the light-heavyweight limit. There is a spring in his step. A weightlifter now, he is in good shape. The son of an Italian father and a Cajun mother, Pastrano has a square-cut face of mottled browns and blacks. Thin lines of scars wiggle through his eyebrows, and long-healed wounds are marked by tiny craters on his cheekbones. Doctors twice have done surgery on his left eye, and now he wears sunglasses because the eye is always red.

And if the eye is red, people think they know. It's a detached retina, but people think the red in his eye means Willie is on the horse again. On the heroin.

He goes to churches now to tell the people without scars on their faces that he was a heroin addict.

He tells them the junk put him in three mental institutions and three hospitals. They wanted to tape wires to his forehead and shoot electricity through his brain. He said no. No electroshock for a world champion. He would beat the stuff on his own.

It's the toughest fight of his life, he says, and he is winning.

Pastrano lost his championship the third time he defended, losing to José Torres in March, 1965. Fighting was the only thing Pastrano ever did right. A fat little kid, shamed by his father, who beat him with a belt for not striking back at neighborhood bullies who taunted him as "jelly shaking on a plate," Pastrano went to a boxing gym to lose weight. In the process, he found talent.

Never a puncher, always a clever stylist, Pastrano fought 18 years before winning the championship from Harold Johnson. On the way up, he had tea with the Queen and Prince Philip while in London to fight; he moved with good fighters such as Kid Gavilan, Benny Paret, Jimmy Ellis and Ralph Dupas, and he had $30,000 in the bank after he lost the title to Torres.

"When I lost the title, I got down on myself," Pastrano said. "I was lonely. I had nobody. I had nothing. So I opened my doors to the wrong people. I let in anybody, just so there'd be people around. For three years after I lost my title, I didn't know who the hell I was."

Who the wrong people were: "Killers, dope dealers, people who sawed up bodies. I didn't know it at the time. I thought one guy owned a gas station and another guy was a salesman. Then one day I went to visit this one guy. I walked through his house and out to the back, to his utility shed, and I saw him through a crack in the door."

What he saw: "He had on rubber gloves and an apron. He had a hacksaw, and his hands were full of blood. I started to say, 'Hi,' and that's when I saw the foot cut off. I puked."

For three years, Pastrano used heroin daily. "It wasn't the heroin I wanted. It was the boxing thing. Boxers should be rehabilitated like Vietnam veterans. Boxers have been to war and are psychologically scarred. You got fighters acting like they're punch-drunk when they're not, just to get attention. Like Beau Jack shining shoes in front of a hotel in Miami. He ain't punch-drunk. He just misses the applause. With the applause, you come to life."

Without that affirmation of existence, Pastrano needed big money for the only high available to him. Heroin.

"I didn't have nothing left from my $30,000, so I was always looking to get money. You needed money because you needed heroin to feel normal. Your body gets to need it like food. I had gin and vodka for breakfast. And heroin. I did 'b and e's' for the money. Breaking and entering. I robbed places across the street from police stations. I robbed houses, I robbed yachts. I never used a weapon, not once. I was sneaking in like a . . . dog."

He went cold turkey in 1969, Pastrano said, and there followed 10 years of wandering. Las Vegas, Oklahoma City, Miami. A trail of tears. Dupas dragged his right leg and became a hermit. Ellis and Gavilan are blind in one eye. Paret is dead, killed in the ring. And Willie Pastrano, their friend, once a champion of the world, worked as a bouncer in strip joints, 2 o'clock in the afternoon 'til 2 the next morning, six days a week. Worked some as a chip runner in Vegas, did some greeting at a greasy spoon in Reno.

Back in his hometown of New Orleans, Pastrano has worked the last year with the city recreation department down at the Magazine Street gym. Yellowed newspaper clippings are stuck to the walls. History is on those dirty walls: Cassius Clay at 13, Tony Galento falling through the ropes against Jack Dempsey, Willie Pastrano in with Archie Moore.

Sitting at the back of the gym, Pastrano watches a handful of plainly pitiable fighters. They should be pumping gas somewhere. They are in Pastrano's gym desperately dreaming. Because a manager reneged on a deal, Pastrano has taken over managing his first fighter, Chubby Johnson, 22, who will be on the Leonard-Duran undercard.

"They say old boxers ought to get away from boxing," Pastrano said. "I don't want to be a manager. But a guy backed out on Chubby and now I got him. Okay, I'm a manager. So all right. Boxing is what I am."

Then Pastrano said, "You know what Duran did the other day during a workout?"

Duran did this: Duran looked into the crowd and raised his gloved fist in salute.

"I looked around to see who he was waving to," Pastrano said.

The old fighter's face left the darkness a moment. "It was for me."

Martina Navratilova

July 2, 1987

London

For a silly little point which meant nothing more than the subtraction of perhaps five seconds from her day's work — victory was inevitable in any case — Martina Navratilova threw herself into the air, suspended horizontally above the hallowed Wimbledon lawn, in the fashion of Boris Becker, diving to her left with the racket extended in hopeless pursuit of a shot.

Hopeless? Not at all, as it turned out, for even at age 30 with seven Wimbledon championships on her ledger, the last five in succession, the fire in Martina Navratilova still burns brightly. Hers is not a consuming fire, not hateful to see; this is beautiful, the glow of a fire warming all within its reach. To see Navratilova diving is to see sport at its best.

And not only diving, but winning the point with a volley angled past the day's opponent, Diane Balestrat. Navratilova crashed to earth. She bounced up right away. Dirt stained her skirt. Her left elbow was skinned. She worked her left shoulder, as if it ached.

"No, no," she said later, "nothing hurt. Just trying to get the grass off my elbow. Only a boo-boo on my elbow, is all."

Here it is, Navratilova winning a quarterfinal match, and the only damage to her in 10 days of her game's greatest tournament is a boo-boo on her elbow. She has not lost a set; she has lost as many as three games in a set only once. If this be the end of Martina Navratilova, as is so widely trumpeted by those smitten with the athleticism of the youngster Steffi Graf, someone needs to persuade Navratilova of it. She begs to differ, and rightly so.

Name the great ones in any game: Bobby Jones and Jack Nicklaus,

Ty Cobb and Pete Rose, Wayne Gretzky and Bobby Orr, Muhammad Ali and Joe Louis, Larry Bird and Michael Jordan. To that list can be added Martina Navratilova. By her physical skills and iron will, she raised the ceiling of possibility in women's tennis. Before Navratilova, no woman was so quick and so strong; no one could play the baseline all day and yet play the net with suffocating precision. She showed everyone a new way to play the game, at a level unimagined before she made it real. She transcended her game. She became so much the best that she breathed the rarefied air of those athletes who are so good it is always their work, not the opponent's, which decides victory and defeat. Playing well, they could not be beaten; they could lose, but only by playing poorly.

For three years, from early 1981 through the U.S. Open of 1984, Navratilova won 235 matches and lost . . . five. Those numbers are evidence of both her skill and her commitment to excellence, a commitment which even in her doddering old age shows no signs of flagging. Now only two victories from a sixth straight Wimbledon championship, Navratilova said, "It's the most exciting thing that could ever happen to anybody. I don't feel it as pressure. I feel it as, 'Wow! This is great.'

"I love it all. This is what all the hard work's for. Playing Wimbledon. It's not the sit-ups, lifting weights, running 400-yard sprints. It's Wimbeldon that's the ultimate, and I refuse to get uptight or nervous. My God, if you can't enjoy it now, after all I've been through, it's time to quit. And I'm not ready to quit."

She first came to Wimbledon in 1973. She was a holy terror, a chubby Czechoslovakian brat who came here "throwing rackets, calling umpires names, getting mad at the crowd for not pulling for me." That year, Billie Jean King won her fifth Wimbledon championship. "I was just in awe," Navratilova said, "and I still am. It's hard for me to think I'm at the same level of those great players. It humbles me."

Navratilova defected to the United States during the 1976 U.S. Open in New York City. "It seemed awfully easy then. Now I look back, I say, 'Oh, my God, how did I do it?' But I know I would do it again. I think at 18 you're ready to take on the world. I had friends here. I had the money and I knew the language. It wasn't like a step for immigrants when they get on the boat and they don't know what's on the other side of the ocean."

She couldn't go home for five years, until she became a U.S. citizen. Her father had told her not to come back, no matter what he might say, because the Czech government might be luring her into a trap. She was 5 years old when her parents and grandparents taught her to play tennis. By defecting, she might have closed the door to ever seeing them again.

In the years since, Navratilova's life has been an open book, even literally with the publishing of her autobiography. We know about the defection, the homosexuality, the fits of temper and her outrageous appetites (for food, jewelry, houses).

"I have been embroiled with all kinds of controversy," she said, and with just the right touch of self-deprecation she added, "I might be more popular with the crowds now because of my personality. They're beginning to realize how wonderful I really am."

Barry Lorge of the *San Diego Union* and I sat with Navratilova late one night, two sportswriters asking informal questions, enjoying her company. Not only is she a passionate athlete in hot pursuit of excellence, a type which is always fascinating in conversation; Navratilova also is a warm and loving person who gives you a part of herself every time you're near her. This night she gave Lorge and me part of her heart, weeping.

I asked if she might go back to Czechoslovakia to see her parents, who had tried to live with her in the U.S. but returned home unhappy.

"I have second thoughts about going back there," she said. "I'd rather do it, I think, once I don't play tennis, because I know it would be emotional going back there. All the friends I had, Czech people that go back, are so depressed when they come out of there. They have a visa for two weeks and they come back after four days."

Then Navratilova said, "My parents can come out anytime they want. So can my sister. And they don't live in the same house we used to live in. So I really have nothing to go back for."

We wrote down her words. I wondered if she meant to sound so cold. I said, "Did your grandmother's death have anything to do with that, your saying you don't have anything to go back to?"

"My grandmother passed away two years ago." Her voice was flat.

Barry Lorge said, "Was she kind of a last link . . ."

"Well, I still have one grandmother, but I'm not as close to her."

Lorge asked his question again, another way, gently, and Navratilova said at a whisper, "Yeah, yeah." And when I asked if the grandmother was her mother's mother, Navratilova said, "No, my father."

Then, without speaking again, she walked away. She leaned against a wall on the other side of the room. She cried for five minutes.

We didn't know what to do. She saw us concerned and said she was sorry, it wasn't anything we had said, it was something she didn't expect to happen. She left then, down a corridor, stopping first to sign an autograph for a small girl. We left Navratilova a note saying we, too, were sorry.

The next day, Lorge and I found out about the grandmother. Her name was Andela Subertova. She had been the soft and loving light of Navratilova's childhood. She called Martina her *Zlata Holcicka,* "Golden Little Girl." At the age of 84, she came to Dallas to visit her famous granddaughter in March of 1979. They hadn't seen each other in almost four years. Navratilova took her to the Czech community in Dallas, where the old woman signed autographs. She introduced her grandmother to Chris Evert.

We found a quote on that. Navratilova said of her grandmother, "She said when she gets home, she's going to brag that she met Chris."

The next year, an aunt in Czechoslovakia sent Navratilova a black-edged card of mourning, a *parte.* She saw a cross in the middle of the page and then she saw her grandmother's name. It was the first word Martina heard of her grandmother's death.

In her autobiography, Martina wrote, "I loved Grandma Subertova so much that she almost did not get into this book. Every time I started to talk about her, I would break into tears, and feel weak and tired deep inside. I still have recurring dreams about Grandma. I see her going into the Metro, the subway, and I call after her, but I can't run fast enough to catch up with her and she can't come back. . . . Nobody has ever loved me so completely, so acceptingly, as Grandma. I can only hope that someday somebody will."

July 5, 1987

Martina Navratilova won her sixth straight Wimbledon championship and eighth in all with a 7-5, 6-3 victory over Steffi Graf. The young loser said to the happy old-timer, "Geez, how many more do you want?"

Navratilova: "Nine's my lucky number."

Bear Bryant

November 9, 1979

Tuscaloosa, Alabama

Three or four years ago some Hollywood types offered Bear Bryant big bucks to make a movie of his life. John Wayne would play Bear. Naturally. Type-casting. American originals both. Mountains of manhood. If Bear grew tired walking across a lake, Wayne would carry him on his back the rest of the way. So Bear said yes to the movie, only to back out on second thought.

"'Cause the family asked me not to do it," he said. "Hollywood. They have the last say on everything. They'll give you any kind of contract. But if they get a lot of money involved, they're going to make something in there to sell."

Something sinful, perhaps?

"Yep."

Such as Alabama losing to LSU?

"Be X-rated then," Bryant said.

Paul William (Bear) Bryant still likes to win. The University of Alabama football coach is 66 years old but looks to be nearer 116. With all the ruts and rough spots, his face looks like a piece of ground that needs water. He doesn't so much walk as he creeps around. It took him most of a minute today to climb the 34 steps of his practice-field watchtower. He held the stair railing with both hands, pulling himself up, one slow step at a time. In his 35th year as a big-time football coach, Bryant is an old man with a dozen pill bottles on his office desk: pills for colds, vitamin pills, pills to get the digestive tract working, pills for his cigarette habit, pills of all colors, yellow, white and blue pills, a pharmaceutical cornucopia.

But he still wants to win.

"I tell you what winnin' means to me," Bryant said. "It means a lot to me. I don't think it means in the same way it used to. I'm a lot more interested now — you know, when you're young and fightin' for your life and tryin' to accomplish somethin', you gotta think about nothin' but winnin' football games — but now what kind of people we turn out means a lot more to me."

Bryant said he doesn't break the NCAA rules the way he used to fightin' for his life. Now if a kid can't play, Bear doesn't *make* him do it; he doesn't get down in a three-point stance and slug it out in the dirt the way he did at Maryland and Kentucky and Texas A&M before coming here in 1958, back to his alma mater. Now Bryant says of that kid, "If we don't help him prepare himself to compete later on in life, we've done a poor job. . . . That's why I think if you do well in that, you're really winnin' whether you're winnin' games or not."

Bryant's teams have won 292 games, lost 77 and tied 16. His Alabama teams have won five national championships, including last year's. From 1971 on Alabama has a 93-11 record, only twice in those nine seasons losing more than one game. Winner of 21 straight Southeastern Conference games, Alabama is undefeated in eight games this year, stretching its winning streak to 17 games. It is ranked No. 1 in the nation.

To hear Bryant's sad song today, though, you'd think he'd never won a game and might never win another one. Poor 'Bama. Injuries galore. Ten men who have been in the starting lineup are injured. Woe is the Tide. The Tide plays LSU in Baton Rouge Saturday night. Even on crutches, Alabama is the better team and figures to win by two or three touchdowns. But if you listen to Bryant for a few minutes, he'll have you in tears over his team's dismal prospects for success.

"LSU will be highly emotional, they'll really be rarin' to go," he said. "And I can never tell about our team. I know we certainly won't be at full strength. We'll be about 80 percent of the team I thought we'd be. I've never had a team as crippled as we were this week. Never been around one as crippled."

Such lamentations, old-timers here say, are signs certain that Bear Bryant is up for the game.

"You gotta watch him," a Tuscaloosa sportswriter said. "All those injured guys will be out there playing like gangbusters." Not all of them, because three have had knee operations; but the idea is the same: the more Bear poor-mouths, the more he's *coaching*.

"It's not recruiting that wins for Bear," said Alf Van Hoose, a Birmingham sportswriter who has seen Bryant's Alabama teams from the start. "He doesn't get the real blue-chippers all over the country. Of his 25 recruits this year, 15 are from Alabama, and most of them weren't recruited by more than one or two schools.

"It's coaching that wins for Bear. It's coaching and spirit. He's often said he doesn't coach football, he coaches people. Give Stonewall Jackson the players, give Julius Caesar the players, they'll whup you. So will Bear."

Paul William Bryant, who became Bear when he wrestled a bear at a country fair, is now wrestling with history. Only 23 more victories will make him the winningest college coach ever. Amos Alonzo Stagg won 314 games in 57 seasons. Bryant, if he were to coach 57 years and win at his current rate of 8.3 victories a season, would win 473 games.

One of 11 brothers and sisters from Moro Bottom, Arkansas — a hamlet described by Bryant as "a little piece of bottom land on the Moro Creek about seven miles south of Fordyce" — Bryant played in the first football game he ever saw. He had a shoemaker attach cleats to his only pair of shoes.

From Fordyce High, where he played tackle, Bryant became Alabama's "other end" opposite All-America Don Hudson on teams that went 23-3-2, won Alabama's first SEC championship and beat Stanford in the 1934 Rose Bowl.

After six years as an assistant coach at Alabama and Vanderbilt, and after three years in the Navy, he became Maryland's head coach in 1945. His team went 6-2-1. Fightin' for his life, tryin' to accomplish somethin', he left Maryland after that one season for lots of money — $4,000 a year — to take over at Kentucky, where he raised a moribund football program to unprecedented accomplishments (still unduplicated there). His teams won an SEC championship and four straight bowl games.

But he worked at Kentucky alongside Adolph Rupp, the basketball baron who by a decade's success had laid first claim to the state's heart.

"I knew it was time to leave Kentucky," Bryant said, "when they had a banquet and they gave Adolph a Cadillac and gave me a cigarette lighter."

After four seasons at Texas A&M, Bryant returned to Alabama and now is in hot pursuit of Amos Alonzo Stagg.

Six or seven years ago, everyone thought Bryant would retire. He'd won everything. He turned down $1 million to coach the Miami Dolphins ("Bet they thank God for that," he said. "'Cause they went and hired Don Shula"). Anyway, Bryant's health wasn't good — friends were worried about the length of his cocktail hours.

"Drifting, is what he was doing," said Charley Thornton, an Alabama assistant athletic director. "He didn't have a lot of personal goals to work for. He's not good at working with a lot of things at once, but if he has one thing to do, nobody can do it better. I started dropping hints about Stagg's record.

"Bear never said a word to show he even heard me. Until one day, out of the blue, he says, 'What did you say that guy's record was?'

"And he didn't say anything again for a long time. At the Birmingham Quarterback Club two years ago, he came to me and said, 'Write down that stuff about those records.'"

And that night, to the Quarterback Club, Bear Bryant announced that he was going after that guy Stagg's record.

"I probably shouldn't have said it, and I didn't mean it as strongly as it sounded," Bryant said. "But every year, we'd go out recruiting and it'd be the same old thing: 'Bryant won't be there next year, he won't be your coach.'

"So I told the club, and it embarrasses me really to talk about it — I mean, just think about everybody who contributes to making a kid a winner and here comes a coach to take credit — I said, 'As long as somebody's gotta have that record, it might as well be me.

And all you guys talking about me retiring might as well quit it because I'm gonna break Stagg's record.'"

So at 2:30 on this afternoon in the 66th fall of his life, Bear Bryant put on a red jacket and white baseball cap, left his office in the basketball arena, walked through a tunnel to the practice field, drove a golf cart across the field and with an old man's struggle climbed up his tower, 30 feet high, from where he occasionally lifted up a bullhorn to send his rolling-thunder voice down: "Wilcox, you're standing around down there. . . . Get more pressure on defense. . . . Perfection now, perfection now. The fourth quarter."

"You keep an eye on him all the time," said David Hannah, a senior defensive lineman, the fourth Hannah to play at Alabama, brother of Charles and John, son of Herb. "It's like the Lord looking over your every move."

Bryant's deification is taken for granted here. Ten years ago, a fast-buck entrepreneur made up a photograph of Bryant walking on water. ("It's silly as hell," Bryant said, but he bought a picture, and he laughed this day when someone told him about the SEC coach whose university president said, 'I've got good news and bad news. The good news is that the Lord called to wish you luck against Alabama this week. The bad news is He called from Tuscaloosa.'")

"Talking to Coach Bryant," Hannah said, "you definitely get a feeling of something great talking to something minor. When you walk into a room with him, he has an awe about him. There are some guys on the team who will fake it and say they don't think that way, but I know that anytime Coach says jump, everybody says how far."

Bryant has a humility fetish. "I'm a simple, old, ordinary barnyard coach," he said. He doesn't quote Virgil, as Joe Paterno does, and he doesn't recite a play-by-play of World War II, as Woody Hayes did. Bryant is extraordinary nevertheless, for he has adapted so well to changing times in four decades that even if he disclaims genius — "I'm dumb, but I can take what somebody else invents and make it work for me" — he yet is a master of his craft.

111

Forty-one of his former assistant coaches and players learned enough barnyard coaching to leave Alabama and become head coaches. Among them: Charlie McClendon, Paul Dietzel, Bill Battle, Howard Schnellenberger, Bum Phillips, Ray Perkins, Jack Pardee, Jerry Claiborne, Larry Lacewell, Babe Parilli, Jackie Sherrill, Danny Ford, Bill Arnsparger.

Bryant loves 'em all. And beats hell out of 'em. His old coaches and players are 5-34 against the Bear and have lost the last 24 in a row. Because he couldn't beat Bryant, Battle was fired at Tennessee; same thing is happening with McClendon at LSU.

Friends say Bryant was in trouble himself at Alabama three years ago, that he insulted the university's interim president at a party (by saying he had approved the president's appointment) and that he was told to control his drinking or be fired.

"Aw, shoot," Bryant said, so disgusted he didn't use those exact words when someone asked if any of that were true.

"I stopped drinkin' for one full year. Used to, every Saturday night after a game, have some drinks and a big meal. But I don't do that anymore. Have milk and cookies. Cigarettes, too. I'm tryin' to cut down on them, too.

"Hell," Bryant said, "when you get to be my age, you gotta cut down on everythin'. I want to live a while longer."

Bryant probably would be allowed to coach past Alabama's mandatory retirement age of 70. "Oh, I don't know how long I'll coach. Some days, it gets late in the year like this, I get tired and think, jeesuz, why do I have to do this? But I don't know what the hell I'd do. I gotta do somethin'. I want to coach as long as I enjoy it."

Bryant is a millionaire businessman, with investments in aluminum windows, meat-packing and hound's-tooth hats. But football owns him, defines him, makes him someone John Wayne would want to play in a movie.

The telephone rang. A radio station wanted an interview.

"It's still early in the week," the coach said for the radio, "but we're badly crippled. Had 10 that didn't play last week, got several more hurt now. Gettin' some back today, but right now, worst crippled team I've ever had."

November 29, 1981

Birmingham, Alabama

When Bear Bryant set the record, they didn't carry him off the field. He's too old for that kid stuff. And he took precautions with his hound's-tooth hat, assigning a policemen to carry the lid to safety. Make no mistake, though. Bryant loved this victory in ways he hasn't loved one for a long time.

"For them to turn it around that way," Bryant said of his Alabama players, who beat Auburn with two fourth-quarter touchdowns, 28-17, "this is one of the greatest victories I've ever been connected with."

It was No. 315. Harry Truman was president when Bryant began winning. Amos Alonzo Stagg needed 57 years to win 314; Bryant has been at it 37 years. Bryant did it by a young man's cheating (self-confessed); did it by works of coaching genius (his wishbone offense is winning while others have died); did it by inspiring his players ("God doesn't see more than Coach did, and Coach probably scares more people," Joe Namath said), and did it by knowing when time no longer could resist an idea driven by truth (Alabama is 116-14-1 with racially integrated teams).

Mostly, he's done it by being Bear. He's good folks, as they say here. No high-falutin' fellow. Loved his momma, loved his poppa, loves his kids. There's a phrase for it in the South: Bear never got above his raisin'. Puts down a bucketful of whiskey, but only the best brand. When the doctor told him to cut the cigarettes down to two a day, Bear thought he meant two packs. Everyone in Alabama would bring the Bear a cake, as a pretty blonde, maybe 20 years old, did this week when she walked into the coach's office with it.

The coach's eyes got real young about then, and when the blonde left his office, Bryant said, "Hell, if this was 40 years ago, I'd have kept her 'stead of the cake."

He is a man called Bear. Begin with that if you would understand the mystique. At 12 he took a shill's dare at an Arkansas country fair and wrestled a bear. Someone asked him 56 years later if he taught the bear to block and tackle. Bryant laughed. "I was the one to learn somethin'. I learned to look for youngsters with good mommas and poppas."

Even at 68, Bryant is a tall, thick man with sledgehammer arms and hands. He once frightened players physically. Later he learned other ways to shape them. In 1963 Bryant suspended the great quarterback Namath for breaking training rules. Alabama had two important games coming up.

"I felt awful," Namath said this week, "but Coach looked worse than I did. When we talked about what I had done, he grabbed his head and fell back on my bed. I thought he was having a heart attack. It scared me half to death. But he was just disappointed in me."

It is simple, Namath said, to understand why Bryant is a great leader. People follow an honest man who earns their respect. Bryant that day in 1963 told Namath that all but one of the Alabama coaches wanted to lift the suspension and allow Namath to play the big games.

Then Bryant said it was up to Namath. He could play. But if he did, Bryant would resign, because such permissiveness was against his principles. Namath accepted the suspension and came back the next spring as the humbled fifth-string quarterback. After Namath worked his way back into Bryant's graces, Alabama won the 1964 national championship.

"A genius, isn't he?" Namath said with a smile.

On this day when he won his 315th game, it's important to know that Bear Bryant doesn't mumble anymore. You win 315 games, you get so you think you can go on forever. "Gonna coach 'til they run me off," Bryant said. To show he's serious, not only has he cut down on the smoking, he has cut out the mumbling.

It's them damn Yankee sportwriters. Every time they come carpet-bagging down here, they make a big deal out of Bear's mumbles. (Down here they understand every word the coach says, as if it were spoken by God in a hound's-tooth hat. Still, the Ford truck people once sped up a sound track so the world at large could understand Bryant.) Them damn Yankees say the coach is over the hill and the proof is the mumbles.

Well, at age 68, with 315 victories behind him, Bear Bryant spoke loudly and clearly after beating Auburn. He shouted across a room to the Auburn coach, Pat Dye, "Governor Carter called."

Like Carter, Dye had grown up in Georgia. "Governor Reagan?" Dye said, thinking Bryant had mixed up his presidents.

"Reagan, too," Bryant said. "But I thought you'd appreciate Governor Carter more."

Dye still wasn't sure. "The president called you?"

"Sure he called me," Bryant said. No mumblin'. Loud and clear. Bear Bryant, who never got above his raisin', was proud that a boy from an Arkansas river bottom had talked to the president of the United States. *Sure he called me.* Bryant raised his chin a notch. His chest came up. His eyes sparkled in the TV lights. The years fell away. There stood the fiery little boy who wrestled a bear.

Bert Yancey

March 24, 1978

Hilton Head, South Carolina

In the winter of 1974, when he was one of the best golfers in the world, Bert Yancey believed he was a messiah handpicked by God and given awesome responsibilities. Yancey was to save God's people from evil, put an end to racial prejudice and find a cure for cancer. The assignment thrilled him and he did his best to complete it.

This week the Professional Golfers Association tour stops here. It is a chance for Yancey to see old buddies. Retired from the tour two years now, he runs a golf instruction school at Hilton Head Golf Club. He also writes for the local newspaper, does a daily radio show and will do two-hour radio interviews of players here this week.

Yancey was a star in the late '60s and early '70s. In 13 seasons on tour, he won seven tournaments and $688,124. Few players were his match. Where Arnold Palmer lashed aggressively at the ball and Lee Trevino seemed the happy hacker, Yancey was a classicist with a club in his hand. His swing was a symphony, each movement majestic in its purity and simplicity. Putting, he was a thief working in daylight, stealing birdies from 20 feet when par was his due.

Only aficionados knew much of Yancey. While he was a winner, he never won the big ones; and while his skills were immense, he did nothing to attract attention to them. He didn't say funny things, he didn't dance on the greens. All he did was pull a white visor low over his eyes and walk slowly around a golf course, walking so smoothly he seemed to float, a man in a dream world. His buddies called him "Fog."

He was a dreamer. He loved golf. He loved its heroes, Bobby Jones and Walter Hagen and Harry Vardon. The rules of golf seemed to Yancey the ultimate guides to honor and sportsmanship. For years he studied films and read books, working on a history of the golf swing. Yancey was bright — some said his IQ was genius level — and he wanted nothing more than to make a lasting mark in the game he loved.

Greatness as a player eluded him. He made a crusade of winning the Masters. When someone told him the only way to win at Augusta was to acquire a feel for the greens, Yancey built clay models of every green. He wanted to run his hands over the contours, to *feel* them. He knew everything about the Masters, including the name of the tailor who made the winner's green jacket. He chose to stay in Augusta at the home of Mr. and Mrs. J. B. Masters.

But he couldn't win the tournament. He twice finished third, once fourth. He was the early leader the first time he played Augusta in 1967, but finished with rounds of 73–73 and lost by four shots. He could have won the U.S. Open in 1968 when he set scoring records for 36 and 54 holes. On the last day, he played poorly and finished third. So in the tournaments that put golfers in the history books, Yancey twice lost when victory seemed his for the taking.

He sat in his apartment at Hilton Head two weeks ago and said his days on tour are over. He'd like to play two or three tournaments a year, perhaps in California and Arizona, just to keep a hand in. The obsession with the Masters is also over. "I had my fun," Yancey said.

Today he is chasing a greater prize.

"I'm not afraid to say I'm mentally ill, and I'm coping with it," Yancey said.

Yancey, 39, has lived the last 18 years subject to the extreme mood swings symptomatic of manic-depressive illness. As thousands like him do, he now takes a drug, lithium carbonate, which acts as a governor on his moods. With the drug, Yancey's behavior is normal. Without it, he likely would go off on another of what he calls "my manic highs."

Those are episodes marked by bizarre behavior. They are generally thought, by Yancey and his doctors, to be defensive reactions to severe depression. Yancey says he wants people to know about his illness because "I think it could do a lot of good for people who would like to know more and understand mental illness. It is, you know, here to stay."

* * * * *

In the winter of 1974, Yancey was floating on a high. As all manic-depressives would, he loved the feeling. The high is intoxicating. The manic-depressive craves it the way an alcoholic craves drink. On a high, Yancey said, he felt smarter than everyone else. No one else could see what he could see. In a comb, he saw evil; he saw good in a brush. No one else could do that. He was smug.

The best part, he said, was the realization that he had been chosen to do God's work against evil, prejudice and cancer. This honor came to him after he completed the 1974 season with money winnings of $84,692, his best year ever. The PGA asked him to do exhibitions and clinics in Japan.

"I was a messiah rising out of the PGA," Yancey said. "I was going to the Orient to bring an end to the evil of communism and bring the religions of the Orient into line with Christianity."

Manic-depressives on a high cannot sleep because they are physically and mentally excited. It was 3 o'clock in the morning in Tokyo when Yancey, in his hotel room, heard a message delivered to him by his radio. A song came on, "Take a Walk, Take a Walk."

"So," Yancey said, "I took a walk."

In the three years since that walk in the dark, Bert Yancey has lived a nightmare. He has been in a straitjacket face down overnight on a jail-cell floor after being arrested on four counts: indecent exposure, "peeping Tom," resisting arrest and destroying government property. He has been chained by all fours to a bed in a psychiatric ward. His wife left him, taking their four children. The lithium carbonate, so necessary, produced the side effect of hand tremors which ruined him as a tour player.

Leaving his hotel room that night in Tokyo, Yancey thought it right that a messiah walk to the top of a large hill nearby and visit a

Japanese religious shrine. There a guard winked at him in acknowledgment, Yancey believed, of his divine status.

Returning to his hotel, Yancey saw the American singing group, The Temptations. Anyone with such a name must be evil, the golfer-messiah decided. "You're the devil," he told the singers, "and I'm here to take you on." Yancey says he remembers the words exactly. In a manic state, he said, everything is unforgettably vivid.

To take on the singers, Yancey assumed a karate stance, though he knew nothing of the martial art. Before he could attack evil, one of the singers slipped behind him and leveled Yancey with a punch so strong it ripped the corner of Yancey's eye.

Yancey returned to his hotel. There was a Christmas tree in the lobby. He pulled it over. "Here I am with my eye bleeding," he said, "and I'm yanking down the Christmas tree. As the champion of justice, I had lost to evil, and that was no place for a Christmas tree."

Later that morning, Yancey contemplated suicide by leaping from the 40th floor of his hotel, only to discover to his dismay that the windows were sealed shut at that level. A friend, tending to Yancey's wounds, then took the golfer to an Air Force hospital. From there Yancey was taken to a mental hospital in Philadelphia where he spent the first 2 1/2 months of 1975.

No one diagnosed Yancey's illness then, just as no one had in the summer of 1960.

A son of the city manager of Tallahassee, Florida, Yancey was a third-year cadet at the U.S. Military Academy in 1960. He made the Dean's List, was a nationally ranked college golfer, had a girlfriend and was proud to be at West Point.

"I was loving the whole thing," he said, "when — boom! — in less than two weeks I was in a padded cell."

He didn't know what to make of it in 1960, but now Yancey recognizes the symptoms of his illness.

"I couldn't sleep. I went for three nights and four days without sleeping. When you're high, your mind just works and works and works constantly. That's why you're creative. You get really charged up. But I'd stand plebes against the wall and say, 'What is truth, mister?' Or, 'What is love?'

"A couple of guys noticed it and asked me to go into a doctor and talk about it. I did, and they committed me. Right away."

For nine months, Yancey was in a hospital at Valley Forge, Pennsylvania. He underwent two series of electroshock treatments. Within a year, he joined the PGA tour briefly, dropping off for two seasons to work as a club assistant pro.

In 1964, he went on tour full-time and for Yancey that step into the sunlight by a man who had seen the darkness of a padded cell was a great victory. For the next decade, he walked with Palmer and Trevino and Nicklaus. His best friends were Frank Beard and Tom Weiskopf, two of that era's most prominent players.

* * * * *

"I want to be on Bert's side," Beard said. "Unless your entire story is going to be positive, I don't even want my name in it. The thing is, the Bert Yancey story is a story with an answer and it's never been printed.

"All these damned assassins in the press are interested in is putting 'Peeping Tom Yancey' in headlines on the front page. Somewhere human decency has to take over. The boy has been raked through the coals. His life has been made a hell.

"The pathetic thing is, he's not a man who needs to be locked up. He's not a crazy man, not a raving lunatic. As long as he takes his medicine, he's as normal as you and I. And he's got a lot to give. He has a wonderful golf mind and he's wonderful teaching with both low and high handicappers."

* * * * *

"When Bert was out here, he was probably my closest friend," Tom Weiskopf said. "He and Frank and Tony Jacklin and I would play all day every Tuesday. He had a tremendous sense of humor, but at some point there was a personality change. His humor turned to a serious nature. It wasn't a bad change; it was just different."

Weiskopf said Yancey was "very, very intelligent and intense." On airplane trips, Yancey worked mathematical puzzles and prodded Weiskopf to describe symptoms of an illness, which he would diagnose. Once a pre-med student, Yancey always was ambivalent about his choice of careers. He loved golf, but believed he might have made a real contribution as a doctor. It worried him.

"My best year in golf, I'd been having trouble with my putting," Weiskopf said. "So Bert spent hours with me developing a putting system that would work for me. He'd stand at the putting green and say, 'Yeah, you're doing it.' 'No, you're not doing it.'"

Beard said Yancey's great obsession was the Masters. "Obsession really is not even the word for what he had at Augusta. Had I ever been as intense on any objective as he was at Augusta, I couldn't have got out of bed."

Weiskopf said, "Not winning at Augusta hurt Bert, but what hurt more than that was not winning the U.S. Open in 1968. He broke all the records for 36 and 54 holes. Then, the last day, his wife Linda and I went out to watch him play the last five holes.

"He had the most discouraged look I've ever seen on anyone. Defeated. Even before he was finished. Right after that, as I look back, the personality change began."

* * * * *

Once the leader by six strokes in the 1968 U.S. Open at Oak Hill in Rochester, New York, Yancey shot a 76 the last day and finished third. Lee Trevino won. The memory seems painful even a decade later, for Yancey speaks of that day and Trevino haltingly.

"I lost it. He just had . . . he beat me. He had more . . . he had more . . . well, he was concentrating somehow with . . . he knew what he wanted to do. He knew he wanted to win. He knew he was going to win and I could feel that . . . and I couldn't get it out of my mind.

"I just felt like he was going to win the tournament. There's so many of those blue-collar workers in Rochester and they were all rooting for Lee, boy, and he would tee off and they would go and I would have to tee up when everybody was moving. Stuff like that. I just never could catch him, the son of a gun."

Those who knew of Yancey's travail at West Point saw in the Rochester defeat evidence that Yancey would never win again. Too much pressure, they said. In fact, Yancey would win three PGA tournaments after Rochester, two on great courses: the 1970 Crosby at Pebble Beach and the 1972 American Golf Classic at Firestone Country Club.

By the fall of 1974, Bert Yancey was a respected member of his profession. Players elected him to a responsible position in the PGA hierarchy. An insurance company paid him well to do golf clinics for its executives. Every week at each new stop, Yancey did clinics for tour sponsors. He was a member of the President's Council for Physical Fitness in Sports. As an elected delegate to the national meeting of the PGA, Yancey went to Hawaii. There he was asked to give the invocation.

"Now, that's how far I had come from that padded cell," Yancey said. "I had it licked again, right? It wasn't the parade field at West Point, but I was sitting on top of the world. And the roof fell in again."

From Hawaii, Yancey went to Tokyo, where the dark journey resumed. It hasn't ended yet.

* * * * *

The third week out of the Philadelphia hospital early in '75, Yancey finished second in a tournament at Miami. In six months, he won $35,000.

He did it while believing he was marked for murder.

Because he voted in favor of a PGA decision to abandon a tournament played at a club thought to be controlled by mobsters, Yancey experienced "a real and honest fear of the underworld. . . . I felt they were out to get me."

After a tournament at Westchester, New York, in August of '75, Yancey ordered a painter down from a ladder inside LaGuardia Airport. Yancey then scrambled up the ladder, near the airport's roof. Hoping to convince the roomful of puzzled witnesses that racial prejudice was foolish, he called out orders.

"I was saying, 'All right, all the whites over here, all the blacks over there, we're going to have us a Chinese fire drill,' or something like that," Yancey said.

"Which meant a great deal to me at the time. And people were laughing, right? That's high, right? Literally and figuratively. That's a natural high. That's manic-depressive illness. You're uninhibited. You do things that have a great deal of meaning to you but they don't have any meaning to other people. They don't understand your meaning.

"So in comes security and takes me down off the ladder into a quiet room. And down there I was spitting on a light bulb, thinking if I watched the saliva burn, the different colors and shapes, I could find the key to the cure for cancer.

"The doctor's there, they give me medication and I'm in the hospital in 10 minutes.

"And in the hospital, within two days, Dr. Jane Parker of the Payne-Whitney Hospital diagnosed my case as manic-depressive illness and put me on lithium.

"That woman saved my life."

• • • • •

For his life, Yancey gave up his golf swing. Not that he knew it then. Among the thousands of manic-depressives on lithium who function well, the limited side effects of the drug are no bother. A small dosage produces a hand tremor so slight as to be invisible.

For a professional golfer, the smallest tremor is damaging. It changes everything because the hands connect the player to his work. A diamond cutter could not work with a tremor; neither can a professional golfer. At the tour level of golf, where four strokes a day are the difference between success and abject failure, Yancey in 1976 became a pathetic figure. Once as elegant as any player on tour, he seldom was able to break 80.

He earned no money that year and quit the tour to set up the Bert Yancey Classic School of Golf at Hilton Head.

So many times up, so many times down — from the Dean's List to a padded cell . . . up to his biggest year and down in Japan . . . back to finish second in Miami only to wind up spitting on a light bulb — so many times up and down, Yancey was now away from the tour, free of that pressure that demanded repeated successes, and now, he assumed, he would be fine.

Not so.

"What happens," Yancey said, "is that when you succeed, believe it or not, you become depressed because your body feels now it has to succeed again and again. And the manic highs are a reaction and a defense mechanism against that depression. So my body was saying, 'Man, I'm tired, I'm tired of this, I'm depressed because we can't keep up this pace.' So a manic episode follows."

On tour, golfers play through various levels of success, each small victory requiring a larger one to certify it as real.

"You win a tournament, you got to win another, then three or four. You win three or four, you got to win a major. You win a major, you got to win another major. I mean, there's no end to it."

The tour, Yancey said, intensified his illness, but he doesn't say it caused it. "How could I? What the heck, I'm the only manic-depressive touring player in the history of the world."

Teaching golf at Hilton Head, Yancey felt safe.

But then his estranged wife demanded he sign divorce papers. Never gregarious — his few friends on tour remember him as a loner who always seemed lost in thought — Yancey was now painfully alone.

And he became high. Some people suspect Yancey stopped taking the lithium in order to get his game back. Without the lithium, he might also find the manic-high escape from that fall's depression. Yancey denies making any change in his medication.

Still, on Halloween night of 1977, he was arrested and taken to jail in Hilton Head.

The police account: responding to a prowler call, they arrested Yancey at 1:30 in the morning outside his apartment. He had peeked in on a neighbor and exposed himself to her while standing outside her window. He struck police officers and, from the back seat of the squad car, kicked out a screen partition.

An account by friends of Yancey: he asked the neighbor for cigarettes. She had none. So he went back to his apartment. Ten minutes later he saw a police car. Wearing a jogging suit with a hood, he told the police he was Robin Hood and playfully extended a leg toward an officer. In quick response, the policeman hit Yancey with a flashlight. At that point, Yancey resisted arrest. By this account, Yancey never was a 'peeping Tom' and never exposed himself.

Yancey won't talk about the episode, other than to admit he was high that night.

"I don't want to knock anyone," he said. "I don't have any feeling of revenge or malice against anybody — because I'm the one responsible. No one else is responsible."

The police put Yancey in a straitjacket, face down, in a jail cell overnight. By court order the next day, Yancey was taken to a South Carolina state mental institution.

"There I was strapped to a bed, chained all fours to a bed, and after three days I was moved to another ward that . . . it was incredible.

"I spent three of the most unbelievable weeks of my life in that ward. I had human feces all over the wall of that cell. And it was a cell, it wasn't a room. Bugs, roaches, flies, just crawling all over and I was tied down. I spent a couple of days cleaning up the cell."

* * * * *

Billy Palmer, 27, the vice president of operations for Hilton Head Golf & Racquet Club, renewed Yancey's teaching contract even after the island episode. The criminal charges are pending, but all sides seem content to do nothing about them.

"Bert scared me at first and I thought we might ought to dissociate ourselves from him," Palmer said. "I thought it'd be bad for business to have somebody like Bert around. But then I got to thinking I couldn't kick a man when he was down. And finally I took the attitude that people with any sense at all wouldn't pay attention to what had been in the newspapers."

* * * * *

The foundation theory of golf that is the key element in Yancey's teaching is what he calls "the pre-swing motion." He teaches students to adopt a rhythmical routine that precedes the moment the clubhead moves away from the ball at address.

It was a cold and gray day, maybe 45 degrees, when Yancey moved beside an old woman and said, "Now, Margot, the oldest truth in golf instruction is, 'So goes the waggle, so goes the swing.' Let's try again."

Waggling the club behind the ball helps set up a rhythmical swing, Yancey says. With more documentation, he hopes to write an instructional book on the pre-swing. He once studied films of top golfers, including Bobby Jones, to see if they had an established routine prior to each swing.

"And they all did, whether they realized it or not," Yancey said. "I put a stopwatch on them. Bobby Jones would take the same amount of time, within two-tenths of a second, every time he walked up to a shot. By setting up that rhythm, he was programming his body for the swing."

·····

Yancey lives under heavy burdens: the club vice president says Yancey must make the club money to stay on the job; the criminal charges are pending if anyone wants to make something of them, and the roots of the manic-depressive illness are unchanged. Heavy burdens, but Yancey says he is up to carrying them.

"This story can be helpful," he says, "if you get the point across that mental illness is not something to be afraid of. But it's something to be handled with care, both by the mentally ill person and by the people around him.

"I'm not talking about brain disease, and I'm not talking about tumors. I'm talking about reactive mental illness. It's part of people's existence and that's why I feel a responsibility as a mentally ill person to do a good job, to just say, 'Heck, I'm normal, like a guy with one arm. I can exist.'"

May 23, 1987

Bert Yancey, 48, once a star, has won $472 on the pro golf tour this year. The pittance came in one check for finishing 52nd at Hattiesburg the week the big shots worked at the Masters. The $472 puts Yancey 239th on the money-winning list. He is, he wants you to know, very happy.

"You couldn't believe my story the last three years," he said. Yancey sat by the 18th green at the Georgia-Pacific Atlanta Classic. His rounds of 80 and 75 failed to qualify him for the last two days of the tournament. No big deal, that.

"You can't believe how many people tell me they're happy to see me out here. I'm a touring professional again. I do the corporate outings and the clinics. I'll play in 12 to 20 tour events. My goal now is to make a cut. It's like I'm a rookie again. Now I'm here to stay. I'm here to play."

For nine years, beginning in 1974, Yancey took the drug lithium carbonate to moderate the extreme mood swings of manic-depressive illness. First effective, the drug later failed. "I had two episodes a year for the nine years I took lithium," Yancey said this day by the 18th green.

Finally, in 1983, he was hospitalized. "The Union Carbide plant had blown up in India, and I figured the Mafia did it. I was in Charter Broad Oaks hospital in Macon, Georgia. I thought the Mafia would gas the hospital. I'm laying in my bed and I can smell the gas. I made a decision right then. I said, 'If I ever get out of this, I'm going to start over.'"

A new doctor diagnosed him as "part of the 23 percent of people who are 'non-respondent' to lithium," Yancey said. "The doctor prescribed Tegretol."

Yancey spelled the drug. He waited while it was written down. He looked across the 18th green toward a soft sunset. Yancey then said with a smile, "It'll be three years August 6, my birthday, and I haven't had an episode. The small-muscle tremors that come with lithium, they're gone. I'm sleeping well, my concentration has been great and my game is coming back."

After the illness drove him off the tour, Yancey became a teaching pro first at Hilton Head, South Carolina, and then at Jacksonville, Florida. When the Jacksonville club went bankrupt a year ago, Yancey decided to try the tour again full-time. He bankrolled himself by selling investment properties.

He moved slowly, not able to contend even in mini-tour events designed for players a cut below the PGA Tour level.

"Then I made a cut in a mini-tour event and finished last and got a check for $50. You don't know how happy I felt. I said, 'Don't get elated, don't lose any sleep, keep your pace even.'"

Early this year at Cocoa, Florida, Yancey won a mini-tour tournament, first prize $2,300, his first golf victory of any kind since 1972. "It was fun. Now, every day that goes by, I'm hitting it better. These kids out here are saying, 'Hey, this Yancey is hitting it, he can play, he's not chopping it around.' Now I just want to make a cut."

In August of 1988, when he turns 50, Yancey plans to move to the PGA Seniors Tour.

Len Bias

June 21, 1986

We should weep for Len Bias, but not because he is the poet's athlete dying young. We should weep because a life has been wasted; death diminishes us all. We should be angry, too. Bias had to know that cocaine kills. How can anyone celebrate, as his coach said Bias did, by using cocaine? How could Len Bias not *know*?

Because Bias could put a ball through a hoop better than most people, he became famous. By drafting him No. 1, the Boston Celtics promised to make Bias a millionaire. At one of the University of Maryland's last basketball games this season, a student lifted up a sign that said "Bias is God." And maybe that's what we want; maybe we make athletes into gods because they are strong, fast, beautiful, altogether better than us. "Gods don't answer letters," John Updike wrote of Ted Williams's refusal to tip his cap to fans.

However fallible and weak we mortals be, so are these . . . gods. Philadelphia Flyer goalkeeper Pelle Lindbergh, drunk, was killed when he drove 100 miles per hour into a wall. Now Len Bias is dead when he ought to be alive. Cocaine killed him. His coach says someone invited Bias to celebrate with cocaine. Some celebration. Put a gun to your temple. Same thing.

What will it take before we know about cocaine? Really *know*. When will we know cocaine the way we know a car wreck at 100 mph? Cocaine kills. Sometimes the killing takes years. Sometimes it takes an hour. It never fails to kill you if you keep at it.

Cocaine messes with the heart, causing it to pump too fast. Blood pressure rises. Body temperature goes up. The heart's rhythmic

129

contractions become twitches of panic that send blood rushing through arteries not designed for the tidal waves caused by cocaine.

Machinery so beautiful on a basketball court can fail under cocaine's demands. "My alternative to a cure was death," said Carl Eller, an old Minnesota Vikings football player who spent $100,000 a year on cocaine before taking the cure. Don Reese went from the Miami Dolphins to jail: "Cocaine dominated my life . . . and almost killed me."

So many people don't know. Micheal Ray Richardson can tell you. Keith Hernandez calls cocaine the devil. Talk to Steve Howe, Chuck Muncie, Lonnie Smith. John Lucas can tell you. These are people, not gods, all of them weak, some pathetic examples of delayed adolescence seeking instant gratification of every sense.

What did Pelle Lindbergh need that he found in alcohol and fast cars? We can weep for the hockey star, a nice-guy hero in his town. But mostly we weep for ourselves; we weep in regret at this world we've made for our athletes. We set up mirrors of illusion. We want our heroes to be gods forever. No wonder some athletes think themselves safe from life's touch even at 100 mph, even with cocaine killing them.

Someone asked Bias about drugs this week. He said he was a born-again Christian and drugs were not part of his life. He also said he could understand how athletes get into drugs; there is so much money in pro basketball and so much free time. Someone asked Bias how he would stay away from drugs, and he said, "I guess I'll go shopping a lot."

The day he signed a $1 million contract to wear a company's shoes while playing for the Celtics, Len Bias returned from Boston to his college dorm room. Now he had money. Now he had free time. At 2 o'clock in the morning, he left his buddies for an hour. When he came back, they said, he was so excited he couldn't sleep. He talked until near dawn when he fell back on a couch, dead.

Erk Russell

September 19, 1986

Statesboro, Georgia

Amorning soon after Len Bias died, Georgia Southern College football coach Erk Russell stopped in at Snooky's cafe in Statesboro for coffee.

Russell is the old bald dawg who decorated the sidelines as Vince Dooley's top lieutenant for 17 years at Georgia. To fire up his Junkyard Dogs defensive unit, Russell from time to time would butt heads with the guys. Because they wore helmets and he didn't, Russell would do some bleeding. He liked it. Cut the rhetoric, give 'em something to see.

On the morning at Snooky's soon after Bias died, Russell said he had coffee "with the 6 a.m. group of philosophers. They got to talking about the Bias thing."

A lot of people talked about Len Bias because of the way he died, killed by cocaine the week he had been drafted No. 1 by the Boston Celtics. Contracts were in the works to make Bias a millionaire. He was said to be a born-again Christian.

And there he was, dead. Killed by the killer he never feared. A witness in the room that night said someone had pleaded with Bias not to take so much cocaine. But Bias went ahead. The witness said Bias's last words, spoken defiantly, were, "I'm a bad . . . I can handle anything."

The 6 a.m. philosophers at Snooky's had an idea. One told Russell, "Messin' with that cocaine stuff is like stickin' your hand in a rattlesnake's mouth."

Russell thought about that for a while. He wanted to make the words come alive for his football team, the way a good head-buttin' can make your shaved scalp bleed and let your guys know you're serious.

"Talking to Snooky's 7:30 group of philosophers," Russell said, "I wondered how I could get my hands on a rattlesnake. By the time I got to the office — well, people are anxious to help out around here. They told me to call over to Claxton," a city that plays host to a rattlesnake roundup every fall.

"Two fellas from Claxton brought me a rattlesnake in a cage, with one side mesh so you could see in there," Russell said.

Then Russell gathered his players for a team meeting. Like all coaches these days, Russell has warned his athletes about drugs. Len Bias had been warned. He had been tested. At the team meeting, Russell spread baking powder on a table and told his players the white powder cocaine can kill you. Len Bias probably heard such a speech himself. Maybe Bias even saw the anti-drug TV spot in which a frying egg is used as symbol of a brain on drugs.

Maybe Don Rogers also heard the rhetoric and saw the symbolism. Rogers, a Cleveland Browns defensive back, died a week after Bias. Cocaine killed him. He was about to be married. He was celebrating. He did coke. Killed by a killer he invited to his wedding.

Russell called his Georgia Southern players around the table with the white powder on it. He warned them, and they listened, and maybe they even heard him. Maybe they didn't think he was just another old goat trying to ruin their fun. Maybe the rhetoric made them afraid of the cocaine.

They certainly were frightened by what came next.

Russell, telling the story: "I turned to a door behind us and said, 'Bring him in, boys.' And the boys from Claxton carried in their cage with the rattlesnake. That rattlesnake was singin', buzzin', and as soon as those boys got through the door, my players started to scatter. That snake was five feet long, six feet long maybe. A big-around snake. I'm talking a *real* rattlesnake."

Russell then told his players to come back closer to the table. At which point the Claxton fellows took the rattlesnake out of the cage and dropped it buzzin' and writhin' on the table.

"They left it there for just a second," Russell said, "but people really scattered this time. I started backing up myself."

Russell told his players to ask themselves two questions.

"How many famous athletes have died recently of a rattlesnake bite?"

Silence.

"And how many," the coach said to the players, "have died of cocaine?"

Len Bias. Don Rogers.

"My main point," Russell said later, "was that everybody scattered and screamed when we brought the rattlesnake into the room. I told them, 'When that white stuff comes into a room, you're not nearly as apt to leave as when that rattlesnake comes in. Look. They'll both kill you. If that white stuff comes into a room, you get out like it's a rattlesnake. Because it is.'"

Bushfield's Filly

April 3, 1975

Goshen, Kentucky

Like all the buildings at Hermitage Farm, the foaling barn is painted black with red trim. At midnight Saturday, under a black sky angry with storm clouds, the barn was visible only in outline when lightning flashed behind it. A single light bulb burned in the barn corridor and in its pale glow Tom Shartle did his beautiful work. A little past 1 o'clock in the morning, he helped a newborn filly stand.

About five minutes before midnight, Walter (Pete) Daniel, an old and toothless night watchman in the foaling barn, got on the intercom to Shartle, the farm manager 18 years for Hermitage's owner, Warner Jones. A chestnut mare named Bushfield was ready in Stall 2.

Bushfield is an eager mother. She has been in foal 11 straight years (when seven of 10 is a good average). For $27,000, Jones bought her in foal to Graustark in 1971. He then sold the Graustark colt for $50,000 and later sold two of Bushfield's fillies for $35,000 and $7,000. "She hasn't had any stakes winners," Jones said, "but every foal has been a winner. She's a good moneymaker."

She was at work at midnight on her side in the straw of Stall 2. The stall is maybe 15 feet wide and 20 feet long, room enough for the expectant mother to move about. Bushfield alternately lay down and rose up, a process designed by nature to help move the foal into position for birth.

Bushfield, at 12:16, was wheezing loudly. "That's not a normal sound," Shartle said. "She's got a growth on one side of her side that's part way closed a nostril." The growth appears as a large lump under the mare's right eye. "They say eventually it will shut off all her air, but it hasn't got any worse in — how long, Uncle Pete? A year?"

"Year and a half, maybe," the night watchman said.

Two hooves of Bushfield's foal appeared soon after the night watchman called his boss. "They usually start contractions about 10 minutes after the water breaks," Shartle said. It had been almost 20 minutes, and the night watchman, Daniel, said, "Not like her to do like this."

Shartle could pass for the Marlboro man riding into the sunset. He wore brown denim jeans and a red, faded flannel shirt. To look at him is to think he could carry Bushfield in his arms to the nearest hospital if need be. At 12:26, he knelt down in the straw and took hold of the foal's exposed legs. He tugged steadily. "Just to encourage her," he said.

Bushfield did the rest. The foal moved slowly toward Shartle. Earlier, the farm manager had split the placenta and now, as the foal moved, the night watchman Daniel peeled the placenta from the foal. The foal's nostrils appeared and Shartle used a small towel to wipe clear the openings. "To make sure nothing was stopping them up," he said.

Suddenly, magically, the foal's head appeared, tucked slightly against the forelegs. The ears were laid back until Daniel used a large towel to rub them dry. Then they popped up. In no more than two minutes, with Shartle handling the foal, encouraging the mare, and with Daniel rubbing it dry, Bushfield finished the work she began 11 months and three days earlier when she was bred to No Robbery. It was 12:28.

With a piece of twine, Shartle tied up the mare's afterbirth. The foal was Hermitage's 37th this year (with 33 to come). Earlier that night, they'd had a filly. "What'd we get?" Shartle said, and Daniel answered, "Another filly. It's been a filly night."

The Bushfield filly was "good size," Shartle said. A chestnut, the filly came with a blaze that resembled a starburst. At 12:42, the farm manager took hold of the filly's forelegs and pulled her through the straw. "Wanna see your mommy?"

135

When he put the filly near the mare's head, the mother licked the newborn's face. Shartle has seen it hundreds of times. He was in the foaling barn when T.V. Lark was born. Silky Sullivan, too. Maybe he has seen a thousand mares and newborn fillies. But it always seems like the first time, he said, when a mare reaches back to nuzzle her little one, as Bushfield did at 12:44.

For a half-hour, Bushfield rested in the straw. The filly grew restless. With her skinny front legs, she tried to push herself up. Nothing doing. She made it halfway up at 12:49, only to topple over sideways. At 1 o'clock, when the night watchman's radio played the national anthem, Bushfield stood up.

Three or four minutes later, Shartle spoke to the foal. "Want some help?" he said, and he took hold of the filly's tail and lifted the 140-pound baby out of the straw. She teetered from side to side and Shartle stood behind her, touching first one side, then the other, to keep her straightened up.

"It's a long way from here to the Derby," he said with a smile. The filly dropped back to the straw. At 1:12, by herself, 44 minutes after birth, the filly raised up. Her forelegs were splayed wide apart. Her rear legs were close together. She walked with the grace of a drunk on stilts. It was a gorgeous sight.

The Derby

April 5, 1986

Louisville, Kentucky

The best time at a racetrack is the morning, just after dawn. The rising light suggests that everything is possible.

As beautiful as a horse is in the afternoon running, it is a dream at dawn.

After the horses returned to their barns, carrying little men who could have passed as princes so great was their dignity, a bunch of us moved over to Barn 42. We leaned against a railing to watch the old man at work. He crouched down, the way baseball catchers do. He rubbed a hand the length of a horse's leg. He did it gently. We kibitzers later would learn that the old man depends on his touch to feel the first heat of infections as well as to discover flaws in bone and sinew.

He performed the act so gently it seemed more than a diagnostician's touch. I made a note: "He touches the horse as if it would break. Lovingly."

The old man rose and said a few mumbled words to a stablehand. Then he saw us at the railing and he explained his work because he knew sportswriters seldom get out of bed before dawn. There came a happy glow to the old man's face.

He said, "Ain't nowhere else to be, 'cept with horses in the morning."

Dawn comes softly at the racetrack. There is the mystery of a morning mist over the churned turf and the grass shiny with dew. Birds make music soft and sweet. We see the horses come out of the mist, a dozen horses, back from a gallop and slowing now to a walk. Even walking, their musculature is so efficient that every step is an

137

airy strut suggesting speed if not flight. Steam rises from a chestnut's shoulder, and the rider in pink reaches down to pat her horse's neck.

Comes the dawn at Churchill Downs, softly, and the rising sun plays golden light off the twin spires high on the grandstand. We stand with the old man in Barn 42. He has been a horse trainer for 50 years, since he grew too big to ride. We wanted to know what the Kentucky Derby meant to him. We knew it to be a fabric woven of such romance and myth, spectacle and drama that the Derby is now the rarest of sports events. It transcends its game and reaches millions of people who don't know a fetlock from a furlong.

The old man's face was a series of crevices hollowed out by the years looking for a warm place to stay. "The Kentucky Derby is, and I s'pose I shouldn't say this, 'cept it's true to me, an ol' hardboot out of Midway, Kentucky — the Derby is like going to church," said the old man, the great trainer Woody Stephens. And the bunch of us sportswriters wrote it down because this was a morning after Stephens had won the Derby a second time, winning it in May of 1984, when he was 71 and so sick he spoke of it as his last Derby, maybe, maybe not, good Lord willin' and the creek don't rise.

"This ol' hardboot," Stephens said, "has had his good times and bad, but let me tell you, fellas, if I ain't dreamin' about a Derby horse, I won't be dreamin' about nothin'."

I am asked to write about the Kentucky Derby, a happy chore, and I think of many things. I think of how much fun it is in the morning to talk to Horatio Luro, the duelist who danced with Lana Turner. During Derby week, I have eavesdropped on King Kong. I have heard a jockey, Don Brumfield, win the race and shout, "I'm the happiest hillbilly hardboot you've ever seen." I also knew Peter Fuller.

Dinner, the Tuesday before the first Saturday in May, 1968. I sat with Fuller, Harvard class of '46, a Cadillac dealer from Boston who had a Derby horse, Dancer's Image.

"We're going to win it," Fuller said, and I made notes for a story on this fellow so brash as to announce he intended to leave the Kentuckians in the dust.

"People say," Fuller went on, "'my God, here's another new one with a lot of money and not much sense.' But this is it. The Derby is what it's all about. . . . I'm going to tell it the way it is, pal, and the way it is is this: I know the Derby is made for this horse. I'm here to win."

On Derby Day, Dancer's Image won the race. Fuller, who had asked directions and practiced the route early in the week, rushed to the winner's circle to lead in the horse he called "my friend."

On Tuesday of the next week, Dancer's Image was disqualified because urinalysis showed he had run with an illegal drug, phenylbutazone, in his system. That week I stood in a hotel room with Fuller. He said, "It's a dream that has turned into a nightmare. It touches everything — your heart, your name, your honor."

Four years later, when Fuller's legal appeals were used up and another horse had been given the winner's purse, I ran into him in an airport somewhere. All he could do, Fuller said, was wait. The pain was old yet new every day. He said with a wry smile, "I'm waiting for the Dancer to sire a fine colt, the kind you can win the Derby with. I'd like to name it Dancer's Revenge."

Morning, a day in May, 1981. We were about to the part where the trainer Horatio Luro decked the French nobleman. They had fallen into a dispute about polo ponies when the Frenchman grabbed Luro by the lapels. So Luro socked him. Next thing you know, the Frenchman whipped a card out of his pocket and said to Luro, "You will hear from my second."

Sportswriters don't often get to talk to a dashing Argentinian who once danced the night away with the movie goddess Lana Turner. Nor do we often run into a great horse trainer who 50 years earlier arranged to duel a Frenchman in the countryside outside Buenos Aires. In Horatio Luro, whose horses twice won the Kentucky Derby, we had both the dancer and the duelist.

"Very attractive, Lana was," Luro said. "I took her to South America with me. Hard to control. You could not hold on to her for long. Too much, too much for me. Ah, Lana." The señor, in what seemed to be a wistful reverie, lifted an eyebrow of salute to the goddess.

Back to the duel. "We could not decide which man had been first offended," said Luro. "So we flipped a coin for the right to choose weapons. I won. For me, this was a happy circumstance. The Frenchman had been shooting mountain lions in Brazil. I chose a conservative weapon: swords. My strategy was evident. I would take advantage of his national infirmity by inviting him to mount a hot-blooded and foolish attack. First, however, some brandy for me. It was very good, that."

The duel was over quickly. "He rushed within range of my blade, and I cut him on the arm. He started to bleed like hell. Of course, they stopped the duel. Ah, the duel. Lana and the duel. These are things in life you have to face."

Ah, the Derby. Heywood Hale Broun once said, "The Derby is a shared delusion. All over the world, people care about the Derby. Late on the first Saturday in May, monks at their prayer wheels in Tibet stop turning them to ask, 'Who won the Derby?'"

Delusion, illusion, fantasy. Whatever, I woke up in my Louisville hotel one morning of a Derby Week and in the atrium there was a six-story-tall Pillsbury Dough Boy balloon. The hotel maid wore jockey silks. I asked her, "What's the Pillsbury Dough Boy doing outside my room?"

"Derby parade," she said. Of course. A man with a thimble has container enough to carry away all the common sense in town during Derby Week. Of course. A parade would form up in a hotel atrium.

At noon downtown, folks gathered to bet on the Derby clock. The clock had statues that went racing around it every hour on the hour. I bet on Daniel Boone carrying his rifle. He lost to a steamboat.

That night, I went to a Derby party at a horse farm. The party was in a circus tent set up in a pasture. Two young women, nude save for three fig leaves, swung from trapezes. They were attended by a giant wrestler in gold bikini shorts. I danced. On the dance floor, I overheard a conversation between a man dressed as King Kong and a woman who carried an eight-foot bullwhip and wore a chastity belt (padlocked).

"Isn't the Derby fun?" the chastity belt said.

King Kong looked at her lock. "Where's your key?"

Ah, the Derby. As Woody Stephens stood by his barn that morning and spoke of his dreamin', I made a note that the old man's voice trembled when he said those words that might have been his life story. Hardboots, their shoe leather turned stiff by shedrow mud, love the mists of dawn, love the smells of straw and manure, the liniment in bandages, the cool freshness of the grass. *Ain't nowhere else to be.* For whatever else the Derby may be — sports classic, civic celebration, business enterprise, shared delusion — it is always this: someone's dream.

"Four springs ago," Joe Palmer wrote in 1948, "two men, not now identified, laid plans which are about to come to fruition. One was planning the mating which led to the winner of the Kentucky Derby. The other was lighting a fire under the mash at the Brown-Forman distillery. Strength to them both."

On winter days three years ago, on spring days such as this, on long nights in foaling barns, more than 44,000 dreams wobbled up on matchstick legs beside their mothers. "Breed the best to the best," the Kentucky horseman Bull Hancock said, "and hope for the best." Of the tens of thousands of foals, no more than 20 make it to the most famous race in the world. They danced in meadows as babies, came to the bridle eager, took a rider's first weight in a stall and walked to the starting gate as if born to the moment.

The thoroughbred was born to run. Poetry becomes bone and muscle. The falling of hooves against the dirt is a sound mesmerizing as it approaches, the sound growing full now, then fading with the horse's passing, the rhythm unforgettable. They are born to run, those who go from the sweet mists of dawn to the chance of a lifetime in the Derby.

It is the chance of a lifetime, Dan Fogelberg's song says, in a lifetime of chance. Old men live with dreams of a lifetime, dreams dreamt in the mists of dawns forgotten. Horses are born to the dream. And the little brave man in kewpie-doll colors atop the horse, the man named Laffit Pincay, says, "The horse, he so high."

Small boys in Panama know of the hero Braulio Baeza, a jockey who won the Kentucky Derby in 1963. Now they know of Pincay, only 13 when he first was lifted onto horseback. The little men perch atop the high horses, legs tucked tight against the muscle, the leather reins tied in a ball, the little men so delicate and yet so strong. Others hear the poem, others smell the morning, others see the blur of color. Only the little men know. Only they touch the horse's side. Only they press their knees against the muscle. Only they know.

"I moved on the air," Pincay would say of his 1984 Derby victory, 20 years after his first ride. He moved on the air, through the mists of a hundred tracks. "If you ask all riders what race they want to win the most, they say the Kentucky Derby," Pincay said. Then the boy from Panama smiled, as the old hardboot from Kentucky smiles, everyone smiling, all those who come here the first Saturday in May, dreamers together.

Pincay said he prayed to God before the '84 Derby, which he rode for Woody Stephens. "I say, 'God, I never asked you to win a race. But if you could give me push, I would appreciate it.'"

It is the chance of a lifetime in a lifetime of chance. There are so many blind turns. Of the thousands of foals, who knows how many came with bad legs? How many refused the rider? How many were frightened by the steel of the gate? "If it was easy," said the trainer Wayne Lukas, "everybody would be here. It takes a very, very special horse to win the Derby."

The Texas oilman and cattle baron W. T. Waggoner once offered a blank check to Sam Riddle for the purchase of the greatest racehorse of the 1920s, Man o' War. To Riddle, the offer was a blasphemous act by a shameless heathen.

Riddle's reply to the oilman: "You go to France and bring back the sepulcher of Napoleon. Then go to England and buy the jewels from the crown. Then to India and buy the Taj Mahal. Then, Mr. Waggoner, I'll put the price on Man o' War."

For every Man o' War — ". . . as near to a living flame as horses ever get, and horses get closer than anything else," Joe Palmer wrote — for every Citation and Secretariat who knock your eyes out, heaven only knows how many yearlings fall in the pasture, hurt. We know only that a dozen or so will wake at dawn on the first Saturday in May and find no feed in the stall. No feed in the morning means one thing to these horses born to run. They will run that day.

More than 125,000 people will be at Churchill Downs on that day, wonderfully eccentric Churchill Downs, where uneven brick paths meander under a maze of wooden grandstands. The dawn will turn to brilliant afternoon. The music of birds will be replaced by the raucous clamor of the crowd. Then the place falls silent. The horses that first ran in pastures with their mothers will move to the starting gate. And when the doors clang open, the dream will run in a rainbow's blur of colors, in a cacophony of shouts, and the dream will run two minutes, two full minutes, lovely minutes.

Woody Hayes

March 14, 1987

Obituary writers seem eager to defend Woody Hayes by careful placement of the word "but." The obit writers tell us that Woody hit people when angry, "but" he loved his players. Woody ran mad across the plains, "but" he stopped by hospitals to cheer up sick people. Even President Reagan got into the balancing act. He called Woody controversial, a soft way of acknowledging that the coach could be a vile, vulgar bully. "But," Reagan added, Hayes was a great American.

There is no need to defend Hayes by weighing good against bad. The good and the bad, it was all Woody, the incomparable Wayne Woodrow Hayes.

He refused to resign the night he struck Charlie Bauman, a Clemson defensive lineman, and not because he believed it was his right to hit anyone. To resign would have been to deny what he was. To quit would have been to deny the forces of energy and commitment that moved him all those years. If being Woody Hayes meant you wind up at age 65 taking an old man's feeble poke at a kid who beat you in a football game, you had to figure that was a small price to pay. Whatever Woody Hayes was, he was always himself.

Hayes apologized to Bauman, who better than most of us knew what the punch meant. It meant that Hayes had grown frustrated and, in the manner of men who live by the use of physical power, had struck out at the cause of his anger. It is interesting to read, eight years after the incident, that Charlie Bauman passes the punch off as a trifle. "I never even felt it," Bauman said.

Without condoning Hayes's punch or the tantrums of decades, we can understand all of it. Coaches create teams in a cauldron of competition. They ask athletes for fierce work. When John Thompson, the Georgetown basketball coach, said, "There are no saints in the pivot," he meant that our games are little wars disguised as civil behavior. Sometimes the disguise slips.

How many football coaches have put a hand on a player? From sandlots to the NFL, hundreds of football coaches have done what Vince Lombardi once did to a Green Bay Packer tackle, Steve Wright, a bright anti-authoritarian child of the '60s who once was asked what he'd miss most about Washington after being traded away from the Redskins. Said Wright, "Central Liquors."

Lombardi's frustration with Wright grew until the coach took up fists against his sea of troubles. "He was mad about something I had or hadn't done," said Wright, then half Lombardi's age and strong enough to dismember the raging tyrant, "and he was mad that I didn't care about him being mad. He screamed at me and started pounding on my chest. I said, 'Vince, let me know when you're done.'"

Long before fate put Bauman within reach of Hayes, long before a punter brought suit against Frank Kush because the coach jerked him by the face mask, back in the early 1950s the new Texas A & M coach, Paul (Bear) Bryant, loaded two buses with proud Aggies and drove them away from Texas A & M to a desert camp where the furnace sun was the least of the punishments.

"One Sunday, Coach Bryant asked if anybody wanted to go to church," said Gene Stallings, now coach of the NFL's St. Louis Cardinals, "and we all thought that would be a great way to get out of practice. So everybody's hand went up. Coach Bryant said, 'I'm proud of you boys. The church'll have a big collection today. And after church, we'll have a good, *hard* practice.'"

Woody Hayes was 65 when he struck Charlie Bauman. Though sick with heart disease even then, the old coach had not considered retirement. And no one at Ohio State had asked him to quit. We ought to assume that the people closest to him saw Woody Hayes for what he was and not what he seemed to the nation in inevitable caricature. The people nearest him saw bedrock integrity in a man

145

who wanted only the simple things Americans love: honesty, loyalty and excellence.

Friends of Hayes wish the coach would have retired in time, before an anonymous lineman came his way with an interception in a second-rate bowl game. Yet those friends also know that Hayes wanted nothing but to coach.

The curmudgeonly Kentucky basketball coach Adolph Rupp was near his state's mandatory retirement age of 70 when he took his team to Ohio State one winter. Rupp stopped by the men's room, where, next spot over, Woody Hayes stood. Hayes said, "Adolph, they gonna run you off?"

"Goodgodawmighty, no," said Rupp. "I'm gonna die on the bench stompin' my foot at some SOB in a striped shirt."

Bobby Cremins

March 11, 1985

"Bruce, you're my MVP, you OK? You got stomach pains?"
"I'm tired, coach."
"Bruce, c'mon. I don't want you to end it like this."
       — Bobby Cremins and Bruce Dalrymple, at halftime

When they weren't beating on him with steel rulers, they were preaching hell's fury at him, and skinny little Bobby Cremins didn't think this was much of a way to get through high school, let alone life. The brothers at Irish Christian had kicked him out of school for getting five F's. His father, the old longshoreman, grabbed him by the hair and threw him down on the principal's office floor, begging the brothers to give the kid another chance. That was before military school. It was before college at South Carolina, before pro ball in South America, before he became a coach at Georgia Tech — long before March 10, 1985, a day on which life's thunderstorms gave way to rainbows for Bobby Cremins.

Eight seconds to play yesterday.

Tech leading North Carolina, 53-52.

Mark Price to shoot free throws for Tech.

Those of the 16,723 fans at The Omni who came dressed in gold, white and black — and those such as Tech grad Gerta White, up in Section 205, who once worked in Africa and had Tech game films shipped to her because "I bleed gold and black" — all those fans so long waiting filled the place with a happy noise, a waterfall's roar, and there was Bobby Cremins in his heaven, hugging tight to him his assistant coaches, Perry Clark and George Felton, the three men aloft on the ether of joy.

On court, Tech guard Bruce Dalrymple crouched low in a cat's night walk, moving slowly, a smile this wide. He would touch hands with buddies in a low-five celebration. The giants John Salley and

Yvon Joseph embraced at the far end of the court. Mark Price sat on his haunches with his eyes closed. He said a prayer of thanks. And then he threw in the free throws.

"To see them fight like that," Cremins would say of his team which once was 11 points behind, "that's why I love coaching and why I love college basketball." He might have said that's why he loves life, too, for what we saw was life coming full circle for Bobby Cremins.

The New York neighborhood called Highbridge, near Yankee Stadium, is a cesspool of hate. The young Bobby Cremins learned basketball there. He was distinctive there. He was white. Most of his basketball friends at Highbridge were black, and most were lost forever in that jungle. South Carolina coach Frank McGuire loved New York players, especially white guards made of barbed wire.

South Carolina was good in Cremins's time there. But it couldn't win an Atlantic Coast Conference championship. In 1970, with the tournament championship at stake, South Carolina lost to North Carolina State in two overtimes, 42-39.

Basketball was Cremins's life, and to lose then was to lose what meant the most, and so Bobby Cremins ran away that night. He went to a cabin in the mountains somewhere. No one saw him for two weeks. *Bruce, c'mon. I don't want you to end it like this.* The coach could say those words. He had lived such a defeat and 15 years later it still hurt like hell.

Bruce Dalrymple is a sophomore at Tech. Maybe he'll get another chance at winning an ACC tournament. But if you've been near it once, as Cremins was, and had it taken from you, you know how much even one chance means. Dalrymple played superbly in two tournament games, only to play so poorly against North Carolina that Cremins wondered at halftime if he were sick. The coach benched him early in the second half.

Cremins sees himself in Dalrymple: a New Yorker, street tough, a gym rat who'd rather go one-on-one in 110 degree heat than go to the beach. One man is white, one black, both fighters. "Bruce is somebody really special to me," Cremins said, and Dalrymple has said, "My coach, I love him." So Cremins, who had been there in

1970 and who would see Dalrymple struggling this day 15 years later, did the harshest thing he could.

"Take the basketball away from him," Cremins said. "Put him on the bench. He'll do anything then to play."

Dalrymple took a seat on the bench.

For all of 41 seconds.

"Coach, I'm ready," he said to Cremins.

Of Dalrymple's 12 points yesterday, all but two came after he sat on the bench for 41 seconds. When Tech fell behind, 38-30, Dalrymple scored on a rebound. Then he made a 17-foot jumper. And a minute later it was 38-all.

Bobby Cremins was 45 hours short of graduating at South Carolina. He was a basketball bum, looking for a job anywhere, in South America, in Europe, even in Pittsburgh. He came home in 1972 because he had run out of obscure teams in Godforsaken places willing to give him a tryout.

Cremins: "My father said, 'I went to high school and you went to college. And I'm getting you a job now, and it's the same job I do.'" Cremins's first job: bellhop at the Waldorf-Astoria. His father's last job: elevator operator on 86th Street.

Shamed, Cremins earned his degree at Columbia University, looking to coach, maybe coaching someday in his old league, Frank McGuire's league, the ACC, maybe coaching someday in the championship game, the game that once sent him to hide in a mountain cabin during one of life's thunderstorms.

"I thought as I sat on the bench," Bruce Dalrymple would say later, "'Am I going to sit here and be a quitter?'"

Whatever fires burn in Bobby Cremins are at full flame now. The heat touches those around him, and Bruce Dalrymple long ago knew the answer to this question, and he knew then he didn't want it to end like this, as it had ended once for Bobby Cremins. Tech's last points in its 57-54 victory came when Dalrymple stole an in-bounds pass and, fouled, made two free throws with two seconds to play.

They would win this time, Cremins and Dalrymple and Georgia Tech, and this time Cremins wasn't looking to hide. "What bar's open around here?" the coach called out, his smile a rainbow of joy. "We gotta go somewhere."

Casey Stengel

October 13, 1969

New York

I had old-timers, guys who couldn't play, and I paid $100,000 for
each of 'em, couldn't give 'em away on the street, and they were
racing horses, and I remember the day when they won two races
in California and Chicago, won $125,000 both races, but they just
used the Mets' name to fill crowds, so I asked 'em why not spend
some for players who could play?"

Casey Stengel said that. What it comes to in translation is that
when Stengel managed the newborn Mets he was equipped only
with has-beens while the owners, the Whitneys of horse racing
note, tended more to the stables than to the baseball team.

Casey Stengel said much more, too. For four hours the other
night, he sat at a table in a hospitality room at the World Series. For
four hours, he talked. He is an old man, 79 now. His baseball career
is legend. He played for the Dodgers and the Giants. In 12 seasons as
manager of the Yankees, his teams won 10 pennants and seven times
won the World Series, the first five in a row.

And then, fired by the Yankees when he was 70, he went with the
Mets, an expansion team, and finished 10th three straight years.
The fourth year, 1965, he broke a hip midway through the season
and retired. Soon after, he was named to baseball's Hall of Fame.

In town for the World Series, Stengel is writing (with a ghost) a
daily sports column. He also is to throw out the first ball tomorrow
when the Mets, of all teams, play in their first Series. Stengel's face
is full and crisscrossed with wrinkles. His elephantine ears dangle
near his jawbone. His face is so mobile that now it is flint-tough and
then it is open and laughing. His voice is Jimmy Durante's, the

151

words coming in no particular order. Here's Casey Stengel talking
. . .

"Now, how can I say I thought the Mets would be here today
when I already told you the St. Louis Cardinals were the best team I
saw all spring with that big bull at first base and who knows why the
Cardinals turned out to be saps? The redheaded manager made the
dumbest move in Atlanta, which he had his lefthander pitch to the
righthander with a base open and damn if they don't let the right
fielder, who's a great one but I don't know if he's Mays, who was the
greatest who ever lived for a while, hit another one, pow!

"Maybe the Cardinals had too many outside interests, so I'm glad
they kept that manager because I remember when we played the
Indians I went out and told the pitcher how to pitch to that Easter
and, goddam, he hit a home run before I got back to the dugout and
I didn't see it but I can still see it. Anyway, the owner has that beer
and it's still good but he don't play."

Then — having discussed the bullish Orlando Cepeda, the great
one Henry Aaron, the manager Red Schoendienst, slugger Luke
Easter and beer baron Augie Busch — Casey Stengel talked about
the Mets again.

"We were no good at the start and how could we be with Hodges
and Snider and guys who couldn't play no more except for Ashburn
who hit .300 for us but the only one he threw out was the one that
ran backwards that time.

"But these Mets now can pitch and they can make the cutoff play
and they can make the cutoff play with two strong arms and throw
people out, and they're all young and married and that helps, too.

"Mostly, Hodges has pitching, Seaver and Koosman, but what
he's done best is give them the winning spirit and that's what it
takes, you gotta think you can win and he's got them thinking they
can win."

During the conversation, Stengel was interrupted twice. First, a
fellow from Denmark wanted to ask a question. He said he was a
radio reporter.

"What sport?" Stengel said.

"Soccer," the Dane said.

"Fella, you ain't gonna make no money here."

Later a newspaperman from Akron asked Stengel a question, and when the man left with his answer, Stengel said, "Now, he wanted to know the life history of Cleveland and I told him we had some good clubs, too, you know, and that one year I thought if I won 93 games we'd be in and we won 103 and I was almost discharged because Cleveland won 111."

And then — having dealt with fading heroes Gil Hodges, Duke Snider and Richie Ashburn, young pitchers Tom Seaver and Jerry Koosman, and the 1954 pennant race — Casey Stengel got up to leave. It was midnight.

"I gotta skip now," he said. "Because whenever I hurt, I fell and broke my hip twice. It's always in the morning."

But the old man stopped for one more question. Practically every reporter has a local angle with the man whose career road map includes stops from coast to coast.

"Sure, I played in Shelbyville, Kentucky," Stengel said to a Kentuckian. "I was at Kankakee, Illinois, and the league blew up, so I went to Shelbyville with Miller and Collins and the team was owned by a plumber. Later I moved with the team to Lexington and then to Maysville. That was 1910. I wasn't as old then as I'm old now. Gotta skip now."

Al Campanis

April 18, 1987

T he anecdotal proof of baseball's racism is piled high in this spring of the 40th anniversary of Jackie Robinson's entry into the major leagues. At the law's insistence, the civilities of racism have changed since Robinson's first year with the Brooklyn Dodgers; the reality of racism hasn't changed. The lords of baseball believe blacks have a place and that place is mostly in the outfield and certainly not in charge.

Al Campanis is not an evil man, as testified to by many blacks who spoke up for him after his unwitting self-indictment on ABC-TV's *Nightline*. The sorrow of his fall is that he didn't know what he'd done. Asked by Ted Koppel why there are so few blacks in baseball's front-office jobs, Campanis reasoned in racial stereotypes. He said black people lack "the necessities."

It is bad enough that the Dodgers' general manager — in charge of all baseball operations — would think that. To say it out loud and to repeat is when given four chances by Koppel to recant is to expose such thinking as the foundation rock of the Campanis racial philosophy for the 50 years he had been a Dodger, first as a player and later as an executive.

There is a piece of children's rhyme the last line of which is, "He who knows not and knows not he knows not is a fool, shun him." The irony of the Campanis affair is both painful and obvious: Jackie Robinson's Dodgers are built on a fool's rock.

Campanis was fired the day after his TV appearance by team owner Peter O'Malley, on whose watch such a fool was allowed to create policy. The next step, after the expedient jettisoning of his loyal employee, was for O'Malley to apologize, which he did even as he promised to do better in the hiring of blacks for responsible jobs in his organization. We'll see about that.

Baseball commmissioner Peter Ueberroth promised to resign if the game doesn't do better for blacks. "Initially, I think (Campanis's) statements hurt," Ueberroth said. "But I think in the long run they will bring about important changes. I think most everybody in the game wants to improve the situation."

One begs the commissioner's pardon, but where is the record of anyone in baseball wanting to improve the situation? Fifteen of the 26 teams have no blacks in the front office. Of perhaps 870 management jobs in baseball, blacks hold no more than 10, most of them jobs in stadium operations and only indirectly involved with the game itself.

The Atlanta Braves' farm system director is Henry Aaron, the game's greatest home-run hitter. He is the highest ranking black man in any baseball organization. You might think, if baseball is so serious about improving the situation, that the Braves, of all people, would have a black manager in Henry Aaron's farm system. There is none.

Only one team has a black manager in its system. The Oakland Athletics have Tommy Reynolds at Modesto of the Class A California League. The only other black manager in the minors is Dan Norman of Miami, an independent team in the Class A Florida State League.

Baseball's leadership is virtually all-white in a game where hundreds of blacks are stars. The limp explanation is that blacks won't put up with the low-paying drudgery it takes to become a big-league manager. Of baseball's 26 managers, 23 first managed in the minors.

Perhaps, yes, a George Foster, to name a $2 million-a-year player, wouldn't manage for $18,000 a year. But lesser players who love the game might take half that just for the chance to chase a dream. Sparky Anderson knew he couldn't play in the big league, so he decided to be a manager. Dozens of banjo hitters had done it, and Anderson followed the path they carved.

For black players, that path is closed. No black major-league manager first managed in the minors. Frank Robinson, Maury Wills and Larry Doby moved up from big-league coaching jobs. Absent any role models in leadership jobs, the black man knows the game is over for him the day his physical skills are used up.

"I'll review the situation at the end of the year," Ueberroth said, "and I think it will be pretty obvious if things haven't gotten better." One wishes him luck. He'll need it in a game whose leaders don't know what fools they be.

Isiah Thomas

June 4, 1987

I f we're going to blister Al Campanis for racist ignorance, the
same heat ought to be applied to Isiah Thomas, who said Larry
Bird "is a very, very good basketball player. . . . (But) if he were
black, he'd be just another good guy."

Dennis Rodman, Thomas's rookie teammate with the Detroit
Pistons, started it with an extraordinary critique of Bird in which he
said the Celtics' star has been the league's Most Valuable Player
three times because he's white. "Larry Bird ain't God," Rodman
said. "I don't think he's the best player in the NBA. I know he isn't.
He's a smart player. . . . other than that, he's (just) a decent player.
He's slow and he jumps this much."

Rodman put his fingers two inches apart as a measurement of
Bird's leaping ability. On the firm belief that such a measurement
better applies to Rodman's attention span, we can ignore Rodman,
who is a small-bore hot dog with a wind tunnel between his ears.

Not so easily can we dismiss Isiah Thomas, a great player whose
opinion carries weight. The unsettling part of this is that Thomas
cannot believe that Bird would be *just another good guy*. No one with
the smallest exposure to Bird doubts his greatness; yet here is a man
intimate with Bird's work demeaning its value.

Why do it? Maybe Thomas was depressed by losing to the Celtics
in Game 7 that day. Maybe he was angry. Here was a guy who had
played poorly when his team needed him to play well. It is Thomas's
reputation, also, that he seeks to divert attention from his failures.
In defeat he took a shot at Bird, who, you may remember, played
terrifically when his team needed him to be terrific.

157

The next day, Thomas issued the inevitable apology. He blamed the newspapers for failing to convey the texture of his words. He was, he said, only kidding about Bird. "In print, you don't get the laughter," Thomas said. "In print, you don't get the sarcasm. In print, you get what you get."

As Al Campanis learned, apology is not the answer. It is sad that Campanis built a 50-year career without learning the difference between stereotype and reality; it is also sad that Thomas, laughing or not, reached into the black racist's bag of self-pitying slurs.

Maybe reading the Boston newspapers — "Larry Legend," they call Bird — moved Thomas to a general anger that found its focus on Bird. Such deification has convinced many blacks, Thomas and Rodman not the first, that they would never be treated so generously by the press; they would be treated as *just another good guy*. It's Bird's whiteness, they believe, that gains him disproportionate credit.

It's the Celtics' whiteness, many blacks believe, that makes the Celtics so favored with the predominantly white press and fans. The Celtics start the most white players (three) and have the most whites (eight) on their roster. "South Africa's team," say people who regard Boston as America's most racist city. "The white boys are tired," said my neighbor after Game 7, assuming I understood he meant the Celtics.

The Celtics' history in black basketball is powerful. They had the league's first black player (Chuck Cooper), the first all-black starting team (in 1963), the first black coach (Bill Russell) and now are coached by another black (K. C. Jones). Georgetown University coach John Thompson, seen by some as a black racist, played for and pays homage to Red Auerbach, the Celtics' boss, a white man. And Georgetown, the blackest team in college basketball, plays identically to the NBA's whitest team: both are athletically gifted, selfless, relentless and intelligent.

What bothered Thomas, and there is truth in this, is the idea that Bird is called great because he is smart and works hard, as if he were not athetic at all but only a bundle of white-boy intelligence and dedication. A black player, Thomas said, is presumed to come naturally by his greatness, the way lions and tigers learn to hunt.

"It's like I came out dribbling out of my mother's womb," Thomas told Ira Berkow of the *New York Times*.

So when Thomas said Bird would be *just another good guy,* he didn't necessarily mean Bird was not a great player; he meant only that such greatness, if it belonged to a black player, would be minimized as a gift for which the player never broke a sweat of dedication.

True, some people think that way. Some people think in stereotypes because it's easy. They are fools. Only fools think Bird is an average athlete. He is big, ambidextrous, indefatigable, quick for a step and has hand-eye coordination denied to most mortals. And only fools believe Thomas is not smart and not dedicated. Too bad that Thomas gave more ammunition to the fools on both sides.

Gary McCord

June 4, 1983

This March in Florida, Gary McCord sidled up to Jack Nicklaus, who knows that when McCord sidles up next to you, something strange is going to happen. "Uh-oh, whattaya have on your mind now, Gary?" Nicklaus said.

"Jack, I've got a deal that's gonna make you a star," McCord said.

Gary McCord is a man overlooked by fame. He is 35, a husband, father and professional golfer who in his 10th season has yet to win a tournament. By his own estimate, McCord is "a marginal player forever." He has never been better than 59th on the money list. This bothers him hardly at all. He is, you should know, "the best golfing magician who ever lived. Houdini ain't even close. Wanna see my card tricks?"

McCord lists his hobbies as "astrophysics, aerobiology and quantum mechanics." He uses boxing gloves as head covers on his golf clubs "because the places I hit the ball, I may have to defend myself. Out there in them woods, there are things without shoulders."

While such exotica may lead the casual reader of golf news to say Gary McCord is a range ball in a Titleist world, the careful reader of golf news knows better. It was McCord, in a serious moment, who invented the all-exempt tour that pro golf adopted as the answer to a load of problems. McCord loves the game. He just wants us to know that golf and fun are not mutually exclusive terms.

Anyway, he sidled up next to Jack Nicklaus.

And he asked the greatest golfer who ever lived if he would pose nude.

"You could wear a towel," McCord said to Nicklaus. "But, er, you would pose without a lot of clothes on."

"Gary, I can't do that," Nicklaus said. "I'm 43 years old. Look at this body. Who would want to see this?"

McCord sighed. "You may have a point there, Jack."

So when *Golf* magazine, at McCord's insistence, does an August photo layout of five tour players in various stages of undress, Jack Nicklaus won't be there.

Instead, we'll see Peter Jacobsen (the centerfold), Payne Stewart, Rex Caldwell, Keith Fergus and Greg Norman ("in soap suds").

Is this done in good taste?

"Awful taste," McCord said, and his graying mustache twitched in quivering glee.

"We're trying to put the sleaze back in golf. We have to get off our sacrosanct pedestal and get back in the gutter where we belong. These pictures would be first-rate stuff in *Playgirl*. Peter Jacobsen will be signing autographs on his tush. We're all looked at out here as calm, sedate, 6-foot-2 blonds, all clean, effervescent and germ free. We want to destroy that image in one issue of *Golf*."

And what, pray tell, would Bobby Jones think?

"Bobby Jones would go play tennis."

McCord's orchestration of golf's undressing is only his latest contribution to our understanding of the game and its players.

He developed the theory that "GOLF Brain" renders most pros incapable of putting on their shoes without help from a grown-up.

GOLF is an acronym for "genetic overflow of living fluids."

The first year and three months on tour, McCord says, a player sees only the target area on the fairways.

"Then the first couple weeks into the fourth month of that second year, the player starts looking left of the fairway and — damn! — there's a bunker over there!

"That lasts for 11 months. He's hitting everything into that bunker. Then he looks farther left. Out of bounds! Trees! Lakes! Oh, my God!

"So the next 13 months, he starts looking right for some safe place to go. He doesn't even look at the fairway anymore. He's scared as hell of the left. He starts blocking every shot to the right. More trees! Lakes! Houses in some of the country!

"During all this, the brain is working. There are electrical charges going on in the brain. Neurohumors transmit nerve impulses from the left side, the imaginative side, to the right side, where the motor nerves are. These nerve transmissions are going on with the speed of light. Ping, zing! Like pinball. Lights going on and off in the brain.

"As long as these thoughts are positive thoughts, they run cool and everything's fine. You're cooling along like Nicklaus or even a step down from him, like God.

"But negative thoughts are a lot hotter charge than positive cool waves. And what you get then is what you get in one of those nuclear reactors — a meltdown. Yes. The brain melts!

"The brain melts into a living fluid and it starts sloshing around inside your skull. You lean over to putt and your brain starts to run out of your head. You get dizzy. You're like seasick. Think about it. Pro golfers don't go on boat trips. There must be a reason."

They Play Hurt

January 20, 1980

Los Angeles

Jon Kolb took his thumb, the meaty part, and pressed it dead-center against his nose, causing the nose to go flat against his face. After 11 years of pro football, there is nothing left inside Kolb's nose to give it shape. The cartilage has been ground up.

"Near as I can count, my nose has been broken six times," said Kolb, 32, an offensive tackle for the Pittsburgh Steelers.

Offensive linemen carry a distinctive badge of identification. It's a lumpy scar across the bridge of the nose. It's caused by collisions which shove the edge of the helmet down onto the nose.

"The nose gets peeled down, they sew it back up and it peels back down," Kolb said.

He has had four fingers broken.

"Unless you're a concert pianist, it doesn't matter," Kolb said. "I can still shake hands and write letters."

"It's insane, what we do to our bodies."
— Rusty Tillman, Washington Redskins, 1978

This is about pain. Football pain.

The National Football League reports injuries that may keep players out of games. These late-week reports list players as "probable," "questionable," "doubtful," and "out." It is an exercise in sadism to read a season's worth of these reports.

Look at these Super Bowl teams. Twenty-eight different Steelers show up on the injury reports. Those 28 men appear 87 times with Jon Kolb making the list for seven of the 18 regular-season and

163

playoff weeks.

The Rams suffered on a grander scale. Thirty-nine Rams appeared 118 times. Six important Rams, including star wide receiver Ron Jessie and quarterback Pat Haden, were put on injured reserve and missed most of the season.

"After the operation, I couldn't stand to watch Jack play. I thought that every time he got hit, the cancer would come back."
　　　　　　　　　　— Phyllis Pardee, the linebacker's wife

Why would Jack Pardee, now the Washington Redskins' coach, subject himself to the collisions of football after he survived a 13-hour operation to take cancer out of his forearm?

Jack Youngblood of the Rams will play today's Super Bowl on a broken left leg, just as he played two weeks ago against Tampa Bay.

"I'm paid to play, is why," Youngblood said. "I'm a football player and I'll play if I can."

These men play war games. There are flanks and bombs and blitzes. These are combatants, not players. If Jack Youngblood were at war under gunfire, a little old broken leg wouldn't keep him from his duty. Anyway, Youngblood says, it's not that big a deal, playing on a broken leg.

"It's the fibula and it's not a weight-bearing bone, and so the doctor says I can't hurt it any more," said the defensive end, a 10-year veteran.

"It's a matter of mind over body. It doesn't hurt anywhere near what it did at Tampa Bay (when his lower leg took on a blue color). Pain is something you can control. You get into a conscious flow of the game and you forget about a lot of little things."

"In San Francisco once, I was kicked in the groin early in the game and again before halftime. It hurt terribly, but I kept telling myself I was a coward looking for an easy way out. I brainwashed myself into carrying on. I finished the game. In the locker room afterward, I couldn't untie my shoes. I was in the hospital four days."
　　　　　　　　　　— Merlin Olsen, former Rams tackle

Jack Tatum, in his book *They Call Me Assassin*, says it is his intent to strike such a savage blow against intruding ball carriers that they will never pass his way again without the trembles.

Tatum says he and a teammate, George Atkinson, devised a system in which points were awarded for the effectiveness of a hit, the largest prize going to the man who causes the stretcher-bearers to carry someone off the field.

Mean but legal. Not only legal, advised; not only advised, taught.

Literature can create strange bedfellows. On the television one night, a talk show had sports books as its theme. The author John Underwood stumped for his book on how violence was destroying the football he loved. James Michener, a fan, had done a sports book full of optimism.

Between these men sat Jack Tatum, Assassin. When Michener pointed out the irony of Tatum sitting next to Underwood, the Assassin allowed as to how he really wasn't a bad guy, he was just playing the game the way he was taught, all out aggressively.

Tatum is the ultimate product of football's seek-and-destroy mentality. It is not enough to create the minimum power necessary to stop a man; nothing must be held back. If a man is vulnerable to injury from the force of a legal hit, Tatum believes that is that man's problem. You can call me Assassin, but you can't arrest me.

Small wonder, then, that 28 Steelers and 39 Rams showed up on the NFL injury lists this season.

The larger wonder is that after a season which began with training camps six months ago — the Super Bowl teams are playing their 23rd game of the year — the wonder is that anyone still has the preferred number of limbs and that any of them are in working order.

"I don't know if those collisions would kill the average man," said Dr. Robert Kerlan, for 20 years a sports medicine specialist. "But they would kill me."

Football players survive because they have remarkable bodies at once strong and flexible. They also have an uncommon willingness to accept the trauma their choice of professions visits upon them.

It is, Kerlan said, "survival of the fittest."

He said, "The early selection process begins when they stay in the games suited to their psychological and physiological pursuits. This tremendous elimination process, where millions of potential athletes are pared down to 28 teams with 50 players each, really separates the people who can — and want to — play the game."

There is a common denominator in this group of elite athletes. "We come up with a group of men with a higher than average threshold of pain," Kerlan said.

"If I hurt, I didn't tell anybody except God, and I told Him in language He wouldn't like."
— Billy Kilmer, Redskins, 1977

Gerry Mullins has a "burner."

A burner is a pinched nerve in the neck. The pain in there feels like fire.

Mullins, 30, a nine-year offensive guard for the Steelers, remembers the arrival of this latest in a long series of burners.

"We do a lot of trap blocking here, and so the offensive linemen wind up throwing their heads in the way of people," he said. "I was sticking my head in there and somebody gave it a whack. And when a 260-pound defensive tackle at full speed runs into your neck, giving you like a whiplash, it can get you hurt."

This one pinched a nerve.

"It felt like somebody stuck a knife down into my shoulder. A hot knife. I about blacked out. I lost the strength in my left hand. If you get hit a good one, you go right to your knees. And it lasts a long time. It might last five seconds, which is a long time."

In July, Jon Kolb said, he had a spring in his step. But now, three days before the Super Bowl, 22 football games, a broken nose and a separated shoulder later, Kolb said, "It took me about an hour to come from the locker room to this practice field."

Mullins said the Steelers' offensive line in mid-January is so beaten up that the starting lineup is not a question of who's healthy. "It's who hurts the least." He'll play Sunday with a ring-collar around his neck in hopes it will keep his head upright if a 260-pound express comes by.

"Somebody wrote that I was the Billy Kilmer of linebackers. It was meant as a cut, but I liked it. Kilmer, he was practically killed in a car wreck. His leg almost got cut off. He kept playing and he threw it end over end and he won ball games. Billy Kilmer. Yeah."
— Jack Reynolds, Rams linebacker

"The reasons athletes fight through the pain are complex," Dr. Kerlan said. "They are reasons based on psychological, sociological, philosophical and economic factors."

One man's simple reason: "It's a feeling of being needed that makes you play hurt," said Eddie Brown, a Rams kick returner who as a Redskin remembers seeing the toes and front half of tackle Bill Brundige's foot turn black with frostbite after he played a game in 9-degree cold with the injured foot taped tightly. Brown also remembers Pat Fischer, a little defensive back.

"Pat played with more pain than anybody I ever saw," Brown said. "And he wouldn't tell anybody. He gritted his teeth all day, and he played super. If I had to idolize anybody, it would be Pat Fischer and Billy Kilmer."

Ted Turner

September 1, 1977

Newport, Rhode Island

T he very proper gentlemen of the very proper New York Yacht Club have demonstrated their propriety beyond doubt. Though tempted sorely, they have not drilled little holes in the bottom of Ted Turner's boat. Even when Turner was beating the barnacles off everybody, the very proper New York yachties did not fire even one torpedo against Turner. Their best hope was Jaws, but the big guy is busy on location chewing up more tourists for the entertainment of the theater popcorn crowd.

Against their dearest hopes, the New York yacht folks have chosen Turner to represent the United States in the America's Cup races with Australia beginning any minute. This is a big deal, the Cup. It's the World Series of boatdom. America has never lost in 123 years, and the appointment of Turner to defend our national honor must have seemed to the very proper clubbies the equivalent of asking Willie Sutton to hold the keys to one's safe-deposit box.

Turner is 38, tall and so devilishly handsome with fine features and a thin mustache that he could pass for a young Errol Flynn. He owns the Atlanta Braves baseball team, the Atlanta Hawks basketball team, an advertising company and some television stations. Because he often says and does things that are not altogether proper, Turner has been called (a) Captain Outrageous, (b) the Mouth of the South, and (c) worse, oh much worse.

The son of a World War II naval officer, Turner took up sailing when, as a youngster, he learned he was not good at the traditional ball games. He now is an internationally known yachtsman who has won dozens of the most important competitions. This will be his first appearance as the skipper of an America's Cup boat, but he might have been here in 1974 had he not fallen to fisticuffs with the boat's designer — a bout that led to his replacement at the helm.

By winning 26 of 35 races against other two other 12-meter boats this summer, Turner and his boat, *Courageous*, made it practically impossible for the New York Yacht Club to anoint anyone else as defender. While it is true that Turner called one of this summer's opponents a liar and caused another to say that Turner's race tactics include smashing broadside any boat ahead of him, he has been, for him, very proper. Even diplomatic.

To the suggestion that he and his 10-man crew saw a need to overwhelm the opposition in order to avoid a selection based more on good manners than on how well a 66-foot racer moved across the ocean, Turner said, "No, sir, we just came up here to go sailing."

But, it was pointed out, he did dominate the racing.

"It wasn't by much," Turner said. "The average margin was one-third of one minute. In a three-hour boat race over 24 miles, that's like one-third of a point in a 100-point basketball game. That's all. There was no room for error."

Turner and his crew have made few errors in dispatching other American challengers, first *Independence* and then *Enterprise*. Turner calls his crew "the best ever on a 12-meter boat," and, to keep them inspired, plays onboard the theme music from the movie *Rocky*. No one expects Australia to be the equal of *Courageous*, which means that soon we will enjoy the delicious sight of a victory ceremony in which the New York Yacht Club stiff-collars will say very proper things to a skipper who wears a railroad engineer's cap, chews tobacco, drinks most anything except water and says he might once have been Christoper Columbus.

Turner walked down Thames Street wearing his cap today and everyone recognized him and shouted hello. The sun was warm and bright, and Captain Outrageous was positively feeling good. "A little hangover, the celebration and all," he said. "Other than that, super."

It's silly, he said, all this stuff portraying him as a scofflaw if not an outlaw, as a rake if not a rascal. "The most serious thing that's ever happened to me was a parking ticket," said the man who this summer (a) is said to have offended a very proper hostess by pronouncing, loudly, on what he saw as her twin physical attributes, (b) is said to have offended the very proper city of Newport by choosing to answer a call of nature from off the end of a city pier, and (c) is said to be sailing here to kill time because he has been suspended from baseball this season for tampering with another team's player.

Turner is a showman. Here on Thames Street, walking, he recognized a melodrama in the making. His chin held high, Turner said, "If being against stuffiness and pompousness and bigotry is bad behavior, then I plead guilty."

Voice rising.

"If being friendly and not thinking you're better than anyone else just because you've got more money than them, because God gave you more talent than He gave other people — if that is a crime, I plead guilty as charged."

A pause for breath.

"Oh, every now and then, I open my mouth when it should be shut. But, hey, if not being perfect is a crime, I plead guilty as charged."

He stopped walking.

"You know what it says in the Bible, don't you? About the prostitute who was stoned? 'Let he who is without sin cast the first stone.'"

Captain Outrageous let that one soak in.

"Pretty strong stuff in the Bible."

Walking again.

"I try to bear the blows and keep on smiling. But the more you get beat on, the more sober you get. Not sober like you've been drunk. Sober like it's not fun. I'm fighting that. I have fun going to baseball games. If going to baseball and basketball games and cheering is a crime, then I plead guilty."

The America's Cup series is work, he said, like climbing Mt. Everest, work in which there is more satisfaction than fun, and

170

when someone asked Turner when he began working toward the Cup, the skipper said, "Twenty-nine years ago."

When he first sailed?

"Or it might have been a thousand years ago."

In another life?

"I might have been Sir Francis Drake, Captain William Cook, Horatio Nelson, Vasco da Gama."

Voice rising, to a thunderclap.

"Or Christopher COLUMBUS!"

July 13, 1986

Moscow

A Soviet journalist this week asked Ted Turner if he wanted to be president of the United States.

"No, no, I'm too busy with the world to be president," Turner said.

The Goodwill Games are Ted Turner's biggest stage. He caused this puffed-up track meet to take place. And in case we hadn't noticed the size of his accomplishment, Turner has measured it for us. It is "a major, major undertaking of colossal proportions." And a pretty big deal, too.

Alexander the Great wanted to conquer the world by force. Turner figures it can be done by TV signal. Megalomania goes high-tech. Turner has used his resources — cable-television, big bucks, a sense of athletics — to bring together implacable enemies, the U.S. and the Soviet Union. Everybody hopes to make a buck or two.

Old Alex the G, one of Turner's many warrior boyhood heroes, waged war and claimed it was his divine duty. Turner now wages commerce in the name of peace and nuclear disarmament. Seldom does a minute pass here without Turner announcing that friendship

171

means the end to war. Friends don't bomb friends. He keeps saying it.

He once added, "Am I completely wrong?"

An American newspaperman said, "Not *completely*.

"Well, I'm not saying the Goodwill Games will change things forever," Turner said. "But it can't hurt. We've got to learn to live together or we're going to die together."

Not a decade ago, Turner wanted to win the America's Cup. He did. With money from a billboard advertising company started by his father and driven to great success by Turner, he bought the baseball Braves and basketball Hawks. From a start with a moribund television station whose signal couldn't get out of town, Turner has created a national, even worldwide, cable-television network using satellite relays. "The world's most important network," is how Turner's folks describe it on air.

A group of journalists from the United States and the Soviet Union sat with Turner for an hour of conversation the other day.

"Sitski here, Sovietski," Turner said to the man from a Soviet sports newspaper.

To be in Turner's presence is to be surrounded by him. "Poland!" he shouted when a journalist introduced himself. "Hey, Poland. I like that Polish vodka. Get some of that for me. Here's my room number. Bring me some, Poland!"

Turner is a free-form thinker whose thoughts arrive just in time to be spoken. It is as if he is doing a play-by-play of every sensation and thought in his life, radio station WTED, 24-hour talk. These thoughts are often sentence fragments. They are spoken in a squeaky drawl at gale force. They can be brilliant or foolish, hypocritical or sincere. They can be all those things at once. As Turner has said, "At one time or another, I have offended everybody."

Here are names dropped by Turner in our hour: Hitler, Jiminy Cricket, Francoise Mitterand, Helmut Kohl, General George Patton, Robert E. Lee, Marshal Zhukov, Caspar Weinberger, Jacques Costeau, Carl Sagan, Perez de Cueller, Admiral Horatio Nelson, Mikhail Gorbachev, Howard Baker, John F. Kennedy and Lester Maddox.

Places and things Turner mentioned: Verdun, Finland, the National League, Seattle, Cuba, pigeons, San Diego, the Middle Ages, Nigeria, F-111 jets, $2 billion, Holland, Australia, oxen, elephants, mountain goats ("I killed one here last winter, and they just delivered the stuffed head to my hotel room"), Ping-Pong diplomacy, backpack nuclear weapons and Lester Maddox's ax handles.

The mind reeled. Ax handles in a nuclear war? Robert E. Lee in a F-111? And somewhere in there Turner mentioned that the U.S. and Soviet Union don't much like each other; he proposed a way to fix that, saying, "I think both of us ought to be taken out behind the woodshed and some Big Daddy take a board and give it to us. You know, bend down and hold your ankles. That's what I think. Speaking figuratively. I think it's just time we grew up. Just like segregation in the South. We looked in the mirror and said it's time to move on. To move on to the next challenge."

Someone wondered aloud if Turner, because of his commercial connection and his propagandizing for the Soviets, would be portrayed upon his return to the U.S. as "a Red spy."

"I certainly hope that is not the case because I love my country very much," Turner said. "I love all people. We're all brothers and sisters, and we better start acting that way or we'll blow ourselves to kingdom come."

The idea of nuclear war set off an atomic reaction in Turner's cerebellum. Or something. For he next said, in full cry . . .

"If there's a nuclear war between our countries, we're killing everybody. That's Bermuda, Bahamas, Jamaica, Switzerland, Sweden, Nigeria, India, Ceylon. Ceylon? They call it something else now. Perez de Cueller said it. By what right do the superpowers feel they have the right to decide the lives and fates of all mankind?

"Carl Sagan said it in *Breaking the Spell*. We've been here millons of years, 10 million years, human existence, that we've slowly evolved, that our parents worked to make us better and send us to better schools and get better education and improve airplanes and communications.

"All the things we've done, our books, our art, our literature. And what have we done with our opportunity? Get ready to blow ourselves up. And not just ourselves. What about the elephants?"

Pete Maravich

January 6, 1988

You'd be afraid to take your eyes off Pete Maravich. You'd be afraid that the moment you looked anywhere else, he'd do something you'd never seen before and would never see again. Creative genius works that way. The deed would spring full-blown before the thought occurred to anyone, even Maravich.

Many players moved with greater grace, Earl Monroe for one, but none moved with more purpose than Peter Press Maravich. An inelegant collection of bones, the skinny 6-foot-5 Maravich flailed his way downcourt, all elbows and knees, sharp angles rearranging themselves, that mop of hair flopping in antic rhythm to his gallop, an Ichabod Crane on the fast break, and you dared not blink.

Only Wilt Chamberlain commanded more attention on a basketball court. And even Chamberlain didn't have the ball *all* the time. Maravich holds the NCAA career scoring record of 44.2 points a game. He scored more than 50 points 28 times. In a decade as a pro, he scored 25 a game. Yet he was only secondarily a shooter. Maravich was a ballhandler, nonpareil.

As if telekinesis were one of Maravich's gifts, the basketball did his bidding. We see it spin on his fingertips. We see it move behind his back and over his shoulder. In reports of his death yesterday, we saw a film of Maravich on a fast break, the ball floating ahead of him, untouched, and what does he do? He moves his right hand around the ball, a blur he does it so quickly, making a circle around the ball until he slaps it to a man on the left wing, not so much a pass as a deflection, not a deflection as much as imagination made real.

175

The basketball was part of Maravich, soulmates. Five years old, he could dribble through his house blindfolded. He took the end seat at movies so he could bounce the ball in the aisle. He dribbled the ball on the street from inside a moving car. A Maravich fan called WSB radio and read a poem he'd written on Pete's death, a line of which said, "At night he went to bed with a basketball in his hand."

It couldn't have been easy to be Pete Maravich. His father, Press, was a failed pro player who become a coach. After his father's games at North Carolina State, Pete practiced alone for hours. At LSU, the father now coaching the son, Press Maravich told reporters who compared Pete to Bob Cousy, "Cousy never saw the day he had moves like Pete."

Their obsession exacted a high price in pain. As good as Pete Maravich was, his teams were never good. Many people blamed Maravich, said he needed the ball too much, wouldn't share it. Off the court, it was worse. His mother, an alcoholic, committed suicide. He had only basketball to comfort him, and it was no answer. Too many mornings in too many cities, Maravich woke up lost in an alcohol fog. He would come to say, "The only thing that ever mattered to me was basketball. I sold my soul to the game."

After retiring from the NBA at age 33, a burnt-out case, Maravich began a search for himself. It took odd turns to meditation, vegetarianism, astrology. He painted a sign on a barn roof inviting extraterrestrials to capture him. In time he married and had two children. He said he met Jesus Christ. He preached alongside Billy Graham. He ran basketball camps with religion a part of the daily routine; as deep as the wounds of basketball had been, he loved the game too much to blame it for his failings.

It has been said that Maravich was a white man playing black man's basketball. That wasn't so. Maravich's work was distinctly and only Maravich's. No one, not even Cousy, ever had such hand-eye skills. And certainly no one without such skills could have dared ask that all eyes be on him all the time.

"One of these nights," he said as a senior at LSU, "I'm going to hit all my shots."

A listener said, "Come on."

"Yes, if I take 40, I'll make 40," Maravich said. "I don't know when it's going to happen — in college or where — but it'll happen."

Maravich redefined basketball. His genius stretched the boundaries of the acceptable. In the late '60s only Maravich dribbled between his legs on the fast break; only Maravich threw behind-the-back passes across the court; only Maravich put up odd-angled, off-balance shots, hook shots, bank shots, shots from downtown, thrown from the shoulder, shots from the hip, "Pistol Pete" blazing away.

He died during a pickup game on a basketball court at age 40. Friends said he had become a happy man, the circle closed in peace, "and now," to finish the Maravich fan's poem, "he's gone to heaven with a basketball in his hand." The television news shows ran a film clip of that last pickup game, guys walking through the motions, laughing. The last we saw of Pete, he banked one in from 17 feet.

Pete Rose

August 27, 1975

Chicago

Arriving at the Windy City airport after getting only six base hits in eight games on this road trip, Pete Rose boarded the Cincinnati Reds' team bus only to bump into a civilian who disembarked when he found out it wasn't the 5:35 to Waukegan. "If you can hit," Rose told the man, "stay on the bus." For Peter Edward Rose, all of life comes down to an ash stick colliding with a horsehide ball.

The day before in St. Louis, Rose approved of Ted Simmons's new look in hair. The Cardinals' .330 hitter is distinguished by hair which laps against his shoulders. Said Rose, "What's Simmons doing, trying to be Prince Valiant?" He added, "Wear it down to his back pockets if he keeps hitting like that."

Mario Guerrero, a St. Louis infielder, watched the Reds hit. "Come here," Rose said to the rookie, "and let's talk about hitting. You can tell me everything you know. I got 30 seconds." Rose then proferred his Louisville Slugger in both hands, saying to Guerrero, "This is a baseball bat, and you use the bat to . . ."

At age 34 in his 13th season with the Reds, Rose has a lifetime batting average of .310. A man said to Rose at batting practice, "Pete, about hitting . . ." Rose took it from there.

"I'm not a guess hitter like a lot of guys," he said. "Oh, in certain situations, say with a man on third base and nobody out, I'll try to get a pitch to hit a fly ball. But normally I just go up there looking for one thing. Right, the ball.

"I start concentrating when the pitcher begins to wind up. Prior to that time, I have a little fun, talk to the catcher, look around."

Of the hundred subtle man-to-man contests that make baseball richly intriguing, none is more basic than pitcher against hitter. That contest can be subdivided, too, and part of it is the pitcher's eternal quest to hide the ball from the clown with the stick in his hand.

"Sometimes you can see the ball in the pitcher's hand when he first starts his windup — and you can follow it all the way," Rose said. "But other guys hide it really good."

When does Rose first see the ball on its way to the plate?

"Right here." Rose held his arm high, indicating the top of the pitcher's delivery motion. "I can see it spinning as soon as he lets go of it."

Ted Williams is said to have been able to read the label of a 78-rpm record as it spun. Now comes Pete Rose to say he can see the red seams of a baseball spinning. Try as we might, mere mortals will never comprehend the eyesight and reflexes a great hitter must have to 1) see the ball, 2) judge its flight path, 3) decide its speed, and 4) analyze its spin. Rose says he can identify a fast ball (spinning backwards), a curve ball (spinning sideways) and a screwball (opposite the curve's rotation).

"I've been in the big leagues 13 years," Rose said. "I know what the spin looks like. I could see it in high school, too."

Having seen the spin, having made the necessary computations in the small part of a second available before the arrives at maybe 100 miles per hour, then comes the hard part — hitting it. Williams says hitting a thrown baseball is the single most difficult act in sports, aside, perhaps, from paying off a golf bet.

"I give the ball all the time it wants to get to the plate," Rose said. "I watch it all the way. Some guys commit themselves too early. Hell, you can't hit the ball until it gets here anyway. It can curve out there all it wants. I can't reach it there. So I watch it all the way into the catcher's mitt. I don't give up. I've got a lot of hits out of the catcher's mitt."

What pitcher gives Rose trouble?

"Any pitcher I face and I don't see the ball well. Screwballs at night in Los Angeles bother me. The lights are bad out there."

Does Rose have a pitch he likes to see coming?

"Yeah, one about this big around," he said, spreading his hands to the appoximate size of a mature watermelon, before eating.

Rose went into the batting cage, still talking. "I'm going to hit these hard." A pitch came. Batting left-handed, Rose lined the ball into right field. "That was in on me." Then a line drive to left center. "That was out, so I went with it." With a bat in hand, Rose was a man at peace. "It was a double, maybe three the way I run."

The Eleven

July 29, 1984

Los Angeles

Moshe Weinberg loved it in Munich. He wanted to be home in Israel with his wife and baby two weeks old, but if he had to be somewhere else, the Olympic Village in Munich was it. He called his wife at her parents' home. "He asked me everything about Gouri," Mimi Weinberg said. "He was so happy to have a son."

Moshe Weinberg never saw his baby boy, Gouri. Terrorists killed him with machine gun fire through a door which he held shut against them. The terror ended only when 11 Israeli athletes and coaches were dead. Mimi Weinberg, holding her baby, heard it on the radio at 9 o'clock.

She couldn't believe it. "Something about terrorists," she says now. Only two days earlier, she had spoken to her husband, the Israeli Olympic team's wrestling coach. Small talk. He liked Munich, the village was nice, the food terrific. She could hear his voice still. And then the radio said he was dead. For a day and a half, she was lost in hysteria. She woke to find her parents weeping at her bedside.

She remembers it now. "I asked, 'Why do you cry?' They said, 'Mimi, all the 11 people are killed.'"

At a cost of $5 million, the Los Angeles Olympic Organizing Committee produced a festive opening ceremony Saturday in which 12,000 dancers and musicians welcomed 7,800 marching athletes from 140 countries into a stadium filled with 100,000 people.

All those numbers.

The number that can't be forgotten is 11.

September 5, 1972. Munich. The Olympics.

Gouri Weinberg's father, one of the 11, loved the Olympic idea. "Sport was all his life," his wife said. "I'm the second place." She is 38 now, an election worker in Tel Aviv. She is a survivor. She drank too much, she said, after her husband's murder. She couldn't touch her son, Gouri. "I didn't want him," she said. She wanted to forget.

She took Gouri and left Israel for Montreal in 1978. They moved to Los Angeles the next year. In those places, she was a woman again, not the wife of the martyred Moshe Weinberg. She wanted a life separate from the terror. But then, because Gouri kept asking, she knew she would never forget. More, she came to know this: she must never forget.

"Gouri heard children talking about their fathers, and he would ask me, 'Why don't I have a father?' And I would try to explain to him. And he would ask, 'Why? Why my father?'"

The phone rang one day at Mimi Weinberg's house. A teacher called to say there was trouble with Gouri. "'My God, what now?' I said. But the teacher only had to say, 'Gouri is so good with the cello that we must put him in another school.'" Even now, three years after the teacher's phone call, Mimi Weinberg trembled. Terror is on the radio, terror comes by phone. She can't forget.

"Oh, yeah, it could happen again, here. Who knows? The security is very good here. But who knows? A man with a gun kills people in San Diego. Who knows? Everybody is afraid to go outside. This is the world I give to my children?"

At age 12, Gouri Weinberg plays soccer, tennis and baseball. His eyes are so fine a blue they seem translucent. He will leave many young girls breathless in his time. He came to Los Angeles with his mother for a memorial service to the 11. They came to the Simon Wiesenthal Center for Holocaust Studies, where 300 people sat outdoors next to cedar and olive trees.

Candles, 11 of them, were lit and candles, 11 of them, were extinguished. The names of the murdered were said. Some had moved to Israel from Romania, from the Soviet Union, from Poland, from Libya. "Moshe Weinberg," the reader said. "The first to die."

An Israeli soldier stood before the assembled memorialists and said, "Never again." He said, "We learned well the lesson of Munich and we share it daily with the world. If we don't destroy terrorism, it will destroy us."

In her turn Mimi Weinberg said, "I tell the sportsmen of the world, 'Try to understand each other, and don't listen to people who push you to kill in cold blood.'" Her son, Gouri, came to the lectern and, for the first time, said the *Kaddish*, a Jewish prayer that is an exaltation of God.

And Gouri Weinberg said, "I didn't know my father. I only wish my father could be here today to share in the joy and excitement of the Games and . . ."

Then a little's boy smile, as beautiful as the sun rising,

". . . perhaps to take me to the Michael Jackson show. Wouldn't that be great?"

They gave Gouri Weinberg a medal on a ribbon to hang around his neck. The medal's inscription said, "The Eleven." The boy was proud of it and he touched it and sneaked a look at it now and then. When his mother spoke to reporters later, the boy moved behind her and lifted the medal to rest it on her arm, so the reporters could see it.

"My father," Gouri Weinberg said to a man asking what the son knows of the father, "was a good sportsman and I know he told his students to try, you have to try. If you try, you'll be much better. If you do it, you can win a medal. You must try through the pain. He told them. And they did it and that's why they made it to the Olympics. But they didn't make it back."

College Athletics

December 20, 1987

As for why a college athlete would take money from an agent when such a transaction puts the athlete's eligibility at risk, I am forced to answer, "Why not take the money, doesn't everybody?" My tone is at once cynical, sarcastic and Lord knows weary from use. For as tenacious a hold on hypocrisy as politicians and televangelists have (thinking here of the Messrs. Hart, Bakker and Swaggart), one need move a finger only a short way down the current list of phony-balonies to bump into the stuffed-shirts who run college athletics.

First, a quick disclaimer before we heat up the debate: I love the college games, not only for the passion invested in them by young men and women in pursuit of their athletic dreams but for the societal good the whole enterprise can accomplish by giving thousands of young people a happy reason to crack a textbook more than once (or, in the habit of some folks who became sportswriters, press a book close to the bosom in hope that knowledge seeps into the bloodstream, education by osmosis).

Greed begins at the top. A college coach, if he's much good at his job, has a Rolex, a free car, TV and radio shows, a shoe contract, more ink than a U.S. Senator and so much money he hires people to alphabetize and file it.

The Rose Bowl pays two teams $12 million. The University of North Carolina fired football coach Dick Crum, but will pay him the $800,000 remaining on his contract: almost a million dollars to *not coach*. Television will give the colleges $55 million for basketball games this year.

When everyone in the college game takes the money, how can we expect the most impressionable people in the system not to put a hand under the table for their share? We tempt our college athletes, seduce them and put them in great stadiums and arenas. We ask them to put on shows for which customers and TV networks will pay big bucks. We ask these kids to be boffo box-office and at the same time say, "Lookee here, kid, you so much as touch a dollar bill and we'll fry you on a public spit, barbecued."

Where are we in college sports? This is where: we're now blaming the sins of the system on the players when, in truth, the players are the exploited victims of myth nearly a century old.

Where should we go from here? To a revolution. We need new machinery built for new times. Athletes deserve a better shake from big-time, money-making games which are more professional than amateur.

It may have been a $2 million day at Indianapolis last week for a basketball doubleheader, 40,000 fans at $25 a throw, $600,000 from TV, $25,000 from a bank which paid for the privilege of painting its logo on the court. The athlete? He gets a scholarship and the promise of an education. If he takes a dollar from a booster or from an agent or from his coach (who knows all too well the depths of the exploitation), then all hell breaks loose. We hear, ohmigawd, that the star center at Enormous State U has *broken an NCAA rule.* The star center's picture shows up on page one of the newspaper, as if he were an ax murderer or a self-inflated politician puffed up within an inch of popping.

Yes, a player can get money legitimately. Uncle Sam has a Pell Grant fund for college students from financially strapped families, the maximum grant $2,100 a year based on need. But under NCAA rules, the player can keep only $900 of that money. The school takes the other $1,200 for its use. Vince Dooley, the Georgia football coach, says, "The Pell Grant limitation of $900 is one of the most discriminating things in college athletics. A regular student can get the whole thing, but not the athlete. It's awful."

A player can get money with a summer job; he can get bank loans. But he knows there's something missing. From the coach to the athletic director to the sportscasters and sportswriters, everyone makes money off the player's talent; meanwhile, the player cannot make a legitimate penny. Every cent he takes from people who recognize the commercial value of his work is a cent said to be dirty.

And yet the newspapers of late have been full of stories telling us how players took the so-called dirty money. Why would they do it?

"It's simple why they take it," said Spencer Tillman, 23, a running back out of the University of Oklahoma, now a rookie with the NFL's Houston Oilers. "You're looking at guys who aren't used to those dollars. It intrigues him. And he knows everybody's making money except him. He can sense the unfairness of that. He feels he's being cheated by whoever the powers are. Taking the money is his way of getting back at them for cheating him."

If a player is that one in a million who has a seven-figure deal certain to pop as soon as he finishes school, it's easier to say, as Pittsburgh running back Craig Hewyard, does, "Good things come to those who wait."

Heyward, who figures to be next season's frontrunner for the Heisman Trophy, said, "I'm not getting hooked up with any agent. But I understand how it can happen. Some guys don't have any money. They come from one-parent homes in lower-class situations. Some of them have to work to help out back home. For other guys, it's greed. They get to live in the fast lane. It's a fashion show for them. They've never seen this type money before. Maybe their parents are on welfare. You can't expect them to say no."

These players live in a professional world. But they're expected to never touch the money. Come to the water, but don't drink.

That is an unrealistic expectation, even cruel. College poohbahs will try to persuade you they're doing what's best for the kids. Presidents, athletic directors and coaches think that anyone who can use football or basketball to pay for an education is getting a good deal. The word "priceless" comes into their conversations.

Bob Knight, the Indiana basketball coach, believes identification with a college team is indeed priceless for kids wanting good summer jobs and good starting jobs fresh out of school. At the same time, he believes the NCAA has shortchanged many athletes, and intentionally shortchanged them, to save money.

"The one thing the NCAA doesn't care about is the kids," Knight said. "The schools make the rules. And they don't care about the kids. When's the last time they made a rule for a kid instead of against him?"

Only three explanations are possible for the NCAA's exploitation of players: 1) the NCAA is a conniving slavemaster which wants to maintain its cheap-labor pool; 2) the NCAA is a confederacy of dunces which doesn't know it is abusing people, or 3) all of the above: the NCAA panjamdrums are slavemaster dunces who have bought in so completely to the old-college-try malarkey as to be hopelessly disconnected from the real world.

In any case, the NCAA's abuse of players is reprehensible. The benevolence of certain masters does not absolve them of the collective guilt. Here is a powerful group of people imposing on a weaker class a system of labor which guarantees maximum profits for the boss and minimum wages for the worker. Under this system it is OK for a coach to reap great financial rewards. It is OK for the university to use the money to raise great buildings. But it's wrong for the players to make a buck.

In no other part of American society is such reasoning allowed to work its exploitation. Financial restraints on college athletes are unfair at best, illegal at worst.

So severe are the restraints, and so widespread is acceptance of them as necessary and right, that athletes are held up to public shame if they accept $20 from a fan. When Riccardo Ingram took $2,000 to sign with an agent in his senior season, he was kicked off the Georgia Tech football team. To measure the heinous nature of his crime, let's do some long division. Ingram worked for Tech for four years. He took an agent's two grand. If we divide the $2,000 by four years' work to arrive at a weekly average, it comes to $9.62 a week. Some crime.

The shame is Ingram's; he agreed to abide by rules, then broke them. But the greater shame by far is Georgia Tech's and the NCAA's. The shame is that a gifted athlete who helped fill stadiums is paid so little, and paid not by the school but by an agent, paid not up-front but paid in clandestine meetings by secret agents — and is paid the equivalent of $9.62 a week.

"The NCAA is not representing college athletes, they're misrepresenting them," said Jim Abernethy, the Atlanta agent who signed Ingram. "The critical point is, these guys . . . they're going to have 3.6 years (the average NFL career). They're taking away over 50 percent of their income-producing years by not paying them in college. . . . The players should be paid at least as much as the assistant coaches."

By robbing their Riccardo Ingrams of money the athletes helped produce, the colleges are engaged in a cynical pretense which reveals, in the poet Walt Whitman's phrase, "a hollowness at heart." The colleges pretend to pay obeisance to the god called amateurism. They pretend to be part of the educational system (this guise allows them, under the U.S. tax code, to exist without paying taxes. What a scam. Multi-million dollar businesses paying no taxes. Small wonder athletic departments won't admit being pro sports. Uncle Sam would take a chunk of the pie).

Anyway, by pretending to amateurism in the interest of hiding money from Uncle Sam, the schools also are relieved of the obligation of paying the workers a real wage. That is an outrage. It's a pro game in the colleges. They sell tickets. They buy rich coaches. They take big stacks of money from the TV people. They beg boosters for millions of dollars.

History teaches us that this scam is nothing new. As early as 1900, Yale University enrolled a tackle, James Hogan. The writer Robert H. Boyle said Hogan was lured to New Haven "by giving him a suite in Vanderbilt Hall, free meals, a trip to Cuba, free tuition, a monopoly on the sale of scorecards, and a job as cigarette agent for the American Tobacco Company."

By 1929 the Carnegie Foundation declared college athletics a sorry mess with chicanery afoot at 84 schools. The foundation's annual report called the scandal "the deepest shadow that darkens American college athletics." Payments went to players (some sold $2 game tickets for $100). There was abuse of academic integrity with universities accepting unqualified students and jiggling gradebooks to keep them eligible.

Infuriated by the pose of amateurism, the great sportswriter Paul Gallico wrote in 1937 that college football was coming into its own "as the leader in the field of double-dealing, deception, sham, cant, humbug and organized hypocrisy. . . . Economically, the principles under which the colleges work are sound. Ethically and morally, they smell to high heaven. There is only one conclusion that can be drawn from their stubborn adherence to outmoded principles, and that is that as long as they stick to them they can continue to get football players for next to nothing — cheap labor. . . . The system is rotten from top to bottom."

So commonplace were the revelations of covert aid to players that *Newsweek* columnist John Lardner, in 1937, satirized the subject: "At a certain Southern college, when I told them I had come to expose graft and professionalism, they told me to use the exposers' entrance. 'Around back,' they told me."

It has always been the same. In 1956 *New York Herald Tribune* columnist Red Smith wrote of an affair in which UCLA players were paid $71,000. Smith believe $71,000 was a low wage for such heavy duty. He wrote, "The old question of defining labor's fair share in the fruits of labor is a continuing problem in college football. There is something scandalous about a college collecting hundreds of thousands in gate receipts and paying off the help with a bowl of rice."

What is for Mr. Smith a bowl of rice is nothing so meager in the view of today's college administrators. They see the players being treated to a great feast of goodies. They see athletes strutting in great stadiums; they see athletes guided to college degrees at no cost; they see athletes given first-class training for the pro leagues.

Homer Rice, the Georgia Tech athletic director, says his school kicks in $35,000 per athlete every year. He says his school's athletics budget is nearly $12 million. Dividing that number by the number of athletes on campus, Rice says, "We figure our cost at $35,000 per athlete."

That cost, Rice says, includes $10,000 for out-of-state tuition, room and board, an academic support system, sports medical treatment, equipment, travel, coaching and personal counseling. This is the full package that comes with a Tech athletic scholarship, and it is a nice deal.

Nice, but not priceless; certainly not when you figure that the athlete, by his work, is paying for the whole deal — and paying for more than just that. He's paying for buildings, paying to create non-revenue sports, paying for the jocks and sweatsocks and shoulder pads.

And no one even wonders if this use of the athletes' money is fair. It's been done that way so long that everyone, it seems, assumes it must be OK. Decent men such as Homer Rice say, "It's different in colleges than in the pros. Cities, counties, states build stadiums for the pros. Here we have to build our own."

Did anyone ever ask the athletes what they think of this use of the money they create? Did anyone ever ask an athlete if he wanted his money used to build a better stadium?

No one asks the athlete's opinion about anything. The athlete is asked to run, not think. Kindly people will look after him, teach him, guide him to growth as a person. It's a paternalistic notion, the boy under the father's wing. And that's good. But giving up freedom is too high a price to pay for it.

Some coaches recognize the high cost. Grant Teaff, Baylor's football coach: "People say athletes aren't treated the same as regular students. And they're right. Athletes are treated worse."

It is not extreme to say a player gives up freedom for a football scholarship. An example: if during the recruiting process at a great university such as Baylor the player should want to meets its prominent alumni who might serve as living examples of the school's good work, sorry, no can do, that's against the NCAA rules. You can't meet the alumni until after you enter school. Rules, rules: no longer can a player go to dinner with just anyone. No longer can he talk to everyone he meets. He is under watch. He must take a drug test whenever the paternalistic bosses say so. He must sign papers saying he hasn't signed papers with anyone except those people approved by the NCAA and for purposes which serve the NCAA's interest, not the athlete's.

Life is regimented: breakfast at the training table, study halls, lunch at the training table, go to classes, practice, study hall, dinner at the training table, study hall. It's two jobs at once, student and athlete. To keep his scholarship (issued yearly, no longer a four-year deal, the idea being to keep the kid on his toes), the athlete must maintain a course toward graduation while also playing big-time college sports. No easy deal there. And heaven forbid that he should take a $10 bill from his coach for dinner.

"And he shouldn't take that $10, because I can show you that every rule ever written was written because some coach abused a privilege," said Lee Corso, once the Indiana football coach and now an ESPN television commentator. "These kids are working their way through college, the same as your daughter works at the dining hall. And the education they're getting is one of the priceless things they'll ever have. If you give players anything, then someone will give them more somewhere else. It gets unfair. The rules we have now pretty much stopped the cheating because now they know if you get caught, you're a real crook."

Hold on a second.

A crook?

A cheater?

For being paid an extra $9.62 a week over the length of your career when the university makes millions with your help, you're a crook?

Not in Dale Brown's opinion. "We're calling kids 'cheaters,'" said Brown, the Louisiana State basketball coach. "That has a sour ring to it. 'Cheaters.' Who's cheating whom, anyway? We're cheating athletes of basic human needs. If schools don't satisfy those needs, players will find a way with agents, gamblers, drug dealers and jock-sniffers with the plantation-master mentality.

"We can't continue to legislate against human dignity. Yes, there must be guidelines. But Moses came down with two stone tablets and 10 rules — and we can't follow them. So how can we follow 400 pages in the NCAA manual?

"I'm a coach. I'm offered $150,000 to wear a basketball shoe, $75,000 to schedule a game, $50,000 to dribble a certain basketball. One game with Georgetown will pay our entire scholarship program for a year. Why should we have this and a kid can't get his tonsils out or a kid can't get home at Christmas to see his blind, 82-year-old grandmother who is dying?"

Rules. A zillion NCAA rules, all written to do the impossible, to legislate morality. Cheaters will cheat. What the rules do mostly is make it impossible for decent people to treat their players fairly.

"If it sounds good or feels good, it's illegal," said Mike Gottfriend, the Pittsburgh football coach.

Grant Teaff: "It's frustrating to be slammed up against the rules every day. You can't do anything for the kids. They ought to just let us use common sense. Nobody's trying to rob the bank here. We just want to treat the kids fairly. But you get into interpretations of interpretations of the rules. It gets so when you want to take a deep breath, you call the NCAA office and ask if it's OK to take a deep breath or should we limit it to a shallow breath?"

Duke basketball coach Mike Krzyzewski: "The rules discriminate unfairly against the revenue-producing sports. Why should golfers be able to play year-around and basketball can't? I'm not in favor of play-for-pay, but we need to be fair, we need to face reality. A monthly allotment of $100 or $200 would do it. And it should come out of the NCAA tournament money. If a school can't afford that, maybe it ought to go to Division III and play under those rules."

"Gestapo bastards," Dale Brown says of the NCAA enforcement staff personnel, some of whom conducted a four-year investigation of LSU basketball that uncovered eight violations, none major, for which Brown's program was punished by the loss of two scholarships. "They say rules are rules. Don't give me that crap. There was a rule blacks had to ride in the back of the bus. There was a rule women couldn't vote. There was a rule that Jews had to wear stars on their breast. A rule is only good when it protects mankind, not when it suppresses. And our rules, the NCAA rules, are absolutely, totally ludicrous. We should burn the book. All the rules we need can be written on a 3-by-5 index card."

Players don't get paid beyond the scholarship. In a capitalistic system, this is the next thing to robbery. Pro football players went on strike this year trying to get more than their current 58 percent of all NFL revenues. Let's draw a comparison and contrast here. If the University of Georgia football program brings in $10 million a year and if it pays 100 players with scholarships worth $7,500 each, that means Georgia's players receive 7 ½ percent of the revenue.

And the Georgia players don't get that 7 ½ percent in cash; the money goes straight back to the school's general fund to pay for the scholarships.

What, then, becomes of all the money paid by spectators to see college games? Oh, fear not. It doesn't go to waste. It's used for many things. And here is the true scandal. It's the NCAA, all right. The National Conspiracy Against Athletes.

Besides funding the likes of women's volleyball, men's wrestling and other non-revenue sports, college basketball and football players make possible a grand lifestyle for their masters. Some 40 percent of the NCAA basketball tournament revnue is used to pay 75 percent of the operating cost of the NCAA office in Mission, Kansas. That money is used to fly NCAA executives, college administrators included, to conventions at priccy resorts. While the athlete is limited to a bowl of rice, the NCAA poohbahs pour butter over lobster.

"Cocktail parties," Bob Knight said, a snarl his tone.

Dean Smith, the North Carolina basketball coach, once wrote: "The NCAA takes considerable amounts of revenue generated from basketball, then uses it for travel, committee meetings, non-revenue sports — which I will agree are worthwhile — but notice how well those administrators live when they take those trips for meetings; the meetings are always in some fairly exotic place. And then there's the student-athlete, who doesn't have the spare change for a hamburger, trying to scrape living expenses together.

"The sad thing is that we have the money in Division I basketball and football to help these young men, but the college administrators keep getting in the way. . . . If this sad set of priorities stays intact, then the exploitation of student-athletes will be as difficult as ever to curtail, let alone stop completely."

Big-time schools recruit from coast to coast. More often than not, their players come from poor circumstances and are asked to move into a college life unlike anything they've ever known. Coaches see the stress of that adjustment. They see players who have only canvas shoes and blue jeans.

Gottfried of Pitt: "I see kids who don't have enough money to buy toothpaste. Like Teryl Austin (a Pitt star who, like Ingram, lost his eligibility by signing early with an agent, in his case a New York show-biz agent named Norby Walters). Teryl was thrown out of his dorm for some prank, so he had to live off campus. By the rules we could give him $260 a month living expenses (the equivalent of on-campus cost). Well, his apartment cost $220 a month. That left him $40 for 30 days of food and incidentals. That's why he was a perfect target for Norby Walters."

Gottfried finds fault with Teryl Austin, who knew better, but the coach finds greater fault with an NCAA system that leaves a young man living in poverty when he has a talent which the university uses to make big money.

"Yeah, we wonder why a kid gets involved with an agent," Gottfried said. "I don't wonder anymore. I know."

Gabriela Andersen-Scheiss

August 6, 1984

Los Angeles

Whence is it courage, when is it the human spirit invincible? And when is it a waste, when is it life invaluable slipping away?

We saw Gabriela Andersen-Scheiss. We saw her come through the dark tunnel into the sunlight. We saw her after she had run 26 miles. We fell silent at the horror. She was a dying runner. But she was unwilling to stop. *Unable* to stop.

We come to any coliseum anywhere to see the beauty created when an athlete's talents intersect at a sweet spot in time with a dream. Nowhere is this beauty as well defined as in the Olympic Games, where athletes reach for the one moment built on a life's work. What we almost never see is the pain of that work.

We have seen it now. We have seen it wearing red. Gabriela Andersen-Schiess also wore something white on her head against the sun. A cap? A handkerchief? All we remember is how she looked. She looked like a woman in damning torment. Pain twisted her body and distorted her face. Her left leg was useless. She dragged it behind her. She was a cripple lost in the sun of a desert with no mercy.

A track official wanted to help her. She shied away, moving from the inside lane to the outside, far from anyone who would help her. She had made it 26 miles. She would finish.

By now, Joan Benoit had won the marathon and was carrying an American flag around the coliseum on a victory lap. Cheers rang down, for we loved her moment made real by thousands of solitary miles through the hard winters of her adored Maine, along the

195

steely blue ocean. Her Achilles tendon flew apart once. Her knee locked up this spring and doctors had to fix it with surgery.

"Nobody came," Joan Benoit, 27, said, meaning she moved in front early in this marathon and nobody moved with her. It was easy, she said, and she loved the moment when she came into the coliseum. "It was very, very special," said this small rock of a woman whose life's work has been done in silence and whose dream was certified real by the thunder of a coliseum. "It was something I've dreamed about. So many people to be thankful for."

The thunder came down for her, but not for her alone. Gabriela Andersen-Schiess, 39, is a ski instructor in Idaho, a veteran marathoner who, as a Swiss native, ran this marathon in Switzerland's red-cross uniform. As Benoit circled the coliseum floor in joy, Andersen-Schiess stumbled in pain. One man's notes: "No. 323 in red . . . walks, tries to run, can't . . . like a drunk, weaving . . . crowd cheering, trying to help her along . . . won't let anyone touch her . . . why don't they make her stop?"

Joan Benoit loves the icicles on her eyelashes. They come in the hard winter of Maine. It was 5 below zero last March and she put on thermals under her sweat suit to go running in the snow along the icy inlets of an unforgiving countryside. She comes at you with the big blue eyes of a tiny girl who has sprung full life from a *Peanuts* comic strip. She has a little voice, and she is the picture of a waif, and you wonder how she does it.

"I don't know where my competitiveness comes from," she said Sunday afternoon. "I like challenges, I know that. I feel I still have my personal best in me, and I want to keep running until I get it out of me. . . . Maybe it was growing up with three brothers and it was survival of the fittest. . . . I was a skier and I had dreams of making the Olympics as a skier. I couldn't do that, but I had the dreams."

She broke a leg skiing. To get back in shape, she ran. She came to love the splendid isolation of running. She's a Mainer, a hard case in a soft package. "A wisp of a will," Jane Leavy wrote in the *Washington Post*. Benoit had arthroscopic knee surgery April 25, just 17 days before the Olympic Trials, and Sunday afternoon she came running into the sunlight of the coliseum.

Gabriela Andersen-Schiess began to stagger two miles from the coliseum. She was dehydrated. She started fast in 76-degree heat. After 20 miles, she was only 10 minutes behind Benoit. After 24 miles, 15 minutes behind. But she needed 17 minutes to go the last mile and a half.

"I didn't see her at all," Benoit said. Runner-up Grete Waitz of Norway said, "I don't think Gabriela realized where she was. I see it as a tragedy. She didn't know where she was or what she was doing. I feel so sorry for her."

They gave Joan Benoit a gold medal Sunday. They took off Gabriela Andersen-Schiess's bloody shoes and carried her out on a stretcher. She finished 37th, 24 minutes behind Benoit. Sunday night she was said to be resting well with no permanent injury.

John Riggins

January 16, 1983

Washington, D.C.

Handsome as the night is long, smiling in the sunlight of a day he'll love always, John Riggins took his helmet off at midfield and with a flourish of gallantry did a deep bow, his arm across his waist, bowing first to the folks on the south side of the stadium and then turning to say thanks to those on the north, the 54,000 or so screaming meemies who loved it as much as Riggins did.

Paint a picture of the moment. Get the blotch of mud on his cheek. Leave the grass stains on the white of his jersey. Remember that his pants were ripped, a pad peeking out on his thigh, and when you're done with the picture, hang it somewhere important, like in the White House or, better, in Pig Alley where the hallowed Hogs hang out.

Hang it high and shine a light on No. 44 as he raises a hand to wave his thanks near the end of a 21-7 victory over the Minnesota Vikings that put the Redskins into the National Football Conference championship game.

Riggins ran with the ball 37 times yesterday. No Redskin ever carried so often. He gained 185 yards, most of it in the gritty, little-bitty, chug-chug-chuggin' chunks that caused some customers to blow diesel-truck horns in appreciation. No Redskin ever ran so far in a playoff game. John Riggins never ran so far as a pro. He made the Redskins' first touchdown possible and scored the second on a two-yard run of brutal beauty. When it got to be 21-7, Riggins carried the ball 20 more times to stash away the victory.

Not bad for an old man of 33, an antique in a business where running backs age years in hours. In Riggins' 11th season, he has never been better. The joy is, he knows it. He knew it 10 days ago when he went to Coach Joe Gibbs.

It was an extraordinary thing Riggins did then. He has been called an eccentric whiner. He wore a Mohawk haircut with the Jets, followed immediately by an Afro. Rather than play on the Redskins' terms, he sat out an entire season arguing about money. The music in his ears was that of a different drummer. But whatever anyone said of Riggins, they all said he loved the moment of combat.

So right before the first playoff game, after resting a bruised thigh for two games, Riggins went to the coaches' locker room at Redskin Park. "He came right to me," Gibbs said, "and he just said, 'I'm really getting down the road, I don't have many of these left. I've been out two weeks and I'm ready. Give me the ball.'"

And with a minute to play yesterday, Gibbs, who knew he had seen something special, sent in a new man so Riggins could come off to the standing ovation he earned. Olivier as Hamlet never earned a bow on stage any more than Riggins earned his this day, and the stadium crowd stood to tell him how he had done. As time ticked away Riggins walked alongside the Redskin bench, holding his helmet by the face mask, trading hand slaps with people as happy as he was.

With a hundred reporters wanting to talk to him, Riggins yet stayed in character. Olivier probably didn't do interviews on his motivation as Hamlet. Riggins as Riggins, a fascinating role, came directly from a shower, dripping wet, and picked up his hiking boots. Later he sent a man to get his saddlebags and clothes (a hunter's camouflage outfit). Then Riggins beat it out of the stadium, walking past waiting reporters.

He walked through the parking lot, not a half-hour after his bows, and a woman ran to him. She took off her shoe. Riggins autographed it. Fans who think of Riggins as an 18-wheeler, as an irresistible force, draped a banner over his car: "Run on Diesel Power, High Octane."

Riggins stashed his saddlebags in the car trunk (no briefcase for a man who once rode his motorcycle from Kansas to Washington) and then took a beer from his hometown buddies. One told him, "Best game ever, John. High school, college, pro, anywhere. Best."

Riggins sipped at the beer, threw back a swig of tequila and said to his buddy "Hey" before driving away.

Riggins won't talk to reporters because, and this is a guess because he has never explained it, he didn't like what the newspapers said during his contract squabble with the Redskins two years ago. Two requests yesterday — "Can we talk about the bows, John?" — received only a stare in reply.

So much to ask him. Instead, ask Doug Martin, the Vikings' defensive end, what he thinks of Riggins.

"A Sherman tank," Martin said.

George Starke, the Redskins' veteran offensive tackle: "John is a living representation of an old Hank Williams Jr. song. Hard-drinkin', hard-fightin', ornery. That's what makes him a good runner."

A while ago, Pig Alley got in here. Pig Alley is a row of lockers at Redskin Park which is home to the Hogs, those dainty bruisers of the offensive line who, on seeing Riggins' body, made him the only non-lineman elevated to Hogdom.

"The guy weighs 260 pounds, and he runs like *that*," said Starke, who stretched it maybe 20 pounds but had the proper tone of wonder.

This is the way Riggins runs: truly like an 18-wheeler. Slow at the start, never the butterfly a Walter Payton is. Content to go straight ahead, never needing the egoistic dance of an O.J. Simpson. When the Hogs open a small hole, Riggins then, with his third or fourth step, has put the pedal to the metal. Then he is ready to run over people or run around them.

What to make of Riggins? Here's something from *North Dallas Forty*, the football novel by Peter Gent. The words are from Phil Elliott, a veteran for whom the game, not the sideshow, is life:

"That's what I love about sports, man. There is a basic reality when it is just me and the job to be done, the game and all its skills. And the reward wasn't what other people thought or how much they paid me, but how I felt at the moment I was exhibiting my special skill. How I felt about me. That's what's true. That's what I loved. All the rest is a matter of opinion."

Hank Williams could sing it. John Riggins is it.

Spud Webb

February 12, 1986

Spud Webb, we bow before you. Master of the skies, we worship at your winged heels.

Gravity defeats us, but you sail on. We stand bound to the earth while you rise on the warm zephyrs of imagination. We look up at the rim, an orange ring a ladder's length away from our Lilliputian leaden feet. We look up. And there you are, up there.

Spud Webb, a little man, 5-foot-5 ½, your face is in the net, the orange ring a hand's length away. What we mortals dream, you make real. Spud Webb, the Spudnik of basketball orbitry, you can dunk it, slam it, throw it down, reverse it, 360 it, goodgawdawmighty it.

Maybe there is a better sports story than Spud Webb winning the NBA's Slam Dunk contest, but maybe not, either. When's the last time the NBA had so much fun? Here is basketball's elemental challenge, the ultimate move, reducing the risk of a missed shot to zero. You put your hand inside the rim. It is a visceral moment. The dunk makes a guy king of the world.

A newspaper colleague, when we spoke of man's universal urge to stuff it, said he gave up the quest long ago. "But our daughter, Katharine, she'll be 3 in January," said Jack Wilkinson, "and I have hope for her. Lucy, my wife, is 5-foot-10 ½. Katharine may be the first woman's 6-5 point guard. Anyway, for Christmas, we got her a Dunk-It basketball game. She went right to it. Walked right up, took the little ball — and threw it down!"

"I'm 31 years old," sportswriter Bud Shaw said over lunch when conversation turned to Webb's great feat, "and still, about once a month, I have this dream. In my dream, I'm dunking the ball. I'm floating by the rim. It's so easy." There was a lovely lilt to the old fellow's voice. He is a 6-footer, if you count his curls, which he does, and he plays some hoops yet. "But then I wake up," he said, "and I'm still down here."

Down here. On the ground. His vertical leap is now measured not in feet or inches but by seismographic tremors that suggest a building has collapsed. We watch, then, in wonder at players who work on the high wire. We see Dr. J dunk from the free-throw line. We see Dominique Wilkins dunk from downtown. And now we see the little guy, the Spudnik, Spud Webb, dunk it . . . on two bounces.

To win the NBA's contest, Webb did a two-bounce dunk that began 30 feet out. From there, the Hawks' guard began to move. At 20 feet, he bounced the ball off the floor at such an angle as to send it against the backboard. Then as it bounced off the backboard, Webb came flying up there to catch it in one hand.

At which moment, the little man slammed it down.

What this did, besides make Spud Webb a celebrity, was get a lot of old fellows talking about dunking the ball.

Every afternoon after school back home in Illinois, Legs took me to his backyard basket. Legs was a nickname, short for Frog Legs. This sucker could jump. I would shoot from 20 feet and hope I never missed because Legs got every rebound. The merciless braggart would then dunk the ball on his nine-foot-high hoop.

As foolish and ignorant as I now am in the declining years of my childhood, which is to say I am over 30 and under 50, this ignorance is as nothing next to that of my adolescence. Then I believed, from reading Charles Atlas ads in comic books, that I could change the muscular development of my body by lifting weights in the basement. One night I used anvils. I hooked a toe through the anvil handle and lifted. The theory was that I, too, would spring like a frog into the wild blue yonder. I quit with a sprained big toe.

I was 15 years old the day I went out to our shed which had a rim, maybe eight feet off the ground. It was nailed above an open doorway. To use this entrance to the shed, you took a step up to a landing about a foot off the ground. I stepped up on this landing. From there, the rim was only seven feet away. I crouched low to spring up. I would perform a reverse dunk, the first ever done on Kindred land. I would be somebody.

I sprang up. But not very far. I had forgotten about the door jamb above me. My head crashed into it. I fell to earth.

Muhammad Ali

April 12, 1974

Louisville, Kentucky

We forgive Muhammad Ali his excesses because we see in him the child in us. In all of us a child lives. The child laughs and cries. He asks for the sweets of the world as if they were his alone, and he begs in a hundred ways, a thousand ways, for the attention that is a guarantee of love. We grow old with this child in us and we pretend the child is gone, for we are told to put away childish things.

Muhammad Ali is the child in all of us, and if he is foolish or cruel, if he is arrogant, if he is outrageously in love with his reflection, we forgive him because we no more can condemn him than condemn a rainbow for dissolving in the dusk.

The room was quiet. Ali looked into the coffin where a policeman rested. Behind the heavyweight champion of the world, empty wooden chairs with curved-top backs stood on a gray linoleum floor. The room's only lights were bare bulbs in floor lamps at the ends of the coffin. Ali's face was made sinister, shadows moving each time he tilted his head to see another part of the dead man. Rowhouse funeral homes in Philadelphia ghettoes are repositories for the friendless, and Ali, his Rolls-Royce parked on the street, had come to see the man.

"He got shot during my fight," Ali said. Men had argued in a Philadelphia arena. They had seen Ali fight Joe Frazier on closed-circuit television. The policeman was off duty and he tried to stop the argument and someone shot him. Ali read about it in the newspapers. In front of the coffin, Ali reached out and touched the dead man's hand.

"Cold," Ali said, drawing back his hand.

He would go to the policeman's wife, Ali said, and talk to her and say he was sorry. He would see if there was anything she needed and he would try to help.

The child is good, and he is black, and the policeman was black, and if Ali is remembered for anything, he wants it to be this: "I was a fighter who tried to help my people."

It was midnight, the same night in 1971, and Ali was at home in a Philadelphia suburb. His home was testimony to his wealth and need for gratification that is instant and constant. The walls of his living room were mirrors and he spoke not to a person across from him but to his own reflection. There were 22 telephones in the 10-room house. At midnight in the basement of his house, Ali turned on a record player.

The rock 'n' roll singer Little Richard came on, and Ali said, "Little Richard, he called himself 'The Greatest,' and that's where I got that. Now nobody knows where Little Richard is, but everybody knows me."

A silhouette took shape at the head of the basement stairs, a man blocking the living room light.

"Ali?" The voice was a quiver. The man pronounced the champion's name as Alley. "You there, Ali?"

"What you want, old man?"

"I need money, Ali. I come to Philadelphia from New York to see you. I come on the bus and I come on the bus out here."

"How much, old man?"

"A couple . . ."

"Hundred?" Ali said. "A couple hundred?"

The man stood silent.

"Come down here," Ali said, and the old man moved slowly down the stairs. It was winter and the old man wore rags. Light from the living room played against the man's face, a field of stubble drawn tight by whiskey pain. "What you do if you get money, old man?" Ali said.

"Go home," he said, and Ali handed the man $200 from his pocket, saying, "Don't stop along the way."

"Bless you, champ," the old man said.

The child is good. He takes care of his mother, father and brother. He takes care of hangers-on. He finds on-the-bum fighters or they find him. He cares for them.

He once took a taxi to a home for elderly Jews and wrote out a check for $100,000 because he heard on television that the place was about to be closed down. He has made millions in the ring and he has spent most of it.

It is easy for many people to dislike Ali. The child is loud. He brags. He didn't go into the Army, saying even as Americans died, "I ain't got nothin' against them Viet Congs."

He is a Black Muslim and though he no longer calls for segregation from that hated white man, he once preached that gospel in frightening accompaniment with Elijah Muhammad, who advocated a black state given over to the Muslims by whites whom he called "blue-eyed devils."

Ali preaches high morality, but his second divorce was followed quickly by the birth of an out-of-wedlock baby. He can be cruel. Because the former heavyweight champion Floyd Patterson, a black man, insisted on calling him "Clay," Ali called Patterson "a white American" and tortured him in a fight when Patterson was helpless with a bad back. "What's my name?" Ali spat at Patterson, before, in Robert Lipsyte's memorable phrase, picking another wing off the butterfly.

Ali is a beautiful child, beautiful in form and motion, and anything less is subject to his contempt. He called Joe Frazier "an ugly gorilla." To George Foreman, Ali once screamed, "I'll beat your Christian ass, you white, flag-waving son of a bitch, you." With a mean sneer on his lips, he warned Frazier's manager, Eddie Futch, to stay off the streets of Harlem "because you have been marked by Muhammad Ali."

And Ali, the child in us, says he meant none of those things. He said them, sure. He meant them at the time. He always means what he says when he says it. Later, he is sorry he said it.

"Naw," he said of the Foreman tirade, he didn't say those gutter words. He was on a couch in a dimly lit dressing room. He was tired after a workout. His voice was soft, the tone gentle. "And if I did say those things, I shouldn't have. I got carried away."

But 10 minutes later he was at it again, up off the couch, throwing punches in the air and shouting about the fight coming up with Foreman that year, 1974.

"I'm fighting to represent Elijah Muhammad. This Foreman, he represents Christianity, America, the flag. I can't let him win. He represents the oppression of black people. He represents pork chops.

"I'm the only black man in the world standing up for my people. All the rednecks and Uncle Toms are pulling for me to lose. I'm going to whup George Foreman — not for the money, not so I can have a blonde on both arms — but so I can go with blacks, use it to practice what Elijah teaches."

Rainbows are born of thunderstorms, and Muhammad Ali is both. As it does us no good to wonder why a thundercloud came up — it is there and will ruin the day, no matter what — so we waste our time if we expect to find the sources of Ali's dark and hateful moods. We may guess at them, but they cannot be explained, least of all by Ali. And as rainbows tease us with their wonder, so does Ali, for the more we reach out, the more scattered are the raindrops of his beauty.

First he was a fighter, a prodigy at the mean game. By 18 he was the 1960 Olympic champion. America loved him, as much for his unabashed celebration of victory as for his ability. Given the gold medal at Rome, he wore it to dinner, wore it to bed, wore it on the airplane home and, arriving in Louisville, lifted it off his chest for well-wishers to see. Years later he would say he threw the medal into the Ohio River in angry protest of racial slights which began the day after the glorious homecoming.

First a fighter, then a court jester. Before assassination became our national plague in the '60s, Ali made us laugh. He recited silly poems, the shortest being, "Me/Whee/Muhammad Ali!". "Moore must fall in four," he said, and then he knocked out the venerable Archie Moore in the fourth round. Of the heavyweight champion Sonny Liston, Ali screamed, "Where is that big, ugly bear?" It was fun, all of it.

And then men shot men in America, first the president and later Malcom X and Martin Luther King Jr. and the president's brother. In Vietnam, American men were in a war they would not win. The fighter, the court jester, now Ali became a symbol — anti-war, anti-government, anti-Establishment.

Ali the anti-hero buried the name of his birth, Cassius Marcellus Clay Jr., a name he had truly loved for its noble sound. Announcing his conversion to Islam, he said he wanted nothing more to do with a slaveholder's name. He became Muhammad Ali.

Ali was 22 then, talented beyond explanation, physically attractive and enormously charming. The sportswriters told him he would be good for America the way Joe Louis had been good. And Ali said in answer, "I don't have to be what you want me to be."

We cannot doubt the depth of Ali's religious devotion. For his religion, he defied the United States government. He refused the military draft, and history at full tide engulfed him. His act never changed — the silly poems, the mugging, the overheated lectures on Allah, his childish begging for the sweets of fame. As always, he worked to make himself larger than life. And now history was his sideman. He had stirred the boiling cauldron of racial hatred and now he added the war. The primary social issues of our time somehow were represented in this fighter/clown.

He became, with his refusal to go to war, a hero, a traitor and a martyr. Politicians stripped him of the championship in 1967 and refused him licenses to fight. For three years, a free man while his draft conviction was appealed, Ali was denied the right to work at his chosen craft, denied his constitutional privileges by men invoking the national honor.

In 1970 the Supreme Court said Ali was within the law in his refusal to accept the draft. The comeback was on. Whether he was a conscientious opponent of war in keeping with the precepts of his religion, as he argued, or whether, as many said, he simply feared being shot at more than he feared jail, Ali was back in the ring before the shooting stopped in Vietnam.

It has been eight years now since Ali's exile ended, and Ali has come full circle. It is fashionable again to admire him. For one thing, he had the war right, even if he didn't say it right. For another, he dared boldly for what he believed in. There's now a movie of Ali's life, based on his autobiography. He pops up in TV commercials. ABC-TV pays him $50,000 to tag along on a tour of Russia, where he meets Leonid Brezhnev and pronounces the premier an all-right guy.

In the beginning, a child in Louisville, Muhammad Ali wanted to be somebody. He knew only that much. Maybe his father, a billboard painter and frustrated artist, planted the seed of grandiosity. Given a gift of surpassing athletic ability, Ali then pursued fame until the poor thing fell to Earth exhausted. It is his forever now.

In the summer of 1974, Ali drove a white Cadillac down a one-lane logging road through a forest in the Pennsylvania mountains. He was going 100 miles per hour. It seemed as good a time as any to ask if Ali ever thought of dying.

"You don't want to die," he said. "But you do. The man who built this road is dead. The man who built that house (taking a hand off the steering wheel to point out a farm) is dead. We're nobody. Sonny Liston is dead. Zora Folley's dead. Eddie Machen. These are guys I fought. Now Sonny Liston's rottin'. We ain't nothin'.

"We don't own nothin', we just borrow it. When you die, another man moves in and your daughter calls him daddy. Death is the tax a soul has to pay for having a name and a form."

At 100 m.p.h., one hand on the wheel, the other helping him preach, Muhammad Ali was in full cry as a minister.

"So what are we here for? To serve God's creatures. Ike Williams, Kid Gavilan — they were great fighters and now they need help. I don't need to hire anybody at my camp, but Ike Williams and Kid Gavilan need help. So I hire them and pay them and talk to them. They were great fighters. Did you ever see Kid Gavilan fight? I've got some films of his and . . ."

The minister was out of the pulpit then. The child's turn to speak.

September 28, 1980

Las Vegas

God only knows why, but they rolled in Joe Louis in a wheelchair right in the middle of a Muhammad Ali press conference. The old champ had his heart repaired three or four years ago and he has had three strokes since. The Brown Bomber's skin is yellow-gray, the color of old newspaper clippings. He can't see or speak much. But they wheeled him in, Caesar's Palace did, probably because they still pay him, and Ali hurried around the table to touch him.

"Joe, I'm gonna put a whuppin' on him," Ali said. This was said for the television cameras. Ali said this at a scream for the microphones. A job's a job and he and Joe would do their job. "You gonna be there, Joe?"

Joe Louis sat there in his wheelchair. He wore a cowboy hat. He wore cowboy boots. A man from Caesar's said Joe was to have been at Ali's workout for next week's heavyweight championship fight with Larry Holmes. It took too long to dress the champ, the man from Caesar's said.

"Joe, I watched films of you the other night, Joe, you and Schmeling," Ali said, still at a scream. "Your combinations were somethin' else, Joe. That one-two you hit Schmeling with in the first round, that's what I'm gonna hit Holmes with. One round, Joe, I might do it in one round. So don't be late, Joe, you might miss it."

Joe Louis sat there. The hands that hit Schmeling lay dead in his lap.

Ali touched the old champion's knee. Softly now, not for the cameras or microphones but whispering in the champ's ear, Ali said, "You feelin' any pain, Joe, feelin' any pain?"

There came from Joe Louis an animal grunt. His head moved an inch in a nod.

"You eatin' good, Joe, you eatin' good?"

Another chilling grunt. This one meant no.

For the cameras again, Ali raised up and said, "Thanks for comin' by, Joe, it's gonna be a great fight," and then Ali bent low to this warrior once mighty, saying in a whisper, "I'll try to come see you, Joe, before I leave. I'll come to your house."

They are brothers, Louis and Ali, made kin not by blood but by life, for they rose to fame as inimitable prizefighters, the best of their times, and then they stayed too long at the party. Louis was a sad shell at 37 trying to make money against Rocky Marciano. The kid butchered him. And outside the ring, Louis was sadder yet, a sail without wind. Caesar's paid him to show up. It still does. And if Ali at 38 wonders about the pain of Louis, now 66, it is because he looks at the Brown Bomber and sees himself. It must hurt like hell.

I came to Las Vegas thinking I would see a pitiable Ali. Only three months ago at the Leonard-Duran fight, Ali was a rheumy-eyed whale who slurred his words. His hair was graying and he affected a ridiculous mustache. Against a young Larry Holmes who had defended his title with seven straight knockouts, I believed Ali would be hurt badly.

It is amazing what Ali has done in three months. From 253 pounds this spring, he is down to 220. He looks as firm in the upper body as he has for six years. The waistline is trim. "He came to camp as Fat Albert," said his longtime friend and business adviser Gene Kilroy, "and he left as Muhammad Ali."

Ali now uses "a little black hair rinse" to wash away the gray. The mustache is gone because "I just let it grow to make everybody think I was gettin' old." The fat fell away, Ali says, when he ate a plateful of fruit every day for six months and stayed off pastries. As for the sickly eyes, slurred speech and bloated face that marked him pathetic in Montreal, Ali says, "That was my thyroid glands actin' up. I took two pills a day for a month and it's all cleared up now."

The promoters of the fight called in a doctor to announce that Ali was in excellent physical condition, with none of the brain damage alleged by a London doctor who made the diagnosis by listening to tapes of Ali speaking. Seeing Ali in the ring, hearing him at press conferences, veteran Ali-watchers have been convinced that he is, if not the young Ali, a suggestion of that Ali.

"Nothing has changed with Muhammad," said his trainer, Angelo Dundee, who has worked with Ali for 20 years. "Comes a knock at the door of his suite the other day. It's a chick with a baby in her arms. Muhammad saw her in the lobby and told her to come up. 'Let her in,' he says. A man from Mars comes to the door — beep, beep — and Muhammad would say, 'Let him in.'

"Sometimes I think Muhammad might be a man from Mars himself. He sure ain't a normal human being. No normal human being could have done what he's done to get ready for this fight. I didn't believe he could get rid of the flab around his waist. But he did. He's trim. Muscle tone underneath. No hollow shell. The body's right. The continuing saga of Muhammad Ali goes on.

"We're in his room. And Ali says, 'I'm gonna go until 1985.' So Kilroy says, 'Yeah, and I'll be like this,' and he walks around shaking like a guy 90 years old. And I say they'll have to devise a crane to get me up the ring steps. But Ali, he'll be bright-eyed and bushy-tailed still doing his exercises and getting ready for a fight."

The story was a joke, but the melancholy truth hides in it. Ali doesn't want it to end. In his suite later, Ali watched a video tape of a speech he made at Harvard. He glanced from the TV to a mirror, seeing himself in both places, as if needing the reminder that he existed. The Ali on the TV was saying, "Youth never ends."

Four days later

He had nothing. Muhammad Ali had nothing. No jab, no right hand, no dancing, no nothing. He asked the crowd to chant, "Ali . . . Ali," and the sound came back barely more than a whisper. He touched a glove to his ear, meaning he wanted to hear it louder. Nothing came then. This was a minute before the fight. It was over even then. Ali must have known from the silence. So began the longest night for Ali. "A horrible night," Angelo Dundee called it.

Always a warrior, brave and strong, Ali came to battle Thursday night with no weapons. He would have gone on. He was angry when Dundee, his trainer, stopped the fight. Ali is proud. Warriors suffer. Warriors go out on their shields. Sonny Liston quit 16 years ago. Liston quit on his stool. He gave away the heavyweight championship. Gave it away. Sat on his stool, robbed of his will to go on. Robbed by the young Cassius Clay.

Now it comes full circle. Cassius Clay, now Muhammad Ali, sat on his stool Thursday night. He lost to a younger man. Not to say he quit. No, Ali wouldn't quit. "I'll hit you in the mouth," he screamed at Dundee when he said he was stopping the fight. But 16 years after Liston sat on his stool and gave the championship away, Ali stayed on his stool rather than come out for the 11th round. And Larry Holmes, once Ali's teenage sparring partner, kept the title.

Ali says he will fight again. He says he'll fight Mike Weaver. He says he lost too much weight too fast getting ready for Holmes. He went from 260, he said, to as low as 216. So he had no strength, no energy. It will be different the next time, he said. He'll stay trim now and build up his strength and he will fight Mike Weaver.

This is the warrior talking. Even as he was driven by car from ringside to his hotel last night, even 10 minutes after being knocked out for the first time, even with the night's sweat sparkling against the angry blue/purple/black bruises at his eyes — even when he was less a fighter than Liston on that 16 years ago, a night when Liston hit Ali with hammer blows, a night when the young Clay ripped the old man's face with snake-lick jabs and combinations coming so fast as to be blurs of destruction — even when Holmes had won every round on every judge's scorecard, still Muhammad Ali said he would fight again.

It was awful. Ali was a pug. A prelim fighter. Somebody named Ruffhouse Walker lost last night, too. He was in the casino this morning, a toothpick in his mouth, a bandage on his brow. His face was the color and texture of raw sirloin. Ali, to make a TV appearance, wore sunglasses to hide the kind of damage shared by Ruffhouse Walker — Ruffhouse Walker, a punching bag. And Ali his cousin in futility.

Ali's only plan last night was to throw a long right hand over Holmes' jab. He had seen Ernie Shavers knock down Holmes with that punch. One punch could do it. So Ali hinted at a first-round knockout. This is the warrior who once came to battle with weapons no other man ever owned. But now he believed he had only one chance to win. A one-punch knockout. He no longer was Muhammad Ali. He was, good Lord, Ruffhouse Walker looking to get lucky.

Ali came full of bluster, as always. At the end of the second round, he shouted to Holmes, "You about ready? You ready?" A round later: "You're through." It was empty bravado. Ali hadn't landed a punch, hadn't stopped a punch except with his pretty face. Late in the fourth round, there in the parking lot of a gambling casino, there with Ali's glittery crowd of Cary Grants and Frank Sinatras, there with $8 million all his and the world watching on closed-circuit television — there with all the glamor and drama Ali craves so much — late in the fourth round there was, for what seemed forever, total silence as the fighters worked.

Silence. The dead silence given to sorry pugs. Twenty-five thousand people were silent. They had been silent for Ruffhouse Walker and now they watched Muhammad Ali in silence. At the end of the sixth round, they booed Ali. By the eighth round, Ali walked to his stool in dejection, his head hanging, his arms limp.

The crowd now tried to lift him. "Ali . . . Ali," the customers chanted in the ninth round as Holmes crashed a three-punch combination off Ali's ears, bop-bop-BOP, rattling the old man's brain back and forth. The chant died quickly, and by now Angelo Dundee knew what had to be done.

The night Liston quit in 1964, it was Clay, the kid, who first wanted to quit. "Dirty work," Clay screamed at Dundee. Something had blinded him. Something in his eyes. "Cut the gloves off," Clay screamed, but Dundee threw water into Clay's eyes instead and said, "This is for the title, get your ass out there."

It was Liston, the maneater, the knight of the baleful countenance, who quit that night in Miami Beach. He quit in frustration three rounds after Clay had wanted to quit. Liston's best shots didn't stop the kid and in return came the blur of jabs and combinations that revealed the champion as an old man. It wasn't worth it to him to go on. So Liston sat on his stool, saying no to the eighth round.

By slitting Ali's glove and stopping the fight for repairs, Dundee may have saved Ali's title the night Henry Cooper knocked him down. "It was the nearest thing to dyin'," Ali said of his third fight with Joe Frazier, a fight in which Dundee had to lift Ali off the stool and throw him toward Frazier in the 11th round. Ali knocked out Frazier in the 14th.

And then it came time last night to do what had to be done. Dundee had saved Ali against Liston and Frazier and Cooper. Now he had to save him from himself. He had to stop the fight. He knew it early, he said. He told Ali after the eighth round, "I'm gonna stop it."

"Muhammad said, 'No, don't do that,'" Dundee said this morning. "I did it because I thought maybe the threat would get him going."

A round later, after the ninth, Ali's friend and massuer, the silent, grizzled old Cuban named Luis Sarria, spoke with his eyes only to Dundee. Stop it. Stop it now, Sarria's eyes said. It was love in his eyes, Dundee said. "I told him, 'Don't worry, Sarria, the next round.'"

Dundee had asked the referee for one more round. Holmes even had backed away from Ali rather than hit the man once his idol. Ali was helpless, a sad-eyed bull waiting for the matador's killing insertion. At the end of the 10th round, Dundee said it was over. Ali argued briefly. Pat Patterson, Ali's bodyguard, shouted to Herbert Muhammad, Ali's manager sitting at ringside, "What do you want done?"

Herbert Muhammad nodded yes.

It was over.

"But as soon as we got in the car going back to the hotel, Ali said he wanted to fight Weaver," Herbert Muhammad said this morning. "I tried to talk him out of it. I told him to not even think about it right now. Wait a week at least. I don't want him to fight again, period. And my best feeling is that so many people who care about him are going to tell him not to fight that he won't."

December 13, 1981

Nassau, Bahamas

"I shall return . . ." Muhammad Ali said this morning.

" . . . to Los Angeles, California."

The eternal imp, Ali said goodbye with a laugh.

A reporter asked, "Has Joe Frazier called?"

"Yes, he called last night," Ali said, "and we'll be fighting next month."

He knows it's over now, and he said goodbye gracefully.

Someone asked Trevor Berbick if he learned anything in last night's unanimous decision victory over Ali. Before the Canadian champion could answer, Ali leaned toward the press conference microphone and said, "I taught him to retire before he's 40."

Muhammad Ali, five weeks short of his 40th birthday, lost last night to the invisible opponent who is undefeated now and always. "I couldn't beat Father Time," Ali said. He was flat on his back on a dressing room table. He whispered. "This is it."

His twin daughters, 10 years old, wept. His wife, Veronica, stood in silence. Someone asked Ali if six months from now he would smile at us and say he was only kidding about retirement. "No, it's too late now," he said. "The body can't do it any more."

That was painfully clear to the Ali loyalists in the crowd of 7,000 in a makeshift arena of 11,000 folding chairs and wooden bleacher

217

seats. The ring was set up behind second base on a kids' baseball field in the chill winter air of an island in an ocean. Only one of the 50 U.S. states agreed to license Ali for another fight, so he came here. The promoters couldn't find the ring bell. They went to a pasture next door and took a bell from a cow's neck.

For seven rounds, nothing from Ali. In the eighth, trying to dance, he went up on his toes, circling the slower Berbick. But from Ali's corner came the familiar thunderous voice of his longtime friend, Bundini Brown. "You gotta throw some punches," Brown said.

But Ali couldn't do it. Berbick stopped the dance with a hook to the ribs. Even in the 10th round, when Ali knew he needed a knockout, it was Berbick who finished the fight by rocking Ali with three punches.

It ended then, not with a whimper but with a cowbell. Muhammad Ali, 39 and getting older every second, was done. His record: 56 victories, five defeats. Three times the heavyweight champion. Forever the greatest.

The morning after, Ali was not grieving. Not after losing to Joe Frazier, not after Ken Norton and Leon Spinks, not after Larry Holmes and not now. "I'm happy. I've had a good life in boxing." And no, he wouldn't pop up again in another comeback. "I'm not craaaaaaaazzy," he said.

He thought he'd lost too much weight too fast to get into the ring with Holmes a year ago. He wanted one more chance.

"I didn't show," he said, "and now I know."

In seven words of unwitting rhyme, Ali confessed it was over. Once he could do anything, now he can do nothing. "I felt the timing wasn't there, and the reflexes . . . I could tell I was 40, and I could tell he was younger . . . I think I'm finished as far as getting in the ring. Training was difficult, jabbing was difficult, everything I did was difficult. I know myself better than anybody. I know it's the end."

Ed Schuyler of the Associated Press covered 22 Ali fights, from Indonesia to Zaire, from Ireland to Japan, Malaysia and Germany.

This morning he said to Ali, "It's been one helluva ride." Goodbye and thanks from the ink-stained wretches.

And Ali, a twinkle in his eye, told Schuyler not to be in such a hurry to get off. "I don't know how I'll feel next month," the old champ said, smiling brightly.

May 22, 1983

Las Vegas

At hotels here, you can gamble while you eat scrambled eggs. Keno's the game. It's like bingo, with numbers flashed on boards on the restaurant walls. You use a blue crayon to mark numbers on the pink keno slip. A beefy tourist put a crayon and keno slip in front of Muhammad Ali and said, "Champ, you got a 9-year-old fan in Cleveland. Make it 'To Ian.' He'll treasure this his whole life."

Some stories are fun. You laugh at the way the words come out. This one isn't fun. Some stories are just real. You write them down the way you see them. You see people hand blue crayons to Muhammad Ali, who was a hero, who was an athlete of grace and courage beyond knowing, who said you don't have to like me but I'm gonna make it anyway. Martin Luther King said it one way; Ali said it his way. And we're better because they both said it some way.

For 15 years, you'd seen Ali four or five times a year. Now it had been 17 months, not since December of 1981 when he lost his last fight, a cow's bell tolling the end in a makeshift ring set over second base at a kids' ball field on a scruffy exile's island.

"Ali, you look good," you say on the hotel steps, not knowing what else to say. He is puffed up, maybe 260 pounds. And Ali says, "Come on."

You cross a casino gaming room with him, through a cigar-stinking haze, and people call out, "Hi, Champ," and now in the coffee shop Ali says, "I am dedicating myself to promoting world peace." Hearing a sentence, you know it's worse than before. His voice is a mumble. It is as if the voice came from an attic with all the words muffled by the dust of time. You want him to sparkle. You want him to be fun. You want him to be what he was before a thousand punches hit him.

Ali asks a man with him to get the paper on the United Nations plan. A crude drawing of an airplane is over the words, "Children's Journey for Peace." The plan, Ali says, is to have 50 children from 50 countries meet with the world's presidents, kings and sheiks.

"I've been offered deals to do boxing promotions, to speak, to make business deals. I've turned them all down to promote world peace. We'll be making the announcement of the journey in six to eight weeks at the U.N. It's going to cost $2.5 million. Sheiks of Arabia will donate money, certain people will donate the airplane. It's going to be something, man. Beautiful. Powerful. Boxing was Allah's way of getting me fame to do something bigger. This is 10 times bigger than boxing. Powerful."

You tell him it is wonderful, again not knowing how to say anything else. You've heard it before, about great mosques and apartment buildings for the needy. You've seen nothing. He made a couple of horrid movies and did a series of college lectures, none memorable. Marilyn Monroe couldn't be Marilyn Monroe forever, and when she needed help there was no one at the other end of the telephone. And now Ali is not the Ali he was.

He can get money, if he wants money. His name is money. But you see Ali for the first time since his last fight and you know money isn't what he wants. He wants ultimate, eternal, undeniable fame.

Larry Holmes walks by Ali's table in the restaurant. "I hear you're being ugly about me," shouts Holmes, once Ali's sparring partner, later the champion who pulled punches rather than hurt Ali, his idol and friend. "You want to do it, Champ? Let's make a comeback."

Ali smiles, his voice booming now, "I wannnntttt Hooolmmes."

"Ali's making a comeback," Holmes says loudly, and the restaurant customers applaud.

"This nigger's craaaazy," Ali says, and Holmes drops his voice to say, "One champ to another champ. You'll always be the greatest; I'm just the latest."

Upstairs in his hotel room now, Ali asks if you have heard his lecture on the meaning of life. No, you say, though you've heard it three times. "Islamic evangelist, that's what I want to do," Ali says. He has photographs of himself with Billy Graham, Pope John Paul II, Ronald Reagan, Gerald Ford, Jimmy Carter and Leonid Brezhnev. "The world listens to me."

Now the lecture comes from a portable cassette player which Ali sits on the floor, so eight people can hear it. His left arm, resting on his chair, trembles. The thumb twitches. The taped voice of Ali is flat, lifeless and stumbling. Fame plus faith, Ali believes, will make him the Billy Graham of Islam. His lecture is soporific and simplistic, but someone says, "So wise, Champ," and Ali says, "Thanks. *Powerful.*"

Ali's taped voice says we can never repay Allah except by being good. A man brings a blonde woman to Ali and whispers, "This is the Marilyn Monroe look-alike."

Marilyn Monroe Look-Alike, from a hotel show down the street, kneels next to Ali for a photo. Ali ignores her. He is saying, "This lecture is one of 47 I've done. We're having 100,000 copies made."

He says he wants to hold a spiritual revival in Egypt, Africa and Arab countries, and you say you'd like to hear more but you have to be going, it was nice to see you again, Ali. Before the door closes behind you, you hear Ali say to the people still there, "This next lecture . . ."

January 25, 1988

Atlantic City, N.J.

To enter the 5th Street Gym in Miami Beach 22 years ago, you stepped over a rheumy fetal ball they called "Sweet Red," who was, as far as anyone knew, never sweet to a living soul. You searched a way up a dark stairway so narrow its walls left dirt on your sleeves. A left at the landing and you stood four steps from a boxing ring. The greatest athlete you would ever see jumped rope on the far side of the place, his back to you, working in slivers of sunlight that came around lettering on the gym windows.

Twenty-two years later, in an Atlantic City hotel room, no longer young, Muhammad Ali promised author Budd Schulberg he would cause a bottle of perfume to rise from atop a chest of drawers.

"Levitate it," Ali said. "You watchin'?" And Ali lifted the bottle in demonstration of its intended flight path. "Levitate now. You watch."

He wiggled the fingers of his right hand at the bottle. Every eye on the bottle now, Ali laughed out loud, said, "April fool," and walked away smiling.

Muhammad Ali once was a butterfly on the wing. Now 46 years old, six years past his last fight, he moves with a shuffling gait. He speaks slowly and only occasionally above a gurgled whisper. His face is masklike. His doctors say he suffers Parkinson's syndrome, common to boxers and indistinguishable from Parkinson's disease, a crippling brain disease.

When Ali takes medication daily, he is alert and articulate, friends say. But he is inconsistent with the medicine because he dislikes its side effects. A friend also says, "Being religious, Ali may think Allah wants him this way." Schulberg, Ali's friend for 25 years, sees a pattern: "He never took medication, not even as a kid. Like, 'I don't have to be what you want me to be.'"

The most fabulous, in every sense, figure in sports of this generation and maybe forever, Muhammad Ali was a perfect athlete, all silk and all steel, the most famous man on Earth, weaving a life's fabric with threads of sports, poetry, politics, religion, race and glitzy show biz.

In his Atlantic City room on this day, he autographed flyers which carry a message from the Nation of Islam. By handing them out, Ali says he uses "my boxing fame to deliver God's message. I don't try to convert anybody. I deliver the message. God does the rest."

This was the day after Mike Tyson's knockout of Larry Holmes, no big deal to Ali, who said, "Larry the time he beat me would have beat Tyson," that being Ali's next-to-last fight, late in 1980.

A visitor said to Ali, "You in the '70s, not even at your best, would've beaten Tyson."

"You think Tyson's as good as Joe Louis in his prime?"

"No."

"Rocky Marciano?"

"No."

Ali said, more loudly, "Jack Johnson?"

"No."

Louder yet, the volume near that of the young Ali: "And they're saying I'm better than all of them. At last, they're saying I was the greatest of all time," and here Ali raised high his right arm, as he has done from the 5th Street Gym to Zaire.

That night the New York tycoon, Donald Trump, arranged a 46th birthday party for Ali. Watching a film retrospective of Ali's career, the 500 guests broke into laughter when the irrepressible Cassius Clay interrupted an interviewer who began, "Sonny Liston says . . ."

"Ain't he uggggly?" Clay said. "The world champion should be pretty — like me."

Upon beating George Foreman in 1974 to win the championship taken from him when he refused in '67 to join the Army, Ali was invited to meet President Ford. The retrospective narrator said of Ali, "His social, political and athletic exile was over."

Then the birthday party organizers rolled out a cake for Ali, who, on his way to cut the first piece, stopped and bowed to the celebrants. He said, "I wish I could make a comeback," an imp's smile at the corners of his lips.

As toast to Ali, Tyson's manager Jimmy Jacobs said, "Of the 37 heavyweight champions from John L. Sullivan to Mike Tyson, only one can be the greatest, that one above all the others, Mike Tyson,

Jack Dempsey, Joe Louis — the greatest fighter of all time was Muhammad Ali."

Then to the front came Sugar Ray Leonard, once a great fighter who (like Ali) felt unbound by convention, who was (like Ali) as much showman as fighter. Leonard said, "I loved only two men in my lifetime. My father and Muhammad Ali."

Mischief on his face, Leonard added, "In fact, my father still believes I am the illegitimate son of Muhammad Ali," both fighters now laughing out loud, the mask of Ali gone, and off to one side, watching, a man remembered the sunlight in the 5th Street Gym.

Don King

January 16, 1986

Of Don King's shameless use of Martin Luther King's name, of Don King's hype that he will sell 15,000 tickets for the Friday fight here, of Don King's trip to the state Capitol for sweet words of honor from the Georgia legislature — of all this, there is only one thing to say. But we can't say *that*. So let's start with the man's hair and see where we go.

Don King says his hair stands straight up that way all by itself, with not so much as a drop of stiffening goo. The fight promoter swears he never raises the stuff to its gray skyscraper height by using a pick, brush, blowtorch or cattle prod. "I never touch it," King said, giggly as a peroxide blonde.

It is scary news that Don King's hair just happens, as summer clouds just happen, for it suggests that any of us may wake one morning to find his hair *extremis erectile*. Life would never be the same after that. To quote Thoreau, who to judge by drawings of the time had unruly frizz above his ears, men lead lives of quiet desperation. And now we know why. They're afraid they'll wake up looking like Don King.

Discrimination against the frizzed ones is so complete that not a single president has been elected without first combing his hair flat. Would you, be honest now, buy a used car from a salesman whose hair seems to have permed by a shot of 5,000 volts at midnight? See.

No wonder Don King is a fight promoter. What's left? He was a gambler. He ran numbers against the established runners, who didn't like the intrusion, and soon enough King fell into an ugly street fight with a rival runner. The other guy wound up ugly dead.

Time was served, a pardon was given, King got rich. "Only in America," King is always saying, and some people, on hearing this from this man, have inquired about moving to Pago Pago.

Well, if a guy can't be a numbers runner because he's in prison for killing a man, and if his hair standing on end renders him unfit for used-car sales, there's nothing much left but to get rich by promoting fights in which both men sometimes get out alive.

Don King met Muhammad Ali in 1974, as related in Ali's autobiography, where King is quoted saying he was inspired by Ali. "It came when I first saw your dramatic demonstration of marketable skills when I was Number 4819 in Cell 12, Row 12. They let us see your first 'Fight of the Century' against Frazier in '71, and it was then that I decided not to return to gambling, but to go into show business."

Show biz or boxing, both hold truth in such high regard it is used rarely. "A master of trickeration," King said of rival promoter Bob Arum, which Arum took as praise in the business which he calls "the last refuge of desperadoes." Will King sell 15,000 tickets for the Tim Witherspoon–Tony Tubbs heavyweight championship fight Friday as he boasts? Only if he buys them himself. Sales through Tuesday had climbed to 883.

The Georgia legislature has put a high polish on its reputation for slothful research. It honored King as innovator in 1974 of the closed-circuit television broadcast of boxing. By his own admission, King's only connection to the first big closed-circuit TV show — Ali-Frazier in '71 — was as a viewer in one of Ohio's maximum security theaters. But King, ever grateful to this wonderful land of opportunity, didn't want to ruin the Georgia legislature's party with reckless use of the truth, no more than he wants to be true to Martin Luther King's blessed memory.

This weekend marks Martin Luther King's birthday. Atlanta was King's home. So Don King is using advertisements calling this fight "KINGS' DREAM." Two Kings are pictured on the ads: Martin Luther King in the left corner saying, "I have a dream," and Don King on the other side saying, "Only in America."

Martin and Don together — as if these men, a Nobel peace laureate and a pardoned felon, have in common the dream that Terrible Tim Witherspoon should beat up on TNT Tony Tubbs.

"Don King," author Pete Dexter once wrote, "would pick Joe Louis out of his wheelchair and feed him to Roberto Duran if the money were right."

Only in America.

Only in America could a pardoned felon put on a fist fight and drag into the slime, for a few more dollars, the name of a man who never raised a fist to anyone, not to Bull Connor, not even to a numbers runner.

Memories

November 29, 1984

Newnan, Georgia

Hamilton Arnall, Sr., is 84 years old. He was the football team manager for Georgia Tech in 1918. He has on his office wall a team picture showing him, stern faced, in the same row with John Heisman, an imperious tilt to the coach's chin. When Arnall takes down that picture and talks about it, this is what you do: you listen.

"My family has always lived here in Newnan. I got an engineering degree in '20, but I came home to work in the cotton mill for $11 a week. I made more than that playing baseball every Saturday — $125 a month. That's where I got to chewin' tobacco. Still chew every day. My father thought the insurance business would be good for me, so I started it in '22. Been good to me since.

"You got to pay attention to Tech and Georgia here. Georgia has more folks, but a lot went to school there one term. It takes a little more brainpower to go to Tech. We like to say that, y'know. 'Cause it's true. So there's a natural rival thing.

"Tech and Georgia, it's something else. They stopped playing one year when a fella got run over by a car. Turned out he wasn't a Georgia fella at all. He was from Oglethorpe. But everybody got het up and stopped playing football for a while.

"We'd go over to play Georgia in baseball. I was a shortstop and first baseman. We'd stay in the Georgia Hotel and walk down the hill to Sanford Field. Where the football stadium is now. We'd be walking and they'd rock us in. They'd send buzzards over us. Rocks. Stones. They'd throw at us and they'd let loose those birds over us, like we were dead.

"We had this wooden fence around the field at Tech. They burned it down. They did everything to us. 'Course, I reckon we did about anything to them, too.

"But that's because we were the two big schools. It got hot to stay in 1927 when they were going to be champions of the world. They were 9 and 0. But we beat 'em 12–0 and kept 'em out of the Rose Bowl. Bill Alexander was the Tech coach. The way he did it, he let our quarterback catch passes instead of the end. We liked to kill 'em.

"They beat us some, too. That Charley Trippi, he would beat us. Gawdamighty, was he great.

"Look at this picture. You can pick out Heisman. Always wore those baseball britches. Had his watch on a chain in his pocket. That's the watch chain there. He coached with a megaphone. You could hear him everywhere. That harsh Yankee voice. The word for him is tough. There's the megaphone, by his feet in this picture.

"We had three all-Americans: Bill Fincher, Bum Day and Indian Joe Guyon, who came from Carlisle, Pennsylvania, same as Jim Thorpe. I was the manager and Bum Day quit the team because I wouldn't give him a new belt. He went to Georgia and wound up captain.

"We were good in '18. We won 'em all but one. We beat Furman 118-0 and the 11th Cavalry 119-0 and North Carolina State 128-0. Heisman didn't let up much. The only game we lost was our one road game, up at Pitt. They beat us 32-0.

"We took the train up there. All day and all night. We changed trains in Cincinnati and I had to drive the mules and wagons to take our equipment from one station to another. We'd have craps games going on in the train and I held the money.

"It was fun. At that time of the century, you didn't have big shots, no show-offs, no rich guys. Let me see that picture again. Yep, there weren't any cars on this team. Nobody had any money. At practice, fellas in big cars would drive up to watch and give players rides home. They helped out with money.

"That trip to Pittsburgh, I roomed with Joe Guyon. He was the best athlete ever was. Played baseball, played pro football. In the

Hall of Fame for football now. From the Indian school where Jim Thorpe played. Joe had a woman everywhere he went. He'd get passes to the games and be warming up and look at the girls he'd given passes to. He meant no harm, he never hurt anybody. Everybody liked Joe. Gawdamighty, could he run.

"It was a different world. Our guys lived over stores and in two little ol' houses we called 'the shacks.' There wasn't any spring practice. We started September 1 and wound up Thanksgiving. Joe Guyon carried the football forever and he wore a leather headgear about as thin as a lady's silk scarf. The biggest crowd was 8,000 for Auburn in 1918. We beat 'em 41-0.

"This Heisman stuff, the trophy, I mean, that started up after he went back East. We just knew he was a good man and tough. I can hear that voice through the megaphone. One day Red Barron missed a tackle and he made Red tackle a fella 69 straight times. The guy Red was tackling — he quit the team.

"Look, I'll be 85 this July and I've had everything happen to me. Come by again. We'll chew some tobacco and talk some."

John Thompson

January 19, 1983

Washington, D.C.

T he old house at 14th and W streets had a front window that
protruded, so that if you sat on the inside sill you could look
down the street to the corner and see the bus stop.

Anna Thompson worked days then. This was in the 1940s when
$5 a day was good for cleaning house. She had been a teacher in
southern Maryland, where she met her husband, John, who couldn't
spell his name. When they moved to D.C. for work, she couldn't
teach anymore because she had only a two-year school certificate.

Every afternoon, when Mrs. Thompson got off the bus at the
corner, first thing she did was look up the street to that protruding
window. Sure enough, there would be her baby boy, her only boy
and the youngest of her four children. There in the window, waiting, would be John Jr., who knew that no matter what troubles he
had at school or on the street, he always could feel good in Mama's
arms.

In the bathtub, she'd play with his toes. "This little piggy went to
market, this little piggy went to town . . ." One time he was
bringing in coal from the front sidewalk and banged the can against
his shin. He cried and a neighbror, Miss Boston, mocked his crying.
He said bad words to Miss Boston, who threatened to tell his father,
a stern figure.

When little John saw his father coming home, he ran through the
house and out the back to the bus stop at the corner, and he
returned across the lawn hand-in-hand with his Mama, smiling in
Miss Boston's direction.

However big John Thompson got — and he would get to be

231

almost 7 feet tall and 300 pounds — he felt safest in Mama's arms. He would become famous in a way, a big-time basketball coach at Georgetown University, where his world knows him as a man who can scream his head off at something he thinks is wrong or hug a kid when the kid most needs a hug.

Anna Thompson was 76 when she died last month. The last nine years, after her husband died, she lived with John. They lived all over town in the '40s and '50s. They tried to hide her $5 a day from the projects' office man, because he would raise the rent or move them to a more expensive place. Finally, they moved in with Mrs. Thompson's sister Mary on W Street, and little John slept on a couch in the kitchen.

Looking back now, now that he's 41 years old, and talking about his mother, John Thompson sees how it was. He didn't know it was poverty then. He knows now that his mother and father didn't buy a single thing for themselves. They took care of him. One Christmas they gave him a tool box, because he liked to fix things. He fixed the plug on a radio once and Aunt Mary started calling him Mr. Fix-It. "If Fix-It can't fix it, it can't be fixed," she would say.

That made the young man feel good. John was in Catholic grade school and having trouble. He couldn't read. His mother, the old teacher, would read to him at home. It was wonderful, that part. John remembers that his mother would act out all the parts in the stories. Such a voice she had, dramatic as all get out. She'd find a way, such as with the tool box, to make John feel good about himself.

When John took the box into the back yard, green paint came off on his hands. "Gee, this tool box Santa Claus brought me, I got paint on my hands," little John said, and Anna Thompson said, "Honey, he must have just now painted it." A lot later she confessed to big John that money was short and she bought a used tool box and painted it herself just before Christmas.

At school, the nuns had a Gold Star row. They put a gold star in front of the seats for the smart kids. The Blue Star row was for the average kids. They had a picture of a baby for the Baby Row, for the kids doing poorly. That's where John sat, and he didn't like it, and every time you turned around he was being sent home for acting up.

Some parents told the nuns to beat their kids if need be. Wear 'em out. John got his share of iron rulers across the knuckles. But Anna Thompson wouldn't allow anything else. She talked to the nuns about John, and they told her he couldn't read. They said he might be retarded. They said he might never learn anything. Fact is, they got so fed up with John that they kicked him out of Catholic school after the fifth grade.

About the only hope came from one nun who said John did well on tests when somebody read him the work. And John's sister Mary told their mother, "Don't you believe that. That boy is not retarded. Don't let them convince you of that."

Fat chance, for Anna Thompson was a determined woman, a teacher, a mother who first thing off the bus looked to a window to see her baby boy. She took him to maybe the first public reading clinic in Washington, at 14th and R. From her $5 a day, she paid for a private tutor besides. She took him all over the city, he remembers, and she read everything to him, acting out the parts, and she talked a lot about his Uncle Lewis.

Lewis Alexander, her brother, was a poet. He lived with the Thompsons. Tall and elegant, he spoke in magical words of romance and night and tears. John Sr. didn't know what to make of this guy who daydreamed his life away. John Sr. couldn't read because, at school age, he was chosen from his family to work in the fields. In D.C., he worked marble and tile with his hands.

Little John, who couldn't read however much he tried, was fascinated by the tall, elegant poet. He remembers yet the day his mother said to him, "You remind me so much of Lewis."

One of the great things in Anna Thompson's life, her son would say after she died, was that he finally caught on to reading and school. The basketball made his father cry with joy. They had gone to baseball games at Griffith Stadium together, especially to see the Cleveland Indians' black players, Larry Doby and Luke Easter and Harry (Suitcase) Simpson. What John Sr. always said to his son was, "Boy, get that education because that's something the white man can never take away from you."

The old man loved it, too, that little John grew up to be a basketball star in high school and college. Every morning at 5 o'clock, John Sr. would cuss the paper boy for being so late, and at breakfast he'd have somebody read to him the part about his son.

At work, John Sr. would strut some and ask the people, "See what they say about the boy in the paper?"

His son became a high school coach and John Sr. used to sit on the bench. One time at LaPlata, a player from the other team dove into the bench and John Sr. jumped up, swinging his cane. "He thought we were at war," his son said.

Anna Thompson didn't go to games her son coached. They had a different relationship. She had taught him life, not ball. She taught him: Don't want what you can't have. Keep family problems in the family. Be positive. She taught him — when he sat in the Baby Row, at the hardest time to teach him such a thing — to believe in himself and to speak his mind. A thousand times she must have recited a little poem to him:

> You can do anything you think you can,
> It's all in the way you view it.
> It's all in the start you make, young man,
> You must feel that you're going to do it.

He couldn't figure out why blacks had to sit in the back of the Catholic church at his father's little town in Maryland, and his mother said, "Don't get caught up in that. The world can be very mean sometimes. Just go ahead, ignore it. The people who run the church aren't the same as what is being taught in the church."

Even later, when her grown-up son was angered by discrimination and came to her in low spirits, she would say, "Go forward, John. Ignore it. *You can do anything you think you can . . .*"

In her 50s, Anna Thompson studied and became a practical nurse. There's a painting of her in her white uniform on Thompson's office wall. The time she lived in her son's house, these last nine years, she yet was proud of him as her son, not as a pivotman with the Celtics, not as a famous coach. Still a mama's boy, he would say. Sometimes, her mind confused by age, she would call him Lewis, but they would talk their way back to today.

He gave her baths, as she once did for him, and in the bath he would play with her toes. "This little piggy went to market . . ." She would say, "Stop that, boy," and her son would laugh out loud.

The nuns in Catholic school always told the kids to kiss their parents every time they left home because you never know if they'll be there when you get back. Every morning, John Thompson would peek around a corner into his mother's bedroom to see that she was all right. Last month, leaving on a basketball trip, he kissed her a bunch of times very fast, pecking away until she giggled and said, "Stop that, boy."

He came back from that trip when she was dying, and three weeks after she died, John Thompson woke up one morning and out of love's habit peeked around the corner into her bedroom.

Country Brown

August 20, 1986

T wo weeks ago, when Country Brown began coughing up blood, he figured it was time to see a doctor.

A doctor in Chattanooga took one look at a chest X-ray and said cancer.

"Just blunt, 'Lung cancer,'" said Country Brown.

You get to be 65 years old, after smoking cigarettes most of that time, and it is no surprise to hear a doctor say you have lung cancer.

But Country Brown wanted to hear it twice before he believed it.

So he came to Atlanta to see some doctors.

Ralph (Country) Brown had come to Atlanta 40 years ago to play baseball for the Crackers. They called him Country because he is from Summerville, a little town in the northwest Georgia mountains. The writer Paul Hemphill said Brown likely was "the most popular man who ever donned a uniform in what may be the best league minor-league baseball ever saw . . . a legend in the tiny inbred vested world of Deep South sports."

Country Brown was tall and lean, a knife blade of a center fielder who moved "with antelope grace and Ty Cobb meanness," Hemphill wrote. Such a runner: a left-handed hitter, he could drag-bunt with Cobb. "Draggin' it, I could lay that thing on a dime," Brown said. He sat in a hospital room the other morning.

They had a big magnolia tree in center field at Ponce de Leon Park, the tree up on a terrace, and Country Brown more than once ran clear up there to catch fly balls. "They called it Country Brown's tree," he said with some pride, and he moved his hands on the hospital bedsheet, showing a visitor the shape of the old ballpark, where the fences were, pointing with a finger to right where the great old tree stood.

He hit around .300, stole 35 bases every year. "I lived to run, I loved to run, I ran all the time as a kid, out there in the pastures, out in the open spaces."

Weekends as a kid, Brown walked three miles to the Hansen community schoolhouse where he and his buddies played ball. They brought push mowers to cut the weeds. They dug out basepaths. They filled burlap bags with sawdust for the bases and they sawed a piece of wood into the shape of home plate. Then they edged out some dirt so the plate would be even with the ground.

"We'd play doubleheaders, we'd play 'til dark," said Country Brown from his hospital bed, 50 years removed from the kid's dreaming diamond, "and then we'd walk the three miles home. I loved playin' ball."

His time with the Crackers came to a melancholy end in 1952. In Brown's sixth season, the manager Dixie Walker suspended him. "Insubordination," the manager said. Brown says all he ever knew was that Walker benched him during a slump and refused to use him again. "I couldn't stand it, not playin'," Brown said. "I couldn't sleep, couldn't eat, couldn't do nothin'. Playin' ball was my life."

At his request, Atlanta traded Brown to Chattanooga in '53. ("I *crucified* the Crackers after that. How could one guy *crucify* a team the way I did them? Some things are *meant* to be.") Maybe because of his age, Brown was 27 when he joined the Crackers, or maybe because the Crackers needed him as a box-office draw and so demanded too high a price for his contract, Country Brown never played in the major leagues.

"For anybody from Summerville, Atlanta was the major leagues," he said. "I worshipped the Crackers. I listened to all their games on the radio. The nearest big-league team was, where? St. Louis."

For 20 years, until retiring this June, Brown was the Summerville city recorder. He still works at Best Manufacturing, where they make surgical gloves, and it was there one night he noticed the blood coming up.

He didn't think a doctor could look at an X-ray picture and see cancer. So he came to Atlanta, the big leagues, to Emory University Hospital, where Dr. Joseph Miller said he didn't know what it was, but it was something on the old ballplayer's lung and it wasn't pretty.

A letter from a stranger came to Brown in the hospital at Emory: "Hey Country,

"Heard you was laid up. Sorry to hear that. Just remember, bottom of the ninth, down a run and we need a hit. Go get 'em Tiger."

Soon after that, they took Country Brown to surgery to do a biopsy of the lung.

"I was out, so I didn't know anything," he said. "First thing I knew, somebody was leaning over me. He said, 'Mr. Brown, your lung is not malignant.' Well, with the anesthesia, I'm in another world right then. I don't know what he's talking about even. Back up in my room, everybody was all so tickled. To tell the truth, I'd given up. I figured one doctor flat told me it was cancer, I didn't have much of a chance. When the anesthesia finally wore off, and they told me what the real score was, well, it tickled me, too."

There is no cancer in Country Brown. "They tell me I'm 100 percent OK, there's nothing wrong." A young doctor stopped by room 2122 at Crawford Long Hospital to say those words just yesterday. The doctor said, "No tumor, no cancer, that's the final pathology report," and Country Brown said, "Nothing in there?" The doctor said, "It's what we call a lung abcess."

The doctor prescribed antibiotics. Country Brown will go home to Summerville early next week. It had been 30 years or so since Country Brown last saw the Crackers at old Ponce de Leon Park. The other day, leaving Emory to drive to Crawford Long Hospital for the tests on his lung, the old ballplayer looked out the car window. They passed the spot where the ballpark used to be. The fences are gone now. There's a store there. But Country Brown saw something else. There it was, the old magnolia tree, Country Brown's tree, still alive.

Homecoming!

October 6, 1985

Newnan, Georgia

The night before the high school homecoming game, the son said to the father, "Daddy, I believe I'm going to get a touchdown."

The father said, "Just put your heart in it and you might."

"I've got a feeling I'm going to," the son said.

Eric Geter, the son, is 15 years old. He's a freshman defensive back on the Newnan High School team that is this year, as always, a football power in these parts, here in a small town where Eric Geter's father, Joe, 36, was a linebacker at Central High before integration sent black players to Newnan High.

"I'll get the touchdown on a kickoff, I do believe," Eric Geter told his father, who had been his first coach (with the Blue Eagles in the rec league), the son telling the father he would get a touchdown on a kickoff return, a young man dreaming a homecoming dream.

* * * * *

Homecoming! Bigger than life in Georgia's small towns . . . the homecoming queens circling the courthouse square in a red Mercedes convertible draped with white bunting . . . Newnan's band high-stepping in blue uniforms, Jonesboro's in red, the colors shimmering with energy . . . sequined majorettes and flag twirlers on the field as Boy Scouts raise the American flag and a preacher prays, his pulpit voice distorted by the public address system's acoustics, the voice earnest in asking God to watch over this homecoming game . . . boys and girls flirting at the hot dog stand, throwing ice, giggling in tiny voices, wanting to know where these flirtations are going and half-scared to find out . . . 4,000 mothers and fathers and

239

brothers and sisters in Newnan's stadium down the bank behind the high school . . . and every T-shirt saying, "Cougar Homecoming '85."

Max Bass, the Newnan coach for 20 years: "The night before homecoming, we have 'Sweetheart Night.' The players bring their girlfriends. Used to, I wouldn't put up with a 'Sweetheart Night.' Now I'm older and smarter. I know the girlfriends are No. 1 and me and football are No. 3 or so."

Homecoming! The pretty girls sat on metal folding chairs along the football sidelines, two of the girls to be the homecoming queens of Newnan High, one queen white and one queen black, the girls comfortable with the idea of separate but equal queens. And the black queen, Tonja Snow, 17, bright and beautiful, would say of the moment she heard her name announced on the squawky p.a. system, "Me. ME! I couldn't believe it was ME!"

"I was nervous, it being homecoming, but that's what I like about football — the fans, the crowd, the being around in it," said Newnan's little quarterback, Dexter Holiday, 17, a senior, the first black quarterback for a Newnan team. He is quick, a wonderful runner who grew up banging around with his brothers in the front yard at home.

"We'd throw a football in the air and go at it," he said, and after helping Newnan win on homecoming, 35-2, Dexter Holiday said with a smile, "I always felt like the game was in me, like football was what I was put on Earth to do."

* * * * *

"These chil'en," Max Bass said, "need to know they are worth somethin'. Chil'en everywhere get put down too much, get told they're not worth anything. Football coaches can't *create* players. But we can mold players and create confidence. If I've got one talent, I can make players believe in themselves."

The coach drew up a breath because he knew what he would say next didn't fit with the rest.

"I love these chil'en to death, but I tell you what, I coulda killt 'em the other night at Forest Park. No way we shoulda lost to those people. I'm 47, and you'd think I was past feelin' it, but that damn loss 'bout killt me. You don't say this to the players — you want players to hate losin' — but maybe that loss will do us good. Life knocks you down, you pick yourself up."

Look at Max Bass. He is a gentleman of some 270 pounds and some 5-foot-10. To see him, you'd say there are only two things that gentleman could be: either a football coach or a sheriff, and not only because his considerable belly endows him with awesome authority. There's a look on Max Bass's face that says he flat knows what he's doing and pretty much knows what mischief you're up to.

All it takes to know he's a football coach, and a good one, the kind you want your son with, is to listen to him talk, which he does some days from 4:30 a.m. (up to look at game film) with hardly a let-up before bedtime at 10 p.m.

"I want my coaches to love kids first," Bass said. "This is the most formative age. When we get kids, at 13, if we can get those kids to 17 and influence 'em with character and responsibility — most kids can't get where they're supposed to be when they're supposed to be there — we've done some good. They know if they're a minute late, we'll put their hind ends back up that bank."

That bank is the steep rise from the football field to the athletic building. Football money built the place, put the weight room in, put the locker room in and put Max Bass's office in there where he has this sign over his door:

3 Questions Everyone Wants to Know About Me:
1 Can I trust you?
2 Are You Committed to Excellence?
3 Do you care about me?

The four seasons before Bass came to town, Newnan won three games. His first season, 1966, the Cougars went 9-1-1. Newnan was the 1981 North Georgia champion, losing the state championship game in Class AAAA, the top level.

"The sad part of this job is that you can't help those kids you know could make it they just wanted to," Bass said. "It's disheartening. You think if that kid just had stickability. You push 'em to the

241

hurt point — and they give up. It hurts me then. They gotta learn that life pushes you to the hurt point — and you can't quit in life.

"No excuses accepted. I come from Opp, Alabama, raised on a farm, poor li'l ol' boy who tried but couldn't play much football, only in high school and some in junior college. I went to Alabama and Coach Bryant was good to me, but I couldn't play there. If I wanted to make excuses — 'I was poor, I was li'l' — I could be out now plowin' that mule in Alabama or workin' in the Army.

"So I don't feel sorry for you if you don't have a certain thing — because if you're going to be successful, you'll overcome. You can make excuses forever, but you can't eat 'em. I expect the best you got."

* * * * *

During the 1969 integration of Newnan High, students and townspeople marched around the school in protest.

"Two black players came to my office and sat beside me," Max Bass said. "I'll never forget them, and they said, 'Coach, you ain't done nothin' wrong, we trust you.' To me, all chil'en are the same. I don't see how any person who calls himself Christian can treat somebody different because he's black. Hey, win. All anybody wants is braggin' rights. I don't care if a kid is pink and from Mars if he acts right."

* * * * *

Homecoming! What high school football is, Max Bass said on this homecoming night, this night when the Mothers' Club fried up chicken for the players' post-game meal, on this night when the 10 o'clock dew sparkled under the lights on the stadium turf, diamonds for free — what this game is, is fun.

"College football is business, and high school football is fun," Bass said, "and I've got as much spark, as much spring in my legs as ever, though that damn Forest Park loss 'bout killt me. I'm gonna coach here 'til they run me off. Coach Bryant retired and he died in 29 days. I don't plan on dyin' anytime soon."

It was 11 o'clock on homecoming night, and the coach's wife, Nancy, carried a rose and a clutch of shiny homecoming balloons.

She came by to gather up her man. They would go to their cabin on their lake. "Gotta go watch the scores on TV," Max Bass said.

And Joe Geter, on opening his car door to let in his son, Eric, heard these words, "I did it, I did it."

The first homecoming night for Eric Geter, an honor roll student ("Lessons first, football later," the father tells his son) — and on this homecoming night Eric Geter intercepted a Jonesboro pass and ran it back 50 yards, flying as if in a dream, to get the first touchdown of his high school career.

Cicero Leonard

November 11, 1980

Washington, D.C.

I never knew my father was a fighter until I was already a fighter myself. I was about 14 or 15 and we went back to North Carolina. I heard all my father's old buddies talking how good he used to be. He's something. Hey, put this in the paper. I can still whup him.''

— Sugar Ray Leonard, laughing

First thing Sunday mornings, Cicero Leonard drove the iron stakes into the dirt.

Just a youngster then, a sharecropper's son in South Carolina, Cicero Leonard drove the stakes into the ground and then he went for the plowlines.

Weekdays he walked the fields behind his daddy's mule, Belle, and he tugged at those plowlines to keep Belle between the rows.

Sunday mornings he took the plowlines and wrapped one end around a big old oak tree in the front yard.

Running the lines from the tree, he lashed them to the tops of the three iron stakes.

That way he made a square about 15 feet long on each side.

Only he called it a ring.

A boxing ring.

This was 1935. A sharecropper's son from Alabama, Joe Louis, was the heavyweight champion on those Sunday mornings when Cicero Leonard, dreaming, put on his boxing gloves and went into his plowline ring. Newspaper pictures of Louis taught Leonard how to hold his hands up. What the kid could see on the radio, what he *felt* through the radio when Louis fought — that's how he threw his punches, the way Joe did it.

Sunday mornings, 40 kids came to the Leonard place. They brought their gloves.

Cicero Leonard was a little tiger, never more than 5-foot-8 and 150 pounds. He would fight four or five times on those Sunday mornings, two or three rounds each time. He fought all comers, no matter their size.

Never lost, to hear him tell it now.

Not once.

The champ of his front yard.

If he needed it, and most times he did (even Joe Louis took one in the nose now and then), Cicero's mother fixed up the bleeding on his face. Then they would go to church, the Pleasant Grove Baptist Church, a mile and a half away, just outside Mullins, South Carolina, a little farm town near the coast.

The Leonards worked a farm growing tobacco, cotton, sweet potatoes and peanuts. The fighter's father, Bige, a giant at 6-foot-4 and 240 pounds, could knock down Belle with one punch. Cicero says he saw Bige do it more than once. "Sent that mule right to her knees," the little tiger said 45 years later. "Was I scared of Poppa? Wouldn't you be?" Sally, his mother, picked 200 pounds of cotton the day after giving birth to Cicero's baby sister. Sally lived to be 102.

Cicero quit school after the fifth grade. If you were one of 12 children of a sharecropper in the '30s, you learned how to run a ribbon binder. Never mind readin' and writin'. Bige would tell Cicero to drive that ribbon binder down the road and cut and bind (with the ribbon) the oats for old Walker Walters.

Old Walker Walters. Even today, a generation later, Cicero Leonard remembers that name. He was supposed to stop at Walters's place one day. But he drove past to another fellow's farm to help him out first.

A storm struck, and Leonard couldn't get to Walters's oats that day.

Next day came a letter saying he was to report to the U.S. Navy. It was 1942.

"Never did do Mr. Walters's oats, and, boy, was he mad," Cicero Leonard says today. Thirty-eight years after the fact, Leonard still felt bad about driving past the Walters oats.

Sunday mornings he put on the boxing gloves. Saturday nights at the little dance hall on Clyde Davis's farm, he put on the boxing gloves. Cicero Leonard took the gloves with him everywhere in his old Ford, stringing them over his shoulder when he alighted. "Guys would be drinking and they'd say, 'Cicero, I know you're the best, but I gotta try you,'" Leonard said.

Never lost, to hear him tell it.

Not once.

Champ of the dance hall, too.

The closest Cicero Leonard came to being a professional fighter was in the Navy. In his four years as an officers' cook, he fought in the U.S. Navy's 156-pound division.

Navy champ.

Lost once in 47 fights.

"Only fella who beat me was a little fella from Philadelphia called Little Red," Leonard said. "I could hit harder than him, but he was faster."

Back on the farm after the war, working for his daddy again, Leonard drove down the road past the old Walters' place.

Saw a pretty girl.

She sat in the swing in the front yard under a big shade tree.

Prettiest girl he ever saw.

So he sent his first cousin to talk to her.

The first cousin reported that the girl's name was Getha Elliott. And the first cousin said, "I'm gonna ask her out."

Then Cicero told his first cousin this: "I'm gonna take that girl Getha away from you."

And he did.

Getha Elliott was fresh out of high school. She didn't work in the fields. She told her mother she couldn't stand the heat. She just didn't want to pick cotton. She had her own ideas. She did the cooking and cleaning. And she sat in the swing in the front yard, watching that good-lookin' Cicero Leonard drive by every day.

She didn't know Cicero. She didn't go to the Davis dance hall. Nettie Elliott, her mother, didn't approve. Her little girl didn't go anywhere but to school and to church.

So Cicero Leonard walked up to her car at church one Sunday morning and said he'd sure like to go out with her.

About time, she thought.

A year later they were married.

They moved out of South Carolina, looking for work first in Wilmington, North Carolina, then Winston-Salem, finally Washington, D.C. Cicero had a younger brother working in Washington and the brother told him there was plenty of money to be made there. By then, Cicero and Getha Leonard had six children, with another one to come, and so they picked up one more time.

That was in 1960.

Cicero worked in a wholesale grocery place. He became the night manager of a supermarket where he had to slip a knife under his belt for protection. A nervous man with a sawed-off shotgun once blew away a case of Coca-Cola in his store, the stuff fizzing like crazy while the bandit, who didn't mean to pull the trigger, beat a frightened retreat down the street.

Getha Leonard worked as a licensed practical nurse.

Better than picking cotton in the hot sun.

They survived, these children of sharecroppers did.

He is an old fighter so quiet, so modest he didn't tell his son he ever put on boxing gloves . . . a man who worked so honestly he didn't think a war was excuse enough for skipping an old man's oats. She is a woman who worked and cooked and kept her family together even when families like hers were disintegrating , . . a woman who sings for joy that Saturday is her 32nd wedding anniversary, "and to the same man."

Out of the Navy, Cicero Leonard thought of fighting as a pro. Joe Louis did it. The newest star back then, a little tiger the way Cicero Leonard had been a little tiger, was a welterweight named Sugar Ray Robinson. But Leonard could find no financial help to begin boxing. "So I just quit fighting."

Leonard's sixth child, the last son, was born in Wilmington, North Carolina, in 1956.

They named him Ray.

He became Sugar Ray.

Champ of the world.

"Ray was fighting six months before I ever saw him. I never encouraged him. Boxing is tough. He just had it in him somehow. He was 12 or 13 and he said, 'Dad, I can box.' I said, 'You can't box.' So he got me to come see him. I saw him and said, 'That's me. My God, that's me again.' And what's he saying, that he can whup me? Hmmmph."

— Cicero Leonard, proudly

The Seven

January 30 1986

T he seven dead astronauts held the risk in the palm of their hands, and they found it to be light. They went to the top of a rocket to ride the fire into the sky. So many others had flown away from Earth and come back that their acts of courage became routine, not worthy of our full attention. On a television news show we would see another rocket rising and ask, *Is this the 8:50 a.m. shuttle to Mars or what?*

No more. Now we have seen the consuming fire. Now we weigh the risk in our hands, and it is heavy with death. And we ask why. Why ride a rocket into the sky? Why seek the fire when fire kills?

We want to understand what reward can be worth the risk of death delivered by a computer glitch or by the failure of something called an O-ring. If we civilians had come to think of rocketry as routine, the astronauts knew better. They knew cataclysm was a heartbeat away. Yet we saw them on television the other night, walking to the firestick, every man and woman of them happy.

The five men and two women walked out of a building, dandy in their hero suits of blue cloth with zippered pockets and insignia patches. Their walk was jaunty, even cocky. The laughing teacher strode in lockstep with the fliers, the seven of them electric with joy, and they climbed into a van for the ride to the rocket. We saw videotape of the walk a dozen times. Then we never saw them again.

We saw the fire lift them. The teacher's students in New Hampshire wore party hats as they cheered the rocket's ascent. President Reagan later would tell the nation's school children, "The

249

future belongs not to the fainthearted. It belongs to the brave."

We search our experience for understanding. To know why a man rides a rocket, look at men who pursue risk.

"The Man put us here — and He'll take us," the great race car driver A. J. Foyt once said. "That's a square deal if I ever heard of one. We're all here for a certain length of time and that's it. When your time's up, it's up — not before, not after." So Foyt races at age 50. He has been burned and broken. He has seen death and wondered why.

"In '57, I had a good friend killed. And he just laid on the track while we went by. The thought went through my mind whether I wanted to go on. I had to know in my mind if I wanted to do it. You just have to accept life the way it is — and I went on."

Thoreau said the mass of men lead lives of quiet desperation. There is nothing quiet in life as Foyt defines it. Life at 200 miles per hour makes some people think of death. "Not me. I've damn near went out a couple times myself. It's something you learn to live with."

Why race?

"It's fun."

Mel Kenyon's body is a scar, a pale and blank reminder of fire. His left hand is gone. To race, he wore a glove that attached his stub of a hand to the steering wheel. After an Indianapolis 500 a decade ago, the stub was the color of raw meat. Kenyon dipped it in a bucket of water.

Why race?

"Racing is what I do. That's all."

The world champion Formula One racer Stirling Moss spoke of putting a car through a tight turn on the ragged edge of high speed: "So you stay just this side of that fraction of extra speed, that fraction of extra weight that could ruin everything, and perhaps kill you to boot. You're on top if it all, and the exhiliration, the thrill is tremendous. You say to yourself, 'All right, you bloody blokes, top that one, match it even.' And you feel like a painter who has just put the last brush stroke on a canvas, after years of trying to catch a certain expression — it's rewarding."

At age 70, the highwire walker Karl Wallenda went back up on the wire after a fall killed two members of his family and left another paralyzed.

"To be on the wire is life," Wallenda said. "The rest is waiting." And he, too, died falling from the wire.

"Why does A. J. Foyt race?" said a Tennessean named Gary Baker, a lawyer who races stock cars. "For the same reason we all do. It's a challenge. To go fast, that's the challenge. It's just in some people. It's like climbing mountains. Some people might think that's silly. But to a man who lives to climb, it's not silly."

Jonathan Swift said, "May you live all the days of your life." To do that living, test pilots "push the sides of the envelope," as they say, pushing against those invisible unknown borders of their work where man and machine are at risk. Race drivers put their machines teetering on a balance of friction and power that once lost may never be recovered. Wirewalkers and jet jockeys, race drivers and astronauts share with sculptors, composers and ballerinas the dream that lifts them up, the dream that a man, by reaching, can touch the stars.

Jack London wrote, "I would rather be ashes than dust. I would rather that my spark should burn out in a brilliant blaze than it should be stifled by dry rot. I would rather be a superb meteor than a sleepy, permanent planet." Asked what that meant, the old Raiders quarterback Ken Stabler said, "Throw deep."

More Than a Game

May 10, 1986

They never say it, maybe because it's not the kind of thing you say out loud. It's a thought that comes uninvited in the small hours of the night. Maybe you don't even recognize it. Maybe it's just there and you feel it without knowing what it is. You just know this: *Something's missing and I want it back. Bad.*

Ray Leonard may say he wants to fight again so he can leave his name alongside the great ones. He may say he wants to fight Marvin Hagler to make the circle whole: Leonard beat Tommy Hearns, Hagler beat Hearns, so now who's the best?

William Andrews's knee was shredded in practice two years ago. He may say he owes the Falcons service for their money. He may say he misses the camaraderie of a team. And he will be honest in that. It will be the truth, just as Leonard tells the truth. But it won't be the whole truth.

They come back so they can be the people they think they are.

They come back so the reality of their lives matches the perception.

Ray Leonard wants nothing by coming back except to be Ray Leonard again. We can say, "Leonard's made $40 million. He's famous. How stupid can he be? Does he want to lose that eye again?"

Or we can say, "Why doesn't Andrews take that money and run? What a break. He signs up for $6 million, gets hurt and never has to play but the Falcons gotta pay him. Me, I'd never lift a weight again. But you pick up the morning paper, and Andrews is working out. Crazy."

In this age of supposedly spoiled athletes, it's strange to hear the

Chicago Bulls arguing with Michael Jordan. The strange part is, the club doesn't want its star to play. Jordan insists on coming back. The Bulls said his foot was hurt too bad; even his personal doctor said Jordan's foot was only 80 percent OK. The Bulls said to forget this season and come back next year. Jordan would have none of that. He wanted to play.

"I love basketball like a wife," he said. "I'm going to play basketball somewhere, either in Chicago or in Chapel Hill." Even as doctors had been X-raying his foot, Jordan had played pickup games in North Carolina.

Jordan was not in pickup games for money or history or fame. He played because that's what he is: Michael Jordan, basketball player. The night he came back to the NBA against his own team's wishes, Jordan scored 63 points to beat the Celtics.

Do you think Dennis Leonard, the Kansas City pitcher, worked two years rebuilding a knee just to earn his money already guaranteed to him? Or that Len Barker is mucking around in Triple-A two years after elbow surgery to justify the $2.4 million Ted Turner will pay him?

"If I had it to do over, I don't know if I'd take the money," Don Baylor said early in 1977. The fierce hitter left Oakland to sign a big-money deal with the Angels. His average hung in the .100s. "All I'm thinking is I'm not worth this much. It's affecting me."

Some people think pro athletes take the big money and become full-time loafers. It isn't so. Fans have always perceived major league baseball players as grossly overpaid. You can look it up, from Henry Chadwick's day in the 19th century to Andy Messersmith's free agency in 1976. As Baylor's confession was remarkable for its lack of macho bravado, it also was instructive. These guys care.

They care about who they are. Maybe they call it pride. There is that, a pride in their craft. Mostly, it is their identity they care about. Their idea of self-worth long has been tied to success at what we so casually call games.

A man once said to Joe Paterno when the coach's Penn State football team lost a game, "It's only a game." The coach said, "If a carpenter builds a house and it falls down, do you say, 'Don't worry, it's only a house?'" Games are these people's lives.

Ray Leonard, as a kid, was a fighter. He saw the world as a fighter sees it; the world saw him as a fighter. To change either perception is to change who Ray Leonard is. Leonard, Andrews, Jordan — their lives have been shaped by their work, given purpose and direction by that work. They knew where they were going.

But events outside their control changed their direction. Ray Leonard suddenly was not a fighter. William Andrews was not a running back. They had become different people, and they didn't like it any more than Jordan liked being told he couldn't be a basketball player.

These are athletes at the top of the natural selection chain. Only the fittest survive, only the rare and beautiful animal makes it this far. For them, there is no soul-searching for identity. They know who they are. We may be lost and alone, but not these athletes who have given their lives to their work.

Joe Theismann didn't want to quit, not even after breaking his leg. Only a month after the injury — an injury which everyone assumed would end the quarterback's career — Theismann spoke of coming back. "The bones are popping down there," he said, "and that's a good sign. It's a granulation process where the broken ends grind against each other until they wear off the edges and can start to grow together. I'm looking forward to the challenge of getting ready to play again. I don't want to go out this way. I want to say when it's my time to leave."

Theismann and Andrews and Jordan have used the athlete's certain instincts: intelligence, courage, competitiveness. They believe the locker-room bromides. When the going gets tough, the tough get going. Never say die. Quitters never win, winners never quit. Hackneyed truths, they are gospel to great athletes.

"Everybody keeps saying Muhammad Ali should give up boxing," the Georgetown University basketball coach John Thompson once said. "It's not that easy. His entire life, people told Ali to buck the odds. Now the odds say he should give up boxing. How can we expect him to lay down and not buck the odds this time, too?"

They won't lay themselves down. To do that is to become a different person. No longer Leonard, no longer Jordan, no more Ali. So if they have reason to think they can buck the odds one more time, they will. Wouldn't you?